INVISIBLE CRIMES

Invisible Crimes

Their Victims and their Regulation

Edited by

Pamela Davies

Peter Francis

Victor Jupp

all at the University of Northumbria at Newcastle

First published in Great Britain 1999 by
MACMILLAN PRESS LTD
Houndmills, Basingstoke, Hampshire RG21 6XS and London
Companies and representatives throughout the world

A catalogue record for this book is available from the British Library.

ISBN 0–333–74161–7 hardcover
ISBN 0–333–79417–6 paperback

First published in the United States of America 1999 by
ST. MARTIN'S PRESS, INC.,
Scholarly and Reference Division,
175 Fifth Avenue, New York, N.Y. 10010

ISBN 0–312–22182–7

Library of Congress Cataloging-in-Publication Data
Invisible crimes : their victims and their regulation / edited by
Pamela Davies, Peter Francis, Victor Jupp.
p. cm.
Includes bibliographical references and index.
ISBN 0–312–22182–7 (cloth)
1. Commercial crimes—Prevention.   2. White collar crimes–
–Prevention.   3. Employee crimes—Prevention.   4. Victims of crimes.
I. Davies, Pamela, 1962–   .   II. Francis, Peter, 1968–   .
III. Jupp, Victor.
HV6768.I59   1999
364.16'8—dc21   99–11218
                                                                                        CIP

This book is printed on paper suitable for recycling and made from fully managed and
sustained forest sources.

10   9   8   7   6   5   4   3   2   1
08   07   06   05   04   03   02   01   00   99

Printed and bound in Great Britain by Antony Rowe Ltd, Chippenham, Wiltshire

To
Rory and Callum
Adam and Mark
Arthur and Pauline

Contents

Acknowledgements   vii

Notes on the Contributors   viii

Part I The Nature of Invisible Crimes   1

1   The Features of Invisible Crimes   3
    Victor Jupp, Pamela Davies and Peter Francis

2   White-Collar Crime: an Overview and Discussion   29
    Hazel Croall

3   Crime and Work Connections: Exploring the
    'Invisibility' of Workplace Crime   54
    Pamela Davies and Victor Jupp

Part II Types of Crimes and their Victims   75

4   Health and Safety Crimes: (In)visibility and
    the Problems of 'Knowing'   77
    Steve Tombs

5   Cybercrimes: New Wine, No Bottles?   105
    David Wall

Part III Regulation and Control   141

6   Regulating Fraud Revisited   143
    Michael Levi

7   Regulating the Invisible? The Case of
    Workplace Illicit Drug Use   168
    Peter Francis and Peter Wynarczyk

8   Watching the Workers: Crime, CCTV and the
    Workplace   208
    Michael McCahill and Clive Norris

9   Making Visible the Invisible?   232
    Peter Francis, Pamela Davies and Victor Jupp

Index   246

Acknowledgements

The idea for this book emerged from the University of Northumbria's Annual Criminal Justice Conference held during the spring of 1997. The theme and title of that conference was 'Crimes of the Powerful' and several of the contributors to this volume gave papers at that successful and enjoyable event. Our thanks go to all of those who presented papers at the conference, as well as to our colleagues and students at the University of Northumbria. In particular we are grateful to Clive Norris for the way he enthusiastically chaired the conference and for the administrative support provided by Heidi Robinson.

The theme and title of the original conference has undergone revision and refinement for this publication. The title *Invisible Crimes: Their Victims and Their Regulation* reflects the broader contents of the book as it developed out of the conference.

PAMELA DAVIES
PETER FRANCIS
VICTOR JUPP
Newcastle, November 1998

Notes on the Contributors

Hazel Croall is Senior Lecturer in Sociology at the University of Strathclyde. Her research interests lie in the area of white-collar crime and she has published several articles and the book, *White Collar Crime* (1992). She has also published in the general areas of criminology and the sociology of crime, having contributed to *Criminal Justice in England and Wales* (with Malcolm Davies and Jane Tyrer) (1995); her most recent publication is *Crime and Society in Britain* (1998).

Pamela Davies is Senior Lecturer in Criminology and Sociology at the University of Northumbria at Newcastle. She specialises in the teaching of crime as work, along with victimology and explaining crime and deviance. Previously she worked for Northumbria Police. Her research interests focus upon women who commit crimes for economic gain and how this fits into an informal economy. She has recently edited *Understanding Victimization* (1996) as well as *Policing Futures: the Police, Law Enforcement and the Twenty-First Century* (1997) (both with Peter Francis and Victor Jupp).

Peter Francis is Lecturer in Criminology and Sociology at the University of Northumbria at Newcastle. He has written in the area of criminology, penology and crime prevention. His books include *Prisons 2000* (with Roger Matthews) (1996), *Understanding Victimization* (1996) and *Policing Futures* (1997) (both with Pamela Davies and Victor Jupp). He is on the editorial board of *Criminal Justice Matters*. He is currently researching CCTV and crime prevention; and writing an introductory *Sourcebook on Criminology* and a textbook on *Contemporary Theories of Crime*.

Victor Jupp is Head of the Division of Sociology at the University of Northumbria at Newcastle. He specialises in the teaching of research methods and criminology. His publications include *Methods of Criminological Research* (1989), *Understanding Victimization* (with Pamela Davies and Peter

Francis) (1996), *Data Collection and Analysis* (with Roger Sapsford) (1996) and *Policing Futures* (with Pamela Davies and Peter Francis) (1997).

Michael Levi is Professor of Criminology at the University of Wales, Cardiff. He teaches criminology, policing and law and criminal justice courses, but his major current research interests are white-collar and organised crime, money laundering and asset forfeiture, and jury decision-making in white-collar crime trials, though he also writes on violent crime and on drugs, drink and crime. His most recent publications are: *Money Laundering in the UK: an Appraisal of Suspicion-Based Reporting* (1994) and *Victims of White-Collar Crime: the Social and Media Construction of Business Fraud* (1997). He has also written many articles on a variety of criminological and policing topics and is currently writing *Global Responses to Money-Laundering*.

Michael McCahill received a first-class honours degree in Sociology and Anthropology from the University of Hull in 1994. He went on to undertake an MA in criminology at Hull and subsequently was awarded an ESRC doctoral studentship to carry out a case study of the extent and impact of CCTV surveillance in a northern city.

Clive Norris is Lecturer in Criminology in the School of Comparative and Applied Social Sciences at the University of Hull and has written extensively on the sociology of policing. He has recently completed a two-year study examining the police use of informers. Currently he is writing up the findings from an ESRC-funded project on the operation of CCTV control rooms. His publications include: *The Conduct and Supervision of Criminal Investigations* (1992) The Royal Commission on Criminal Justice, Research Study No. 5 (with M. Maguire); *Surveillance, Closed Circuit Television and Social Control* (with J. Moran and G. Armstrong) (1998) and *The Maximum Surveillance Society: the Rise of Closed Circuit Televisual Surveillance* (with G. Armstrong) (1999).

Steve Tombs is Professor of Sociology in The Centre for Criminal Justice, Liverpool John Moores University, where he currently co-ordinates research activity. His teaching interests include criminological and social theory, and corporate crime. He is working on research projects examining media constructions of crime, and the regulation of the UK offshore oil industry. He is co-author of *Toxic Capitalism: Corporate Crime and the Chemical Industry* (with Frank Pearce) (1998), *Corporate Crime* (forthcoming, with Gary Slapper), and is currently co-editing *Risk, Management and Society* (forthcoming, with Denis Smith and Eve Coles). He has published numerous articles on the regulation and management of occupational safety and health, corporate crime, and corporate responsibility. He is also co-author of *People in Organisations* (with Kevin Gallagher, Ed Rose, Bob McClelland and John Reynolds) (1996).

David Wall is Senior Lecturer in Criminal Justice and Deputy Director of the Centre for Criminal Justice Studies, Department of Law, University of Leeds. He co-ordinates the Master's programme in criminal justice studies and lectures in criminal justice, policing and cyber-law. He has conducted research and published numerous articles on the themes of access to criminal justice, policing, information technology and the sociology of the legal professions. His most recent books include: *The Chief Constables of England and Wales: the Socio-Legal History of a Criminal Justice Elite* (1998) and *Access to Criminal Justice* (with Richard Young) (1996).

Peter Wynarczyk is Principal Lecturer in Economics at the University of Northumbria at Newcastle. His research and teaching interests are in macroeconomics, the economics of crime, and political economy, and he has published several articles in these areas. He is co-author of *A Modern Guide to Macroeconomics: an Introduction to Competing Schools of Thought* (with Brian Snowdon and Howard Vane) (1994) and is presently working on *The Dynamics of Capitalism: a Comparative Analysis of Schumpeter and Hirschman* (forthcoming).

Part I
The Nature of Invisible Crimes

1 The Features of Invisible Crimes

Victor Jupp, Pamela Davies and Peter Francis

INTRODUCTION

A wide range of events and actions is described in this book. This range includes, first, *crimes committed by employees against organisations* for which they work; such as using an organisation's facilities illegally and stealing work-based materials for personal use. A second example is that of *crimes perpetrated by organisations against their employees*; and include breaches of health and safety regulations resulting in workplace injuries, illnesses, accidents and sometimes deaths. Third, there are examples of *fraudulent behaviour*; including the use of another's money for personal or organisational gain without their knowledge or consent, and the use of 'sleaze' money to change the course of events, such as in political life or in the field of sport and leisure. Fourth, the range encompasses hitherto neglected *green crimes*; including the pollution of the environment by industrial organisations. Green crimes extend across international boundaries fuelled by the erosion of geographic and trade barriers between countries, and raise important issues regarding enforcement, regulation and control at the end of the twentieth century (South, 1997). For example, in March 1998 environmental ministers from the world's seven richest countries met in London to plan a strategy for dealing with the rapid growth in the smuggling of toxic waste, chlorofluorocarbons (CFCs) which destroy the ozone layer, and endangered species and products produced from them. Indeed, it has been estimated that such smuggling is worth up to £24 billion per year, making it the biggest illegal trade after drug trafficking. A fifth category addressed in this volume concerns that given the generic label 'cybercrime'. This includes computer crimes, such as hacking, the illegal appropriation of image and likeness and the use of the Internet in order to sell drugs, to publish obscene materials or to advertise services in relation to paedophilia.

The list could continue and would include: the mis-selling of pensions, the selling of infected food products, and the installation of unsafe utility appliances alongside the production and selling of counterfeit goods and industrial espionage, and so on. The above discussion merely represents a general guide to the range of events and actions covered within the various chapters of the book. In a number of the examples there is a clear link between the acts and events and the operation of the market economy and the pursuit of profit, while in others, there is not. In some cases, the acts are committed by organisations, and in other cases by private individuals. In many cases it is both. And finally, in some cases there is an obvious transparency and physical location attached to the act or event – obvious examples here include drug-taking in the workplace and employee theft – whereas others represent 'elusive' examples of criminal activity – such as what has been described as 'net crime' (Mann and Sutton, 1998).

The purpose of this introductory chapter is to consider the commonalities associated with this range of acts, events and activities and in doing so map the contours of invisible crime, victimisation and regulation. One obvious commonality is that, in their differing ways, many of the above examples represent instances of crime in the formal sense of being infractions of the law. However, beyond this formal sense of the term, crime as a reality can be difficult to recognise and pin down (Muncie, 1996). Actions can take on different meanings in different contexts and in different time periods: thus what some see as chastisement others consider to be violence against children; what is for some fiddling at work can be construed by employers and employees alike as a means of maintaining stability in the workplace; while what is viewed as enterprising activity in one era or historical period may be labelled as corporate crime in another.

Beyond such definitional issues there is the additional

point that some criminal acts are not transparent, even to the most vigilant observer. That is, they are not readily visible. The discovery and recognition of certain acts as 'crime' and the labelling of certain categories of people or institutions as 'criminal' depend on a host of factors, perhaps the most simplistic of which is that for certain acts to be defined as criminal, they must be witnessed, detected and/or experienced. This point acts as the foundation for the subsequent discussion – namely that a number of acts and events remain invisible. In particular, the chapters within this collection variously focus upon *degrees of invisibility* associated with particular acts and events, and their relations to mechanisms of enforcement, regulation and control. All of the acts or events described and discussed, we would argue, exhibit some degree of invisibility, or more precisely, what we choose to term 'relative invisibility'. They also remain relatively invisible to sociologists and criminologists and they do so because, in differing ways, and to differing degrees, they suffer from little evidence, literature and research focus.

MAPPING THE CONTOURS OF INVISIBILITY

The degree of invisibility is dependent upon a number of factors, often, but not always, specific to particular acts or events. For our purposes here, we detail a number of characteristic features against which degrees of invisibility can be judged. These include: *no knowledge* (there is little individual or public knowledge that the crime has been committed); *no statistics* (official statistics fail to record or classify the crime); *no theory* (criminologists and others neglect to explain the crime, its existence and its causes); *no research* (such crimes are not the object of social research, either in terms of their causes or their control); *no control* (there are no formal or systematic mechanisms for the control of such crimes); *no politics* (such crimes do not appear as a significant part of the public political agenda); and finally, *no panic!* (such crimes are not constituted as moral panics and their perpetrators are not portrayed as folk devils).

Although expressed in what may appear 'simplistic' and

'headline' fashion, such features, we would suggest, help provide a means of categorising and characterising a wide range of acts and events which remain invisible in everyday life. Moreover, when combined, such features constitute a template with which to assess relative invisibility. The elements of this template (knowledge – statistics – theory – research – control – politics – panic!) can be viewed as independent of one another but there is also the potential for interaction and mutual reinforcement. For example, ignorance of victimisation (no knowledge) often leads to non-recording in official statistics (no statistics) which in turn can have consequences in terms of under-theorising by academics (no theory), lack of policy-making at government level (no politics) and little consideration by the popular media (no panic!). The lack of consideration by the media can have a desensitising effect on awareness of future victimisation. And so on.

Obviously, particular acts or events do not necessarily exhibit all of these features outlined above, nor will they exhibit them to the same degree at any given point in time. The relative invisibility of particular acts and events and their subsequent recognition and identification as crime depends on whether the template fits (do the elements apply?), the degree to which it fits (to what extent does it apply?) and the power of interactive effects (to what extent do the elements reinforce one another?). The latter encourages further analysis in terms of exploring the reasons for mutual reinforcements and also the processes and mechanisms by which such reinforcements occur.

The rest of this chapter offers a discussion of each characteristic feature, before outlining the structure and content of the various contributions to this volume.

SEVEN FEATURES OF INVISIBILITY

No Knowledge

The extent to which we know about the perpetration of crime is very much dependent on the extent to which victims of crime are aware that they are victims, and also on whether they inform the police (or others) of their victimisation. The lack of private and subsequent public recognition of victimisation can depend on a host of factors. First, there is the *awareness problem*. Some individuals, organisations or government bodies may not be aware that a crime has been committed against them. The ingenuity of the fraudster, the complexity of the act and the lack of knowledge and vigilance of the victim can all conspire to render the crime invisible. For example, the organisational structures and processes of the global money market and the skill with which these can be electronically manipulated to transfer capital from one location to another is bewildering to most of us. As Croall points out in Chapter 2, financial victimisation often affects vulnerable groups, such as pensioners, who are perhaps less likely than most to know about and understand, let alone report, such acts.

Second, there is the *normalisation problem*. Even where individuals are aware that an act or event has taken place it can be taken for granted as normal rather than as criminal. For example, workers in hazardous industries may see themselves as doing a difficult job rather then as victims of illicit health and safety practices. Also, as Francis and Wynarczyk highlight in Chapter 7, taking drugs outside the workplace may not be deemed problematic for the worker, but rather part and parcel of recreational life. Finally, employers who are the victims of 'fiddles' by employees may see this as acceptable because it harmoniously bonds workers to the organisation, produces stability in the workplace and offers a relatively inexpensive way of providing extra payment to workers. Provided employee theft does not become too excessive, employers are often apt to turn a 'blind eye', realising the potential benefits. In Chapter 8, McCahill and Norris describe how the introduction of CCTV in the workplace can have the consequence, sometimes unintentionally, of disturbing such equilibrium.

A third point relates to the *problem of ideology*. Typically, specific instances such as those described above are framed within wider ideological mechanisms which operate at a societal level. These are highly influential in determining what is viewed as 'right', 'wrong', 'acceptable', 'legitimate' and 'illegitimate', irrespective of the dictat of the formal letter of the law. The interaction between such mechanisms and formal law can lead to a 'blurring effect' at particular boundaries, rendering certain kinds of criminal activities invisible. In Chapter 3 Davies and Jupp focus on the interface between crime and work, and the blurring between what is seen as enterprising activity and what is seen as illegitimate practice and between what is crime and what is work. Similarly Francis and Wynarczyk in Chapter 7, draw attention to conceptual problems surrounding 'drug use *at* work' and 'drug use *and* work' and of how such definitions are bound up within broader conventional wisdoms about drug misuse.

Finally, there is the *collusion problem*. There are instances where individuals collude in their own potential victimisation, for example by knowingly accepting high wages in compensation for working where there are obvious breaches of health and safety regulations, accepting cheap food products knowing that there is a potential risk regarding their quality, or taking substances which may affect their personal safety within the workplace environs. In effect, the individual enters into an informal contract which renders the criminal activity invisible (unless detected by others). Withdrawing knowledge of such activities, and also failing to report victimisation where it occurs, is a key condition of such informal contracts.

No Statistics

Public knowledge about crime depends to a large extent on official statistics of crime as recorded by the police (Coleman and Moynihan, 1996). Such statistics, which are reproduced annually in the Home Office publication *Criminal Statistics England and Wales* (see Home Office, 1997), provide the basis for political decisions as to what is viewed as problematic and what to do about it (politics); operational decision-making about the mechanisms of detection and enforcement (control); academic theorising as to the causes of crime, and crime of particular kinds (theory); and newspaper stories (panic!). Two kinds of statistics are influential. First, there are statistics on offences recorded by the police and secondly, statistics on known offenders. The latter are contingent on the former in so far as they provide data on the numbers of people charged with offences which have been recorded by the police. Statistics on offences recorded by the police are used as an index of the extent of crime in society (the crime rate) and statistics on known offenders are used as one index of police efficiency (the clear-up rate).

It is well recognised that, despite their use by politicians, law enforcers, academics and the media, official statistics under-represent the full extent of crime. This is something which is well established by surveys of victims, such as the *British Crime Survey* (see Hough and Mayhew, 1982; Mayhew, 1996; Mirrlees-Black, Mayhew and Percy, 1996). Such surveys not only indicate under-recording of crime in general but also how the extent of under-recording can vary accordingly to the type and nature of crime and victim. The types of crime described and discussed in subsequent chapters are characterised by such under-representation, and in many cases, non-representation. This is the result of a number of factors.

It is a well used cliché that official statistics on crime start their life 'on the streets' – an act is perpetrated which is witnessed and interpreted by a police officer as criminal, or, as is much more likely, observed by a witness or experienced by a victim. Typically, the crimes we are concerned with here are not committed on the streets, but well away from public gaze. As a result, knowledge of such acts is more dependent than usual on victims reporting their victimisation to the police. However, as discussed in the previous section, there are reasons for this not occurring. For example, victims may be unaware that a crime has been committed; they may treat the crime as 'normal' and not something to be reported; they may be frightened and intimidated; or they may be unwilling to report the crime to the police because it is something in which they have colluded. Or in the case of drug use, the crime may also be viewed as victimless!

Even where an action or event is reported to the police, the police must be satisfied that a crime has taken place. The complexity of some of the crimes, especially those relating to financial transaction, together with the ingenuity and specialist knowledge of those carrying them out, often means that the police are unable to satisfy themselves that a crime has been perpetrated and therefore should be recorded as such. Even where there is sufficient confidence to record a crime, the same arguments about complexity, ingenuity and specialist knowledge *vis-à-vis* the police severely restrict the possibility of a prosecution. For all of these reasons, we would suggest the types of crime described in subsequent chapters are relatively invisible – that is, invisible to a greater or lesser extent – in official criminal statistics, whether these be statistics on recorded offences or known offenders.

The statistics relating to injuries and deaths at work present particular problems. As Tombs points out in Chapter 4, it is necessary to look at sources of data other than governmental statistics on crime. Even then, it is difficult to know, for example, how many people are killed at work in any given year. There are technical reasons for this such as the fact that health and safety statistics do not cover fatal injuries associated with sea fishing or driving a car in the course of employment. Further, it is not possible to assemble accurate data on the number of deaths at work which can be attributed to criminal actions or negligence on the part of management or employers. Tombs' research relies on secondary analysis of special investigations undertaken by the Health and Safety Executive into fatalities at work, commissions of inquiry about disasters and accident investigation reports. What such secondary analysis provides is an indication of the number of cases where there is a criminal case to answer.

The development of crime surveys, especially victim surveys, has been important in providing estimates of the extent of unrecorded crime. Typically, crime surveys are either community-based and cross-sectional (that is, studying a representative sample at a particular point in time) or nationally based and time series in design (that is, studying different samples at different points in time with a view to examining trends). The Home Office-sponsored British Crime Survey, is an example of the latter. Samples of households, and individuals within households, are selected for interview. The interviewer asks about victimisation during a specified period of time, whether crimes were reported and also about fear of crime. In the main, victim surveys collect data from and about individuals. There is evidence that for a range of reasons respondents are more willing to report victimisation to interviewers than to police. Therefore such surveys are valuable in gaining estimates of the 'dark figure of unrecorded crime'. However, they are unable to collect data on crimes about which victims are unaware, and they also tend to miss crimes where there is a diffusion and multiplicity of victims such as environmental pollution. Further, there tends to be a focus on 'street-level' crime and on conventional crime rather than crimes by or against business corporations and governments or the more elusive green crimes and cyber-crimes. This is partly the result of relying on individuals as the source of data and as the primary unit of analysis and partly because the research design is influenced by the main point of comparison, namely official crime statistics, which also tend to capture the conventional and the visible rather than the unconventional and the invisible.

Other kinds of survey have been carried out. For example in Chapter 2 Croall refers to surveys sponsored by industrial and other organisations with the purpose of estimating the extent of invisible crime. These surveys are aimed at crimes committed against such organisations, and/or in organisations' time and space, for example by customers or employees, and are often used to justify the introduction of crime prevention measures such as CCTV (see McCahill and Norris in Chapter 8). However, as Davies and Jupp (Chapter 3) highlight, such surveys are not as regular or as high profile as the British Crime Survey. Moreover, despite their value, in some instances, as Francis and Wynarczyk highlight in Chapter 7, self-report surveys are open to numerous criticisms. In particular, drawing upon a discussion of illicit drug use at work, these writers draw attention to both conceptual and methodological problems affecting the measurement of self-reported workplace illicit drug use, and stress the need for caution when interpreting such data.

There is one further tradition of research closely associated with investigative journalism and that is the case study, which does focus on invisible crimes. This often takes the form of an exposé which is informative, rich in detail, experiential in relation to victimisation and, above all, critical in stance. Such exposés are invaluable in uncovering crimes, and their causes, which would otherwise remain invisible. However, they do not provide strong bases for making statistical inferences about the full extent of such crimes.

No Theory

The history and contemporary contours of criminological theorising are characterised both by diversity and fragmentation in terms of what is seen as problematic (Nelken, 1994; Francis, 1999). Such fragmentation and diversity are the result of both internal developments in criminology in the UK and of external changes affecting wider social, political and economic contexts, including those relating to law and order and how these have impacted on the study of crime and criminal justice (some aspects of which are discussed in the section entitled 'No politics').

An analysis of the development of criminological theorising demonstrates that, among academics at least, there is no simple conception of crime, nor universal agreement on what are or what should be the central problems of criminology, its key theoretical underpinnings or the primary means of carrying out criminological research (Walklate, 1998). It is, perhaps, best to think not of a unitary discipline entitled criminology but of different 'ways of thinking' about crime, victimisation, criminalisation and crime control. It is also possible to suggest a reflective strategy for examining different 'ways of thinking' (for a more detailed discussion of this see Jupp, 1996). Such a reflective strategy starts from a position of looking at criminology-as-a-form-of-knowledge and seeks to take apart, or deconstruct, that knowledge in terms of its key elements and the relations between them. Two key elements are of relevance here: first, the central problems of criminology, and second, the theoretical approaches used to address such problems. Other elements include the range of strategies of crime control – indicated by theoretical approaches – to deal with what is seen as problematic (discussed in the section entitled 'No control') and also the kinds of research carried out, or not carried out (discussed in the section entitled 'No research'). There is also the potential to further develop this process of deconstruction in terms of seeking to relate those key elements and relations between them, to underpinning institutional and social contexts. In this way the strategy of deconstruction does not simply involve taking apart knowledge, but also involves identifying the location of its production. One of the key themes of this volume, and especially of Chapter 4 by Steve Tombs, is that the political economy of social research (see also Francis and Wynarczyk in Chapter 7) and also the pre-eminence of state-sponsored (and to a lesser extent, business-sponsored) research means that an examination of crimes considered here lies relatively low on the criminological agenda. Without research, or without sponsored research or research which follows traditional outputs (such as statistical indicators) critical theorising alone is wide open to accusations of political bias from those who have a vested interest in the invisibility of certain crimes.

A deconstruction of the main theoretical strands associated with the emergence and development of criminology – that is in terms of what is seen as problematic within each strand and what kind of explanation is put forward – would indicate an overriding concern with so-called conventional crimes such as street-level crimes and especially crimes committed by juveniles, and a preponderance of explanations in causal terms, especially but not exclusively in relation to individual predispositions and early socialisation within the family. Where this has not been the case there has been a focus on crime at the level of the community (see Muncie and McLaughlin, 1996). Within these developments there has been consideration of, and theorising about, the kinds of crimes addressed in this volume; for example, white-collar crime (following in the footsteps of Sutherland's (1949) work), so-called crimes of the powerful (emanating from within a radical tradition; see Pearce, 1976) and drug abuse.

However, overall, theorising about 'invisible crimes' has not held a significant position within the broad sweep of the development of criminology. A number of reasons can be put forward for this. For example, there has been the pre-eminence of what Cohen (1981) has described as conventional or mainstream criminology with its close association to the Home Office and officially sponsored research (see also Hudson, 1993). Its features focus on individual pathology, such as explanations set in causal terms, the correction of individuals and on crimes about which we already have knowledge and empirical evidence. Conventional or mainstream theorising tends to address specific sections of the population. Such sections are singled out because of statistical associations – usually correlational – between criminal behaviour and individual attributes such as social class, ethnicity, age and income level. Such statistical analysis relies very much on official statistics as a form of data (and, to a certain extent, on crime surveys). As was argued in the preceding section such statistics are partial and their composition depends to a heavy degree on 'knowledge' and 'visibility'. In their differing ways criminologists and others have also addressed issues of victimisation and of crime prevention and control (see Walklate, 1989; Mawby and Walklate, 1994; Davies et al., 1996). However, in the main this has been in terms of individual victimisation and of the prevention and control of street-level crime rather than in terms of, say, multiple victimisation of environmental pollution or prevention and control of fraud in financial institutions.

One final point can be made in this section. The sheer diversity of what are termed invisible crimes and also of the 'sites' at which they are committed – at the workplace, on the Internet, in the financial marketplace – probably militates against the development of any comprehensive theory of such crimes. This diversity of act and of site, together with their respective distinctive features and the onset of postmodernism could lead to the viewpoint that criminology as it has developed since the turn of the century – and despite its various contours of 'ways of knowing' – is too narrow and constraining to address the full range of crimes in this volume (see Nelken, 1994). It may well be the case that theorising is better placed outside of criminology in, say, theories about globalisation (see Nelken, 1997) or in political economy (see Taylor, 1997). This is akin to the argument of Smart and others in relation to feminist approaches to criminology (Smart, 1990). For Smart (1990: 462) feminist postmodernism 'starts from a different place and proceeds in different directions' from forms of feminism working within the confines of criminology. It is argued that the promise of feminist postmodernism is such that the question: what has criminology to offer feminism? should be recast as: what has feminism to offer criminology? This advocates a way of thinking beyond criminology.

No Research

To say that there has been no research on invisible crimes would be untrue and would do an injustice to those working in the field, including authors of chapters in this volume. However, in terms of the totality of criminological research output it has been relatively small. There are a number of reasons for this. First, there are the mutually reinforcing effects of the paucity of knowledge, statistics and theory in relation to invisible crimes. With regard to knowledge, or more accurately, the lack of it, there is the obvious point that what we do not know about we cannot research. With regard to official statistics on crime, the secondary analysis of such data is an important and influential aspect of criminological research. The categories of crime and the categories of people represented in official data, together with statistical relations which can be established between them, have been important in framing what is viewed as problematic in criminology and also the kinds of theoretical approaches which are predominant. However, as was argued earlier, such statistics represent only a partial picture of the extent of crime and of the number and range of offenders. Some crimes are under-represented in official data and therefore research based on secondary analysis is not especially feasible. On the other hand, research on crimes which *are* represented is entirely feasible and this is one important influence on the profile of the criminological research output.

Additionally, theory also plays a part especially in relation to framing and identifying what is problematic and therefore worthy of subsequent research (and, of course, theory itself is influenced by relationships found in albeit partial official data). What was described in the previous section as the limited and constraining nature of conventional and traditional theorising – with its emphasis on individual pathology, the search for causes and the prevention and control of street-level crime – draws boundaries around certain activities as legitimate areas for investigation whilst marginalising others.

There are also practical aspects of conducting social inquiry which restrict the feasibility and possibility of researching invisible crimes. Research involves the collection and analysis of data with which to frame conclusions in relation to a research problem. The validity of any research – which to some extent influences its legitimation – depends upon the extent to which the data supports the conclusions. Mention has already been made of the range and type of data, especially to official statistics. Typically, what we have characterised as invisible crimes involve vested interests, often interests which have the power to protect their position. Such protection involves withholding information which could expose the existence of crime, its extent and its perpetrators or producing information in support of particular argument or policy decision. It is often inconceivable that there would be voluntary and open publication of such information. In the absence of this, researchers must go in search of data and inevitably this brings them into contact and negotiation with gatekeepers. Gatekeepers are individuals or groups of individuals who have the power to control access to data required to accomplish research. This may involve controlling access to forms of secondary data such as statistics, documents and records and/or withholding permission for the conduct of primary research such as social surveys of observational studies. Gatekeepers may exercise their control by formal means, for example by use of legal powers, or informally, for example by 'losing' sensitive documents (for an example of effective gatekeeping in relation to a proposed study of police corruption see Punch, 1985). Further, there can be layers of gatekeepers, such that the support of one does not necessarily guarantee that of another. A chief executive may support research in his/her organisation but that, by itself, does not give access to the interior of the informal 'occupational cultures'. Where all gatekeepers exercise their power there is little hope! The veneer of access might be guaranteed only to lead to 'deliberate obfuscation' (see Tombs, Chapter 4) and stalling techniques.

In relation to the crimes covered in this volume there are parties who have vested interests in relation to withholding information about their activities – parties who by one means or another are able to exercise power to deny researchers access to data with which to formulate and support conclusions. In the absence of such data either the research is not carried out or it is carried out by means that are not typically found in standard texts on research methods (Sapsford and Jupp, 1996; Jupp et al., 1999). Indeed there is a case for arguing that the standard methods of research such as social surveys, experimental methods, observation and analysis of official statistics collude in the invisibility of some crimes because of their inability to uncover such crimes. Less conventional and formal methods such as reliance on 'whistle-blowers' exposes research to the claim that it is unscientific and biased. Researchers of invisible crimes find themselves in a 'catch-22' situation. Conventional methods of research hardly touch the issues they want to address but if they do not use them and turn to alternative, less conventional methods their work is open to denigration especially by those who have a vested interest in doing so.

Finally, there are issues to do with the politics of social research (recognising, of course, that matters to do with the conduct of research are inextricably linked to wider issues of power and politics). The politics of social research involves relationships between the subjects of research, the researchers, the sponsors, the gatekeepers and the power relations between them. The exercise of power either to pursue or to protect interest, or perhaps both, influences what gets researched, what gets published and what gets used (for a general discussion of the politics of criminological research see Jupp 1989, and Hughes, 1996). With regards to the pursuance of particular goals, Francis and Wynarczyk in Chapter 7 highlight how the production of research findings may help 'fan the flames' of regulatory developments even when they may not be necessary. That is, those with a vested interest in the development of ever more sophisticated technologies of control may offer findings which in some way or other serve their business interests. We can take just one aspect to illustrate the general issue of the influence of politics on research, namely funding and the carrying out of research. Not all research needs funding, but most of it does. Where there are complex issues to be investigated such as in corporate fraud or health and safety matters, research can be extremely time-consuming and expensive in terms of staff costs. There is an increasing emphasis in the public funding of research on 'milestones', 'deliverables', and 'utility' in relation to who are perceived as the 'stakeholders' in any proposed research. The problems of this for research into health and safety crimes are well illustrated in Chapter 4. As Tombs points out, where research questions and theoretical approaches are likely to be critical of existing social relations and the dominant business ideologies within them, proposed research is unlikely to get funding. The political economy of research, including the public funding of research, 'does not bode well for a critical academic assault upon collective social ignorance of corporate crime in general, and of safety and health crime in particular' (p. 99).

No Control

The crimes outlined in subsequent chapters are characterised by problems of effective regulation, control and enforcement. A wide variety of crimes are covered and the extent to which there are problems of control and the reasons for this can vary from one category of crime to another.

First, a key point is that in many instances there is a lack of knowledge that crimes have occurred. As mentioned earlier, one reason for this is that there is often a close interaction of legitimate and illegitimate activities which not only influences the extent of reporting but also makes detection and control difficult. The blurring of the boundaries between what is 'legitimate' and what is not is discussed by Davies and Jupp in Chapter 3 in relation to the connections between crime and work and is further elab-

orated by Tombs (Chapter 4), Levi (Chapter 6) and Francis
and Wynarczyk (Chapter 7). For example, Tombs argues
that the business ideology which became especially strong
in the UK in the 1980s and 1990s has meant that governments and law enforcement agencies are unable or unwilling to make clear distinctions between some forms of
enterprising entrepreneurial activity and some forms of
criminal activity. Further, as Levi argues, even people on
the inside show an unwillingness to recognise and accept
that what they are doing is illegitimate or that 'people like
us would do such a thing'. This can influence reporting,
regulation control and enforcement. The blurring of boundaries between the legitimate and the illegitimate is further
compounded by the complexity of many crimes, for example
in relation to fraud, but also the location and the diffusion
of offenders. Such diffusion and complexity not only mean
that detection is difficult but also that successful prosecution is problematic. The accumulation of evidence and the
presentation and defence of it by the Crown Prosecution
Service and in the courts is typically time consuming and
costly, and does not result in a successful outcome. Not
only have agencies such as the Serious Fraud Office found
it difficult to gain successful prosecutions, but there is also
the belief that because of the length and cost of such cases
ensuing results are unfair and unsatisfactory for everyone
– including the defendants, jurors, judges, victims and tax-
payers. Second, there are issues regarding the position of
corporate and other such crimes within wider policing pri-
orities. For example, in Chapter 6, Levi notes that while
interest among police chiefs in fraud has increased since
the 1980s, especially in the light of several high profile
cases, 'Nevertheless, outside the City of London, there is
very little appreciation by chief officers of the importance
of policing fraud, whether of the élite or blue-collar kind:
their practical indifference extends to all crimes with corporate victims, and even to most crimes against investors'
(p. 154).

A number of reasons are suggested for this situation including the predominance of a Victorian conception of
prudence which incorporates the belief that people who
do not take sufficient care of their own property deserve

scant sympathy. There are also pragmatic factors relating specifically to policing, such as that there has been little pressure from government or from police authorities to do something about fraud; unsophisticated appreciation and knowledge amongst police officers of the world of business; and the low success rate associated with investigations of fraud.

Finally, mention can be made of the international dimension of much corporate-type crime (Nelken, 1997). Where crime is international, especially in a context of increasing globalisation and fewer barriers between nation-states, the possibility of detection, let alone prevention and control, is made more difficult. Within one country, such as the UK, there can be conflicts between various agencies such as the police, the Inland Revenue and the Serious Fraud Office with regard to regulation control and enforcement. Such conflicts are compounded when cross-national co-operation is required. Furthermore, as Wall speculates in Chapter 5 the prognosis for successful 'governance' of cybercrimes which not only transcend national states but have no obvious physical location, is not especially favourable. The development of the Internet and the potential for cybercrimes in the new millennium throw into sharp relief the key issues regarding the control of invisible crimes, namely, problems regarding effective regulation, control and enforcement (which can be lengthy and costly and often do not work) and the issues of self-regulation and compliance (which rely on 'knowledge' and co-operation and run into problems of blurring between what is legitimate and what is not as well as the deeply embedded belief that 'people like us don't do things "like that" – so what is there to report?').

No Politics

The political agenda is very influential, not only in terms of defining crime but also in terms of the prevention and control of criminal activities. Politics determines the law and order issues of our time. Also, as indicated in an earlier section, politics is also an important element in the political economy of research funding and in determining what kinds of research influences policy and with what effect.

There have been exposés of health and safety issues (see, for example, Chapter 4), major court cases involving fraud (see, for example, Chapter 6) and the use of drugs at work (see Chapter 7) which have resulted in these and other invisible crimes appearing on the political agenda. Indeed, some writers, for example Punch (1997) have suggested that business deviance in particular has emerged as a considerable social problem. However, others, including Croall in Chapter 2, argue that despite high-profile cases and exposés and also the proliferation of victim and pressure groups – such as those seeking compensation in the wake of the Maxwell case – there is no real evidence of corporate business or white-collar misdemeanours displacing street-level crimes as a major public concern.

An analysis of the manifesto of the two main political parties, produced prior to the 1997 general election, would lend support to this viewpoint. For example, the Conservative Party used the following banner quotation as part of its pledge for a safe and civil society: 'People have a right to sleep safely in their homes and walk safely on the streets. Governments have a duty to maintain that security' (Conservative Party, 1997: 35). Specific proposals included ensuring safer communities (by a crackdown on petty crime), improved public order and support for the installation of CCTV in town centres; and tackling juvenile crime (by having more police, targeting persistent criminals, more prison places, extending tagging orders and mandatory sentences for burglars and drug dealers). There is a short section under law and order relating to city (financial as opposed to inner) crime which recognises that 'Crime that takes place through manipulation of financial accounts and markets is as serious as crime on the street' (Conservative Party, 1997: 37). However, this section represents only three paragraphs out of thirty-seven devoted to law and order. What is more there is only one proposal relating to 'city crime', namely to modernise the current system of dealing with financial fraud, out of a total of fourteen law and order proposals.

A similar emphasis on individual and street-level crime, under the banner 'Tough on crime and tough on causes of crime', can be found in the policies and proposals of the Labour Party – the eventual victors of the 1997 election campaign. Key elements of their manifesto pledges involved dealing with youth crime, placing greater responsibility on individuals and on parents in relation to their children's actions, stronger measures to secure conviction, tougher sentencing and ways of dealing with disorder, especially that committed by young petty offenders. In another section there is a pledge to crack down on dishonesty in the benefit system. It would be untrue to suggest that the kinds of crimes covered in this volume are not part of the political agenda: there is increasing concern with environmental pollution, financial fraud, health and safety at work, food safety and animal welfare. However, it would be equally unwise to suggest that these crimes are viewed as central to law and order, as New Labour's first piece of legislation, entitled the Crime and Disorder Bill (1997), highlights well (see *Criminal Justice Matters*, 1998 and Francis and Fraser, 1999 for a thorough review and evaluation of the Bill and its proposed component parts, mechanisms and strategies).

No Panic

The politics of law and order is closely bound up with moral panic about crime and especially crimes and criminals of particular types (Cohen, 1980; Thompson, 1998). The notion of moral panic has been influential in criminology not least because it has established links between the media reporting of crime, public and political concern about crime, fear of crime, responses of law enforcement agencies, the reporting of crime and of victimisation by members of the public and the composition of official crime statistics. In its simplest form, moral panic refers to public reaction, especially media and political reaction, to particular types of crime. It incorporates a model which is organised around media outrage at particular events and actions, the development of wider public surveillance and control, subsequent reaction from those believed to be responsible for the events and actions and confirmation of the validity of the initial media outrage as a result of the subsequent reaction. The creation of a moral panic also involves the creation of 'folk devils', that is, the individual or category of individuals at the heart of the panic. The folk devil is viewed as responsible for the actions and events about which there is such concern and is the symbol of what is wrong with society. It is usually claimed that if society can deal with folk devils by strategies and policies of crime control it will be able to deal with that which is wrong in society.

The previous section has illustrated how individual and street-level crimes are high on the political agenda. There is a close connection between the formulation of such agenda and the construction and amplification of moral panics and folk devils in the media. There has been increased awareness of financial scandals, illicit dealings on behalf of governments, 'sleaze' amongst politicians, breaches of food safety regulations to mention but a few. However, these are hardly the stuff of moral panics. They are often portrayed as scandals which are exposed rather than examples of sustained deviant or criminal activity. They are often treated as 'one-offs' and the fault of particular individuals at particular times rather than the outcome of deep-seated problems. Some activities, for example those which produce hazards and health risks at work, are viewed as social problems rather than fundamental law and order problems (even though, as Tombs points out in Chapter 4, deaths from health and safety crimes far outnumber deaths from homicide). Perhaps, most fundamentally, the complexity of many of the crimes covered in this book and the diffusion of culprits mean that there is no obvious folk devil whose evils can be described in media rhetoric and portrayed visually in front-page photographs, such that we can recognise him or her (or examples of him or her) when we come across them. In the absence of the social construction of moral outrage and of folk devils there is, quite simply, no panic!

INVISIBLE CRIMES: THEIR NATURE, TYPE AND CONTROL

The 'headline' features which have been used in the preceding discussion to categorise and characterise invisible crimes emerge at different points in subsequent chapters. In order to focus discussion we have divided the book into three parts, each focusing upon one particular aspect of

invisibility, although not exclusively. Part I provides discussion
on the nature of invisible crimes and victimisations; Part
II on their form, type and range; and Part III provides
analysis of issues regarding their control and regulation.
Chapter 2 offers a critical review of white-collar crime.
In doing so, its author Hazel Croall raises definitional issues
as to what constitutes white-collar crime. A key starting point
in discussion of such crimes is Sutherland's (1949)
groundbreaking work which emphasises the status and power
of offenders. Croall's theme is that a focus on the criminal
act and its nature rather than just the offender encourages
a much wider analysis in terms of how white-collar crime
is related to other forms of crime and also other forms of
business activity; of the organisational complexity of some
of the offences; of the sites of white-collar crime; and the
victims of crime and the beneficiaries of crime. A central
plank in her argument is that focusing on the nature of
the criminal act rather than solely on the offender does
not mean that issues of power, class and status are excluded
from any resulting analysis. This general theme of changing
and widening the focus of attention is further developed
by Pamela Davies and Victor Jupp in Chapter 3, where
some of the values of considering the location of criminal
activity are outlined. This is done in the context of work.
There is a consideration of the variety of connections between
work and crime and of the blurred boundaries between
what are viewed as legitimate and illegitimate activities. The
crime–work equation is explored in terms of looking at
work-as-crime and crime-as-work.

Part II of the book develops some of the headline themes
in the context of different types of invisible crimes. In
Chapter 4 Steve Tombs considers crimes associated with
lack of health and safety at work. He emphasises the invisibility of such crimes in comparison with the more conventional crimes such as theft from the person or house burglary.
It is argued that such relative invisibility is the outcome of
factors such as the absence of health and safety crimes in
law and order campaigns; the reluctance of the media to
attach a criminal tag to infractions of health and safety
regulations; and the methodological and political problems
of collecting data on health and safety crimes so that

conclusions derived from them attract public and political legitimation. The discussion by David Wall in Chapter 5 focuses upon cyberspace as a new 'risk community' and location for a range of crimes such as cyber-trespass, cyber-theft, cyber-obscenity and cyber-violence. The social impact of cyberspace, according to Wall, raises new issues about the nature of crime, about the distinctions between legitimate and illegitimate activities and about types of offenders. Such issues are at the centre of increasing concerns about the inability of existing law enforcement mechanisms to regulate behaviour in cyberspace.

The regulation and control of invisible crimes is further developed in Part III. In Chapter 6 Michael Levi reviews some of the key themes in the policing and prosecution of fraud in the years since he published his seminal work *Regulating Fraud* (Levi, 1988). These include changes in investigation and prosecution, especially the setting up of the Serious Fraud Office (SFO); the need to locate British fraud investigation in an international context and as the outcome of globalisation of financial markets; and debates regarding alternative mechanisms of regulation and control, such as those which surround the notion of regulatory justice. Peter Francis and Peter Wynarczyk in Chapter 7 critically review developments aimed at regulating workplace illicit drug use. In doing so, the authors show how the case for workplace regulation is in many ways embedded within inconclusive research evidence and conventional wisdoms about the effects of workplace drug use. Calling for a more enlightened approach to understanding the relations between the workplace, risk and employee drug use, these authors stress the need for caution in travelling down what they see as the path of 'regulating the invisible', arguing there is a danger of being sold the drug testing myth. Rather it is their view that 'a better starting point would be to gain an improved understanding of the actual nature of, and relations between, illicit drugs, employee performance and the workplace' (p. 170). In the penultimate chapter, Michael McCahill and Clive Norris document the growth of CCTV as a form of regulation and control and, in doing so, focus on its use in the workplace. They argue that the use of cameras in such locations means that employers can no longer turn a blind eye to the 'fiddles' which earlier writers (see, for example, Ditton, 1976) suggest are functional for harmony and stability in the workplace. Throughout the various contributions to this volume, the overriding theme is in making the invisible visible. In the concluding chapter, entitled 'Making Visible the Invisible?', we raise a number of further issues regarding the nature, form and control of invisible crimes, and highlight also the need for a critical and reflexive approach to the subject area. If collections such as this are to make an impact in refocusing the criminological telescope to cover those acts, events and locations that are all too often neglected, then there is a serious need to provide innovations in both methodology and theoretical exploration, as well as in offering explicit yet informed critiques and evaluation of much current policy and practice, alongside exploration of the power and politics which help construct our knowledge of any particular act or event.

REFERENCES

Cohen, S. (1980) *Folk Devils and Moral Panics* (London: Martin Robertson).
Cohen, S. (1981) 'Footprints in the Sand: a Further Report on Criminology and the Sociology of Deviance in Britain', in M. Fitzgerald, G. McClennan and J. Pawson (eds.), *Crime and Society* (London: Routledge).
Coleman, C. and Moynihan, J. (1996) *Understanding Crime Data* (Buckingham: Open University Press).
Conservative Party (1997) *Manifesto* (London: Conservative Central Office).
Criminal Justice Matters (1998) Crime and Disorder, No. 31, Spring (London: ISTD).
Davies, P., Francis, P. and Jupp, V. (eds.) (1996) *Understanding Victimization* (Newcastle: Northumbria Social Sciences Press).
Ditton, J. (1976) *Part-Time Crime* (London: Macmillan).
Francis, P. (forthcoming, 1999) *Contemporary Theories of Crime* (London: Sage).
Francis, P. and Fraser, P. (1999) *Building Safer Communities* (London: ISTD)
Home Office (1997) *Criminal Statistics England and Wales* (London: Home Office).
Hough, M. and Mayhew, P. (1982) *The British Crime Survey*, Home Of-

fice Research Study, No. 76 (London: Home Office).

Hudson, B. (1993) *Penal Policy and Social Justice* (London: Sage).

Hughes, G. (1996) 'The Politics of Criminological Research', in R. Sapsford (ed.), *Research Methods in Crime and Criminal Justice* (Buckingham: Open University).

Jupp, V. (1989) *Methods of Criminological Research* (London: Routledge).

Jupp, V. (1996) 'The Contours of Criminology', in R. Sapsford (ed.), *Research Methods in Crime and Criminal Justice* (Buckingham: Open University).

Jupp, V., Davies, P. and Francis, P. (forthcoming 1999) *Criminology in the Field: The Practice of Criminological Research* (London: Sage).

Levi, M. (1988) *Regulating Fraud: White-Collar Crime and the Criminal Process* (London: Routledge).

Mann, D. and Sutton, M. (1998) '>>Netcrime: More Change in the Organization of Thieving', *British Journal of Criminology*, 38/2, Spring, 201–29.

Mawby, R. and Walklate, S. (1994) *Critical Victimology* (London: Sage).

Mayhew, P. (1996) 'The British Crime Survey', in P. Davies, P. Francis and V. Jupp (eds.), *Understanding Victimization* (Newcastle: Northumbria Social Sciences Press).

Mirrlees-Black, C., Mayhew, P. and Percy, A. (1996) *The 1996 British Crime Survey*, Home Office Statistical Bulletin, Issue 19/96 (London: Home Office).

Muncie, J. (1996) 'The Construction and Deconstruction of Crime', in J. Muncie and E. McLaughlin (eds.), *The Problem of Crime* (London: Sage in association with the Open University).

Muncie, J. and McLaughlin, E. (eds.) (1996) *The Problem of Crime* (London: Sage in association with the Open University).

Nelken, D. (ed.) (1994) *The Future of Criminology* (London: Sage).

Nelken, D. (1997) 'Understanding Criminal Justice Comparatively', in M. Maguire, R. Morgan and R. Reiner (eds.), *The Oxford Handbook of Criminology*, 2nd edn (Oxford: Clarendon), 559–76.

Pearce, F. (1976) *Crimes of the Powerful: Marxism, Crime and Deviance* (London: Pluto).

Punch, M. (1985) *Conduct Unbecoming: the Social Construction of Police Deviance and Control* (London: Sage).

Punch, M. (1997) *Corporate Misconduct* (London: Sage).

Sapsford, R. and Jupp, V. (eds.) (1996) *Data Collection and Analysis* (London: Sage).

Smart, C. (1990) 'Feminist Approaches to Criminology or Postmodern Woman Meets Atavistic Man', in L. Gelsthorpe and A. Morris (eds.), *Feminist Perspectives in Criminology* (Buckingham: Open University Press).

South, N. (1997) 'Control, Crime and "End of Century Criminology"', in P. Francis, P. Davies and V. Jupp (eds.), *Policing Futures, the Police, Law Enforcement and the Twenty-First Century* (Basingstoke: Macmillan).

Sutherland, E. (1949) *White Collar Crime* (New York: Holt Reinhart and Winston).

Taylor, I. (1997) 'The Political Economy of Crime', in M. Maguire, R. Morgan and R. Reiner (eds.), *The Oxford Handbook of Criminology*, 2nd

177707

28   *Victor Jupp, Pamela Davies and Peter Francis*

edn (Oxford: Clarendon), 265–304.

Thompson, K. (1998) *Moral Panics* (London: Routledge).

Walklate, S. (1989) *Victimology: the Victim and the Criminal Justice Process* (London: Unwin-Hyman).

Walklate, S. (1998) *Understanding Criminology: Recent Theoretical Developments* (Buckingham: Open University Press).

2 White-Collar Crime: an Overview and Discussion
Hazel Croall

INTRODUCTION

White-collar crime is invisible in many different respects. Offences are typically concealed within occupational and organisational routines, are difficult to detect by victims, observers or law enforcers, and few offenders are tried and sentenced in open court. It is also absent from public and academic discussions of 'crime' and criminal justice policy. A major theme in research and literature has therefore been to expose the extent, impact and failure to fully criminalise the crimes of 'the powerful'. This chapter will focus on some key themes and issues which continue to be significant for understanding white-collar crime. It will argue that despite an apparent increase in offending it is still necessary to render white-collar crime more visible. It will then explore the extent to which the concept itself requires modification, particularly by focusing more directly on the nature of offences than on the status of offenders. This directs attention to aspects of victimisation and the relationship between white-collar crime and both legal and illegal forms of business activity and organisation. This will be explored by looking at who suffers and who benefits from white-collar crime, an exercise which also raises issues about the close relationships between white-collar and organised crime. Finally, the chapter will briefly outline some major questions dominating discussions of how this vast group of offences can be controlled.

EXPOSING WHITE-COLLAR CRIME

It is often reiterated that criminology focuses on the crimes of the powerless rather than the powerful, on 'street' crime rather than 'suite crime', and despite 'guesstimates' that white-collar crime exceeds so called conventional crime in terms of its extent and impact, its study remains marginal to criminology. The recent focus on the impact of crime on victims and communities has by and large not included research on the impact of, for example, fraud, corruption, pollution or many other forms of white-collar offending. This is all the more notable in view of what to some represents an increase in its extent along with generalised anxieties about declining standards of business ethics and public morality, exemplified in concerns about political 'sleaze'.

This continued marginalisation, especially in British criminology, requires little demonstration. The biennial British Criminology Conferences typically include only one or two workshops on the subject, and the 1997 edition of the *Oxford Handbook of Criminology* contains thirty-two chapters, only one of which is specifically devoted to the vast area encompassed by 'White Collar Crime' (Maguire et al., 1997; Nelken, 1997). Similarly, 1997 editions of the two main criminology journals, the *British Journal of Criminology* and the *Howard Journal of Criminal Justice*, contain no substantive articles on the subject. In one recent text, Punch refers to those engaged in research into white-collar crime in Britain as 'lone rangers' (Punch, 1996). Despite this there is considerable interest in the subject amongst criminologists. Texts with a more critical perspective do explore the subject – one collection looking at the 'problem of crime' contains chapters on 'crime in the market' and 'state and political' crime (Muncie and McLaughlin, 1996).

The majority of victim surveys, which attempt to provide a more accurate picture of the extent and impact of crime than official statistics, exclude white-collar crime. Some, such as the British Crime Surveys (BCS), focus on individual respondents' reports of personal and property crime, although as Pearce (1992) has demonstrated, they could be adapted to include, for example, health and safety and consumer offences, although they are inevitably limited to crimes of which victims are aware. Some industrial organisations have attempted to carry out surveys to estimate the impact of crimes against industry, although this has tended to be restricted to crimes against business rather than crimes committed by or on behalf of businesses (see, for example, Levi, 1988; CBI/Crime Concern, 1990; Croall, 1998). Despite this criminological invisibility, some argue that there has been an increasing incidence of, and heightened public perception of, white-collar crime, following a series of high-profile cases which need little elaboration. The collapse of the Bank of Credit and Commerce International (BCCI) was followed by the celebrated Maxwell case and the collapse of Barings bank. Several 'respectable' financial institutions have been found to have 'mis-sold' pensions. Reports by the Public Accounts Committee of the House of Commons and the Audit Commission in the early 1990s revealed a range of problems of financial management, fraud prevention and ethical standards across public sector organisations, local government and the National Health Service (Doig, 1996; Hodgkinson, 1997). Currently the issue of 'sleaze', which apart from sexual misdemeanours incorporates concerns about fraud, corruption and dishonesty, continues to dominate headline news. The spate of 'disasters' in the late 1980s such as the sinking of the *Herald of Free Enterprise* and the King's Cross and Clapham rail disasters drew attention to the issues of corporate liability and compliance with safety regulations (see, for example, Wells, 1993 and this volume Chapter 4). More recently, the regulation of food has become a major issue with concerns about the spread of BSE and the death of twenty consumers as a result of consuming meat infected with E Coli. Less well publicised has been a succession of prosecutions for pollution and other offences. One water company, Severn Trent, has amassed thirty-four convictions since 1990 (Croall, 1998).

Such examples can give the impression that white-collar crime is increasing – an increase which is popularly linked to deregulation and the 'enterprise culture' characteristic of free market economic policies (see, for example, McLaughlin and Murji, 1997; Punch, 1996; Taylor, 1997). Punch for example, argues that a combination of the 'shake out' in the business world in the 1980s, the globalisation of financial markets, displacement of industrial activity to less developed societies, de-unionisation and rapid expansion of financial markets have vastly increased opportunities for 'business deviance'. He also argues that such deviance has emerged at the forefront of the socio-political stage as a considerable social and ethical problem (Punch, 1996). Further, business has been discredited, by the apparent merging of illegal and legitimate business interests evident in, for example, money laundering, and successive revelations about the use of tax havens. This was potentially embarrassing to governments advocating deregulation who themselves become vulnerable to business crime becoming a political issue (Punch, 1996). That said, it is important not to overstate the significance of these developments. It is virtually impossible to ascertain whether white-collar crime or corruption are actually increasing as their extent either before or after such changes cannot be estimated (Levi and Nelken, 1996; Nelken, 1997). Nor, despite the proliferation of victim and interest groups, is there evidence of widespread or concerted public reaction against corporate or business activities (Ruggiero, 1996). Nonetheless all these developments are worthy of more sustained research than they have received up until now. There is a continued need to draw attention to the subject.

IS WHITE-COLLAR CRIME A USEFUL CONCEPT?

The status of white-collar crime within criminology is related to the ambiguity which has always surrounded the concept itself. It is, as Nelken points out, a contested concept (Nelken, 1997). Its definition and its status as 'crime' have been questioned as has its relationship to other forms of crime. These problems are well rehearsed (see, for example, Croall, 1992; Nelken, 1997). Many arise from Sutherland's original definition of white-collar crime as 'approximately . . . crime committed by persons of high social status and respectability in the course of their occupations' (Sutherland, 1949: 9). This begs many questions including, how is 'crime' to be defined in the context of business activity? Should the 'respectable' status of offenders or the association with occupations be the key defining factor? Is it to be regarded as distinctively different from, or similar to, other forms of crime? While the thrust of much research has been to expose the criminality of high-status offenders this has, many argue, been at the expense of analysing the activities which offences involve and their relationship to so-called 'conventional crime' and also to organised crime (Ruggiero, 1996; Nelken, 1997).

Is White-Collar Crime 'Really' Crime?

Sutherland's research, which included activities not at the time subject to criminal law but to administrative codes, attracted a stream of criticism centring around the issue of whether white-collar crime was 'crime' (see, for example, Tappan, 1977). Later work addressed this by arguing that the legal status of offences was related to the ability of 'powerful' business offenders to resist the criminalisation of their activities (see, for example, Pearce, 1976). While business activities were criminalised, business groups successfully negotiated a situation in which they were seen not as 'real' but as 'technical' crimes, against which the criminal law was used as a means of effective 'regulation' rather than signifying the moral wrongness of the actions concerned (see, for example, Carson, 1979). This involves an apparently more lenient pattern of enforcement in which prosecution is one among many means of securing 'compliance' to 'regulations' – as opposed to being seen as essential to 'punish' those 'guilty' of 'criminal offences'. This produced the now familiar pattern of regulatory enforcement whereby many offenders are not prosecuted, victims do not see themselves as victims of 'crime', and in court, offenders claim that they are not 'really criminal' (see, for example, Croall, 1988; Wells, 1993). A major feature of much writing, particularly from critical criminologists, has been to challenge this ideological construction, arguing implicitly or explicitly that such offences are 'really' crime.

What is White-Collar Crime?

Thus the concept of white-collar crime has been inextricably linked with high-status and powerful offenders. Sutherland's work clearly distinguishes it from the non-occupational crimes of high-status offenders *and* from the criminal activities of 'non-respectable' occupations – the activities of 'organised crime'. In practice, this creates a number of difficulties. How is 'respectability' or 'high status' to be defined? Employees at all levels of the occupational hierarchy cheat, lie and defraud employers or consumers (see, for example, Shapiro, 1990). Any one category of supposedly white-collar offences, for example, crimes which affect consumers, includes the activities of multinational corporations, otherwise legitimate small traders or 'rogues and cowboys' operating on the fringes of the legitimate economy (see, for example, Croall, 1989), and many have commented on the scarcity of 'elite' offenders and the proliferation of lower-status offenders (Levi, 1987; Croall, 1989, 1992). This raises the question of whether only some of these should be 'counted' as white-collar crime. A major problem with Sutherland's definition and later references to 'elite crime' or the 'crimes of the powerful' has therefore been the equation of a category of 'crime' with a specific group of 'offenders' (Shapiro, 1990; Croall, 1992; Ruggiero, 1996; Nelken, 1997). To others, its major characteristic has been its identification with occupations (see, for example, Quinney, 1977). Thus Shapiro, in an attempt to 'liberate' the concept, argues that it draws attention to the abuse of trust inherent in occupational roles – at whatever level of the hierarchy (Shapiro, 1990). Focusing on the activities also draws attention to the overlap between legitimate and illegitimate occupations and organisations – thus Ruggiero argues that it would 'be more fruitful to focus on the nature, characteristics and methods of these offences rather on the profile of offenders' (Ruggiero, 1996: 5). This enables a fuller analysis of how white-collar crime is related to other forms of crime.

How is White-Collar Crime Related to Other Forms of Crime?

Focusing on the occupational nature of white-collar crime does not necessarily create a cohesive category of crime, and a distinction is often made between occupational and organisational white-collar crime with the former relating to offences committed largely for personal gain by individual employees and the latter to offences in which employees neglect or break regulations to pursue organisational goals (often described as corporate crime). Nonetheless, a number of characteristics are associated with the occupational or organisational location of offences which are often used to distinguish it from other forms of crime (Clarke, 1990; Croall, 1992). A major reason for their invisibility is that they are committed in the context of legitimate occupational routines and offenders are legitimately present at the scene of the crime (Clarke, 1990). Also important is the use of scientific and technical knowledge. Shapiro points out that employees or agents are employed because employers or clients lack the relevant expertise (Shapiro, 1990). This means that offences are often complex, and many participants may be involved. The organisational nature of offences directs attention to the diffusion of responsibility within organisations which makes it difficult to identify the 'guilty party' and enables offenders to blame someone else, up or down the hierarchy, for offences. Victimisation is also diffuse, particularly with organisational offences where there is no direct or intentional victimisation. All of this contributes to the difficulties of detecting and prosecuting offences and to their different treatment by the criminal justice process. Indeed to some, these characteristics necessitate this (see, for example, Clarke, 1990). Focusing on the nature of the activities can, therefore, assist exploring the differences between white-collar and other offences.

It can also draw attention to their similarity to some forms of crime. Locating crime in occupational roles and in organisations draws attention to the fine line dividing legitimate and illegitimate occupations and organisations. Organised crime also involves the use of specialist functions and technical knowledge and is complex and difficult to detect and prosecute. To Ruggiero, corporate crime is a variant of organised crime, and analysis of both would be enhanced by recognising these links. First, they have much in common. In addition to pursuing success and financial gain, offenders engage in frequent and persistent law breaking, suffer no loss of status and rationalise their activities as not criminal. Second, both sets of activities are related to the market economy and to entrepreneurship. Third, both can be examined using economic and organisational theories. Fourth, both involve similar skills and know-how. Finally, some offences, for example, money laundering can be committed jointly (Ruggiero, 1996). Analysis, Ruggiero argues, should therefore focus on the techniques rather than the social characteristics or background of perpetrators.

These kinds of arguments raise important issues. They suggest that the traditional association of the concept with elite, high-status and wealthy offenders can hinder research and analysis. Class and status may be important in determining opportunities for crime and the way in which offenders are dealt with, but should not be part of the definition. In analysing the relationship between crime, business and the law it may well be more useful to look at how different forms of business activity are regulated than to restrict attention to those which are pre-defined as legitimate or illegitimate (Ruggiero, 1996). Focusing on activities can also assist the analysis of victimisation and the organisational nature of offences.

WHO SUFFERS?

A major thrust in the exposé tradition has been to draw attention to the considerable harm caused by white-collar crime, thus challenging the often-held view that it is victimless. Stephen Box famously argued, 'corporate crime kills' (Box, 1983). Victims' lack of awareness of offences, the diffuseness of victimisation and the view that offences are primarily economic have all tended to make victimisation appear less serious and also to preclude reliable estimates of the extent of offending. As will be seen in Chapter 4 in respect of health and safety offences there are few sources of reliable statistics. Literature on white-collar crime has tended to rely heavily on individual case studies, which often involve dramatic examples of victimisation, from which it is impossible to extrapolate. In general terms its effects are seen to affect broad categories such as consumers, workers and members of the general public (see, for example, Croall, 1992; Szockyj and Fox, 1996). Questions could also be asked about which consumers, workers or members of the public are most affected. It can be argued that many forms of white-collar, corporate or business crime have a pervasive impact on the everyday lives of individuals and communities, that this impact is particularly severe on some vulnerable groups, that it can be gendered and reflects structural inequalities.

A focus of research on crime prevention and community safety has been assessing or 'auditing' the impact of crime in particular sites. This has been limited to conventional crime, but a similar exercise could be applied to white-collar crime. Table 2.1 summarises an attempt to explore the impact of white-collar or 'enterprise' crime, adopting an inclusive definition, in the key sites of crime suggested by the Home Office publication, *A Practical Guide to Crime Prevention for Local Partnerships* (September 1993) (Croall, 1998). While this used conventionally constructed crime categories, examples of white-collar crime have been inserted into the headings. All the cited examples have been the subject of recorded cases in the media and government reports. Most are legally defined as crime or, where they are not violations against the criminal law, have been subject to calls for criminalisation. The examples are necessarily selective and many more could be added. This outline of the 'sites of crime' for example, excluded the workplace, let alone the sports field, also an emerging site of crime!

To the Home Office guide, violence in the family is seen as the main crime taking place in the home; yet as Table 2.1 illustrates, many forms of white-collar crime have an impact in the home. Basic utilities such as electricity, gas or water all carry dangers, with tenants having been killed by unsafe gas appliances and consumers having suffered ill-health as a result of polluted tap water (Slapper, 1994; Croall, 1998). 'Cowboy' builders and traders have been said to affect up to 200 000 victims annually (*The Guardian*, 27 August 1994), and the growth of selling via telecommunications has provided opportunities for many different forms of fraud along with the transmission of pornographic images via the Internet (Croall, 1998). Considerable publicity has also surrounded the issue of physical and sexual abuse in residential homes for the elderly and children,

Table 2.1   The Impact of White-Collar/Business Crime in Selected Settings

IN THE HOME
Improperly installed or maintained electrical and gas appliances.
Dangerous furniture, electrical goods, toys.
Polluted tap water.
Fraud and dangerous work carried out by 'cowboy' builders and traders.
Sales frauds – for example doorstep sales; telecommunications sales.
Computer pornography.
Physical/sexual abuse and fraud of residents in nursing homes, children's homes and other institutions.

HIGH-CRIME RESIDENTIAL AREAS
Pollution – chemical discharges and other emissions.
Waste disposal.
Noise pollution from construction sites and commercial enterprises.
Safety of construction sites and roadworks.

CRIME: PUBLIC AND PRIVATE TRANSPORT PROBLEMS
Public transport problems:
Safety of coaches, railways, aeroplanes, boats.
Pollution and noise.
Private transport problems:
Car sales and service frauds.
Car safety; counterfeit parts.

CRIME AGAINST SCHOOLS
Safety and child abuse in adventure centres and play centres.
Safety of coaches/minibuses.

CRIME IN TOWN, CITY AND SHOPPING CENTRES
Adulterated, unfit, misdescribed and counterfeit food.
Food poisoning.
Frothy beer; watered-down beer and spirits; short-measure beer.
Dangerous products.
Counterfeit goods.
Sales frauds – e.g. bogus bargain offers; one-day sales.
Deceptive packaging.
Misleading descriptions – e.g. 'green' labels; orange 'juice'.
Illegal trading – squat-shop traders; bootleg beer.

and residents can also be defrauded (Croall, 1998). To the plight of residents in so-called high crime areas could be added the impact of pollution – including illegal emissions of toxic chemicals, the dumping of rubbish and waste, and the considerable noise pollution caused by commercial activities such as road or building works – complaints about which in at least one local area exceeded complaints about 'noisy neighbours' (Croall, 1998).

While vandalism, theft of and from motor vehicles are typically seen as the main 'transport problems', one need only mention some of the cases cited earlier, such as the sinking of the *Herald of Free Enterprise*, to illustrate the many other 'transport problems' associated with corporate and organisational misconduct – many so-called disasters have involved transport and involve a complex combination of factors leading to the neglect of worker and passenger safety. The heading of 'car crime' could also include the enormous costs to consumers of frauds perpetrated through car sales and service, with car 'clocking' having been estimated by the Automobile Association to cost consumers £100 million in one year. Schools and schoolchildren are not only endangered by vandals or intruders threatening violence but by the neglect of safety considerations in school transport or adventure centres – one of the few convictions for corporate manslaughter in recent years involved the death of four teenagers in a leisure centre in Lyme Bay, England in 1994 (Croall, 1998).

High streets and town and city centres are a major site of crime prevention measures directed at public vandalism, assaults and shoplifting and many public places are now subject to surveillance by CCTV. Yet the commercial activities which this is designed to protect can involve a host of frauds and other forms of commercial crime. Food can be adulterated or can contain 'foreign bodies' which injure consumers, and food poisoning has been the subject of recent concern following the outbreak of E Coli in Scotland in 1996. Food and other goods can be misdescribed and subject to counterfeit – one case involved the sale of counterfeit tea bags (*The Scotsman*, 8 June 1995; Croall, 1998). Counterfeiting involves a vast array of products from 'designer goods' and jewellery, through football shirts, Walt Disney videos, CDs and computer games to more mundane items such as soap powder and food. It can involve multinational 'criminal industries', the laundering of drugs money, or may be produced by local 'cottage industries' making fake perfume, clothes or food. It thus provides a good example of the involvement of both legitimate and illegitimate businesses (Henessey, 1994; Wassell, 1994; Croall, 1998). Counterfeit goods can also be dangerous and cause injuries, as can unsafe products (Croall, 1992, 1998). These selected examples illustrate the widespread and pervasive effects of many forms of white-collar and business crime and, as they affect people in similar sites to 'conventional crime', they contribute to multiple and repeat victimisation.

LOCATING VICTIMISATION

While the impact of white-collar and corporate offences is often assumed to be indiscriminate and to involve 'consumers', 'workers' or the 'public' irrespective of class, age or gender, more detailed exploration reveals that they can affect particularly vulnerable groups, such as children and the elderly. The elderly have been particularly vulnerable to food poisoning and to the sale of shoddy, often dangerous products. Pensions frauds, such as the notorious Maxwell case, affect the elderly and middle-aged as do investment frauds which play on the need of these groups to invest to enhance their savings. 'Little old ladies' have long been the archetypal victims of both non-white-collar and white-collar fraudsters due to their assumed lack of financial competence (Croall, 1995). This vulnerability is related to wider economic factors. Recent revelations about the 'mis-selling' of pensions emerged following the development of privately marketed pensions plans, and abuse in residential homes for the elderly has been found to be greater in homes run for profit (Jenkins and Braithwaite, 1993). Children are also vulnerable, not only to offences in residential homes but also to the dangers of counterfeit and substandard toys and clothes, many of which can be dangerous. Each Christmas sees recurrent warnings about the dangers of counterfeit toys, one example being a batch of musical Santas which blew up when plugged into the mains as they were supplied with unsafe electrical transformers (*Daily Record*, 21 December 1994).

Victimisation can also be gendered and recent work has explored the vulnerability of female consumers and workers to many forms of corporate crime (see, for example, Croall,

1995; Szockyj and Fox, 1996). Some of the most notorious cases of corporate crime have involved attempts to 'improve' women's bodies by, for example, controlling reproduction or altering bodies to conform to idealised notions of beauty (Finley, 1996). Some women died, many were rendered infertile and others suffered long-term health effects following the use of the Dalkon Shield contraceptive which was widely marketed on the basis of falsified test results, despite its dangers being known a long time before it was withdrawn (see, for example, Croall, 1992, 1995; Finley 1996). In respect of silicone breast implants, a ruling in the United States found that Dow Corning acted with 'fraud, malice and oppression' in failing to disclose information about the product's hazards (*The Guardian*, 10 November 1993; Croall, 1995; Claybrook, 1996). Perfume is easily counterfeited and fake perfumes, widely on sale in a variety of markets, can injure consumers (Croall, 1995). Recent calls have been made to regulate the 'diet industry' which some see as inherently fraudulent with some diets and dietary products also carrying health risks (Croall, 1995). As workers, women may be vulnerable to a variety of offences including working in modern 'sweat shops' and working with dangerous substances in the food industry (Miller, 1985; Croall, 1995). This is not to argue that women are more vulnerable to corporate or white-collar crime than men. Male consumers may be defrauded or harmed by consumer products directed at men, and work in 'dangerous' industries such as building or the North Sea oil rigs is often seen as 'man's work'. Further analyses could usefully reveal many more gendered aspects of victimisation which could assist our understanding of the relationships involved in offending and victimisation.

These points also suggest that victimisation also involves wider structural relationships of class and power, albeit more complex than those assumed in the notion of the 'crimes of the powerful', which implies a powerless victim. Shapiro's (1990) analysis, for example, directs attention to the power attached to occupational expertise – some forms of offending may involve the power of the 'knowledgeable' agent, employee or service provider over the 'lay' employer or client. Employers can be defrauded by employees and clients, irrespective of socio-economic status, are vulnerable to the activities of occupational groups from 'cowboy' builders and car mechanics to lawyers and accountants. Nonetheless those with more resources can take steps to prevent victimisation. The middle-class householder is probably less vulnerable, being less likely to buy cheap or counterfeit goods, to resort to 'cowboy' builders and able to afford alternative financial and legal advice to avoid the worst excesses of pensions and other frauds. This does not, however, ensure protection as the cases of the Lloyd's 'names' demonstrated. When victimised they can afford to seek legal compensation and to start victim groups. These aspects of victimisation require much more systematic attention and further analysis could assist the development of what Ruggiero has called a 'political economy' of victimisation (Ruggiero, 1992).

WHO BENEFITS?

Analysing offences also involves, suggests Ruggiero (1996), exploring the issue of *cui bono?* – who benefits? The assumed high status of offenders has often been used to challenge theories linking crime to poverty and social disadvantage, with 'greed' rather than 'need' being seen to generate offending (see, for example, Box, 1983; Punch, 1996). Offending has also been linked to the prioritisation of profits at the expense of the interests of consumers, workers or the general public, a tendency which was arguably exacerbated in the 'enterprise culture'. Thus offences can be interpreted as representing 'normal' rather than 'abnormal' business activities. This suggests that analyses of offences must relate them to the nature of business and entrepreneurship and to their location within organisations, issues pursued in recent work by Punch and Ruggiero (Punch, 1996; Ruggiero, 1996). This may also involve, as argued above, exploring the relationships between legitimate and illegitimate organisations (Ruggiero, 1996).

The association of white-collar crime with 'greed' and the selfish pursuit of profits assumes that individuals, corporations and organisations benefit economically from offences. This may be somewhat over-simplistic as not all offences are motivated by or result in economic gain. Braithwaite (1984), for example, has argued that corporate crime may not ultimately enhance profitability – if offenders are caught or companies manufacture goods which harm consumers, profitability and survival can be severely damaged. Punch argues that some cases involve destroying the organisation – Maxwell, he argues, 'plundered' the organisation for his own personal benefit (Punch, 1996). Others have pointed out that profit may not be the only or major goal affecting the sub-units of organisations where many offences originate and that efficiency, personal ambition or the survival of an organisational unit may be equally important (see, for example, Punch, 1996). Furthermore, 'rule breaking' occurs in organisations in the public sector for whom profit is not a major goal. In these organisations efficiency and the speedy processing of cases may lead to innovative ways of avoiding rules – as might, for example, be the case also in the police where the interests of crime control may be prioritised over those of due process in respect of obtaining confessions and guilty pleas (see, for example, Ruggiero, 1996). At the same time, however, a climate in which profitability and efficiency are prioritised is important – the privatisation and marketisation of public services has been associated with increasing opportunities for fraud and 'misuse' of public funds (Doig, 1996; Hodgkinson, 1997).

To Ruggiero (1996), applying the question of 'who benefits?', derived from organisation theory, to deviant organisational behaviour reveals a more complex situation than might be assumed. For example, health and safety offences not only enhance profits but also lead to lower prices for consumers and maintain jobs for employees. Similarly, counterfeiting can be seen to benefit consumers who could not otherwise afford the goods, and the manufacture and sale of counterfeit goods also provide employment. While legitimate manufacturers are victims, they may benefit from the enhanced reputation of their 'brand name', and have even been reported to have released products at lower prices to compete with the counterfeiters (Ruggiero, 1996). These arguments can provide rationales for offending.

The 'enterprise culture' also provides rationalisations for many different forms of entrepreneurial activity – whether it be legal, illegal or on the fringes of legality (see, for example, Hobbs, 1995; Punch, 1996). Historically, as Ruggiero (1996) points out, entrepreneurs have been seen as 'mavericks', as marginal and eccentric figures, and the term has often been applied to 'newcomers' and foreigners rather than to 'establishment' figures. Entrepreneurship has been associated with speculation and risk-taking – entrepreneurs are innovators. Innovative behaviour is in turn often portrayed as 'deviant' – thus Merton's use of the term to describe the 'criminal' adaptation to anomie (Merton, 1938). Indeed, argues Ruggiero, 'economic innovation and deception are almost one and the same' (Ruggiero, 1996: 54). This underlines the argument that corporate and conventional organised crime should be analysed jointly. Before exploring this further, it is also important to look at the organisational context of offences.

The pursuit of profit and the diffusion of responsibility within organisations, where no one person has sole responsibility for complying with rules, has led to organisations being portrayed as 'criminogenic' (Gross, 1978; Clinard and Yeager, 1980; Punch, 1996). To Punch (1996), the organisation is the offender, the means, the setting, the rationale, the opportunity and also the victim of corporate deviance. Behind the 'front' of orderliness and rationality, he argues, are shadow organisations in which 'dirty activities' flourish. Managers, removed from the consequences of their actions, can draw on a variety of ideological rationalisations to justify breaking the law such as that they were 'only following orders', that 'business is business' or that breaking regulations is justifiable as 'government is stifling enterprise' (Punch, 1996). Within organisations, individual feelings can give way to organisational 'group think' in which personal morality gives way to loyalty to organisational goals and individual managers may deceive themselves by denying the immorality, for example, of continuing to market an unsafe product. This conflict between personal and organisational morality can lead to managers becoming 'calculating, manipulative, devious, heartless amoral chameleons' (Punch, 1996: 244). Rarely he argues, do managers see themselves as engaging in deviant or criminal activities. Rule-breaking behaviour therefore may find many moral justifications within and without organisations.

Professional and organised crime is also business activity, and an increasing number of writers have drawn attention to the links between legitimate, semi-legitimate and illegitimate business activities (Passas and Nelken, 1993; Van Duyne, 1993; Hobbs, 1995; Ruggiero, 1996). Ruggiero explores different aspects of these relationships. Organised crime can provide a service to legitimate enterprise – an example of which is where organised criminal enterprises offer a complete service to legitimate industries by arranging for cheaper, and illegal, ways of disposing of toxic waste (Van Duyne, 1993; Ruggiero, 1996). It can also be seen in what Ruggiero describes as 'people trafficking' where, after being provided with passages to Western countries, illegal immigrants are employed by legal businesses (Ruggiero, 1996). In this way organised crime performs an ancillary role in the official economy, providing a clandestine 'tertiary' sector. Legitimate businesses also knowingly or unknowingly assist organised crime – a classic example of this being money laundering, which requires the involvement of legitimate financial institutions (Ruggiero, 1996). In 'mutual enterprises' organised crime and legitimate industry work together. This is seen in the case of frauds on the European Union. One example involves agricultural subsidies which have provided a major source of finance for both legitimate and criminal enterprises. In such instances partnerships are useful as illegitimate entrepreneurs require access to officials and to legitimate business activities (Passas and Nelken, 1993; Ruggiero, 1996).

Whether or not these boundaries are increasingly blurred is difficult to determine, although it can be suggested that the economic factors which have been linked to the assumed growth of white-collar crime may also have brought the legitimate and illegitimate sectors closer together by widening opportunities for fraud and changing the environment of control (Nelken, 1997). The growth of the drugs industry has had profound effects on organised crime and created the need to launder profits into legitimate business 'fronts' such as counterfeiting. Hobbs (1995) in his research with contemporary 'serious' criminals, also suggests that such activities can no longer be distinguished from normal businesses and that in post-industrial global and local economies the 'upperworld' and 'underworld' are increasingly merged as individuals take advantage of a plethora of legitimate and illegitimate money-making opportunities. To Ruggiero, pariah forms of organised crime are distinguished from more prosperous ones by their respective degree of involvement in the official as well as the illegal economy – to conventional organised criminals a major means of avoiding detection and reducing risk, the aim of entrepreneurs, is to 'go legit' (Ruggiero, 1996).

ISSUES OF CONTROL

The final section of this overview will briefly outline some of the major issues surrounding the control of white-collar crime. Discussions of control have been affected by the ambiguity so characteristic of white-collar crime and by the tendency to focus on the status of offenders. From Sutherland's work onwards a major theme has been to expose the apparent leniency of the treatment accorded to offenders by law enforcers, courts and the law itself. This has typically been attributed to the status of offenders with the explicit or implicit implication that treatment should be made more equal by greater criminalisation, by more stringent law enforcement and by heavier sentencing policies. Focusing on offences rather than offenders, however, draws attention to the difficulties of such approaches. Some argue that as white-collar offences are intrinsically difficult to detect and punish, they require a different form of law enforcement and punishment. These kinds of arguments have aroused considerable controversy (see, for example, Clarke, 1990; Hawkins, 1990; Pearce and Tombs, 1990; Croall, 1992; Nelken, 1997). While these are often presented as opposing arguments, suggesting *either* tougher punishment *or* different forms of regulation, it can be argued that they are not incompatible. This section will briefly explore how they relate to law enforcement, sentencing and the role of the criminal law.

In respect of law enforcement what has often been called the 'regulatory debate' has hinged around the 'compliance' style of enforcement referred to above. Many studies in the 1980s illustrated that enforcers perceive their main aim as being to secure compliance to the law, and that to them, the benefits of prosecution are weighed against those of persuasion, education, negotiation and agreeing out of court settlements (Carson, 1971; Hawkins, 1984; Hutter, 1988). While strategies vary within and between agencies, prosecution is often seen as costly and possibly counter-productive. A prosecution strategy could alienate businesses with whom enforcers often wish to build up a 'continuous' relationship and the small fines which result do little to ameliorate the situation. However, to critics these arguments reflect the assumption that offences are 'not really crime', and are based on the ideological distinction between white-collar and conventional crimes (see, for example, Pearce and Tombs 1990). Arguments about cost effectiveness can be seen as ideological in that they are not generally used with 'conventional' crimes such as burglary where prosecution may be equally costly and counter-productive, and not publicly prosecuting white-collar offenders can decrease the deterrent power of the law. The outcome of these processes, whereby very few 'known' offenders are publicly prosecuted, can be interpreted as institutional class bias (Croall, 1992). A logical extension of this argument is that more offenders should be publicly punished to enhance the deterrent power of the law and raise public consciousness of offending – in addition to making treatment more equal.

Class bias has also been associated with sentencing, with small fines and a scarcity of prison sentences being taken as an indication of leniency (Croall, 1992). Again this is often attributed to class bias and to the superior resources of offenders, although a number of studies have suggested that direct class bias is difficult to establish (see, for example, Weisburd et al., 1990; Croall, 1992). Here again, the nature of offences is significant. Victimisation is often indirect and diffuse which reduces the severity of penalties and offences are often presented as being 'one off', isolated incidents. On the other hand ideological factors also play a major role – offenders can use the assumption that offences are 'not really criminal' in court, and to the extent that sentencers accept arguments that offenders have a lot to lose they are, albeit unconsciously, discriminating against conventional offenders who have nothing to lose (Croall, 1988; Levi, 1989; Cook, 1989). On the other hand, it is also argued that organisational offenders cannot be dealt with in the same way as individuals – the only possible sentence is a fine, as they cannot be imprisoned or rehabilitated – they have no 'guilty mind' (Croall, 1992; Nelken, 1997).

These different approaches produce an apparent tension between stricter criminal law enforcement and enhancing the use of 'regulatory' strategies. It is possible nonetheless to accept that arguments about 'regulation' are ideological *and* that the offences do pose problems for control. These problems are not unique to white-collar crime – diversionary strategies and out of court mediation have been suggested for conventional crimes and it has been accepted that public prosecution and sentencing play a limited role in reducing crime. Braithwaite and Pettit, for example, have argued that equal treatment need not involve treating white-collar crimes more like conventional crime and that conventional crime need not always involve prosecution and public punishment (Braithwaite and Pettit, 1990). Ayres and Braithwaite's argument for the use of enforcement 'pyramids' with informal sanctions at the base and tougher punishment at the apex can apply equally to conventional and white-collar crime (Ayres and Braithwaite, 1992). It also implies that while some regulatory strategies can be and are appropriate, tougher punishments can be devised for persistent and serious corporate and organisational crime. Offenders, Braithwaite (1989) argues, can be subjected to publicity and shamed. Also, corporate probation and community service orders can be and have been developed in some jurisdictions (Braithwaite, 1989; Fisse and Braithwaite, 1993). Others have also suggested a variety of ways in which the criminal law could be made more effective: it could be better adjusted to take account of corporate manslaughter; individuals within organisations could be given clearer responsibilities and made liable for prosecution; tougher licensing arrangements could be introduced; and companies, like drivers, could be subject to laws making 'dangerous' or 'reckless' corporate activities offences (Pearce and Tombs, 1990, 1997; Fisse and Braithwaite, 1993; Wells, 1993).

At the same time it is important to recognise that criminal law, and what Braithwaite describes as 'establishment criminology', has severe limitations in dealing with white-collar crime although it remains significant as a symbolic means of expressing public disapproval of corporate activities (Nelken, 1983, 1997; Braithwaite, 1995; Pearce and Tombs, 1997). There is now a growing recognition of the potential role of pressure groups, including trade unions, workers, local communities, victim groups, consumer and environmental pressure groups (Snider, 1996; Braithwaite, 1995; Pearce and Tombs, 1990, 1997). Organisational structures and routines can also be addressed by the encouragement of 'compliance cultures' within organisations and 'whistle blowing' (see, for example, Fisse and Braithwaite, 1993). As Pearce and Tombs, in relation to the chemicals industry argue, 'effective regulation is never a question of punitive versus compliance-oriented regulatory approaches, nor based upon deterrence in any simplistic fashion, nor one which entails a strict dichotomy between state or market mechanisms' (Pearce and Tombs, 1997: 99).

CONCLUDING COMMENTS

What can be concluded from this exploration of some of the major themes and issues which continue to affect analyses of white-collar crime? There is clearly a continued need, in the face of its invisibility, to 'expose' it both in the public domain and within criminology, especially in view of its assumed increase and links to other forms of crime. As Nelken (1997: 920) has argued:

> The potential of criminology to contribute to shaping public policy concerning the best way to regulate white-collar crime is likely to increase in importance . . . there will also always be a need for denouncing the 'crimes of the powerful' and their many illegal (as well as semi-legal and legal) ways of causing harm.

The concept itself remains surrounded in ambiguity

although it can be argued that freeing it from its automatic association with high-status or 'powerful' offenders can assist analysis, particularly of offending and victimisation. Whether as Ruggiero (1996) suggests, corporate crime should be seen as a 'variant' of organised crime is more problematic. Nelken (1997) argues that they might rather be seen as a continuum, with some forms of white-collar crime clearly lying in the legitimate sphere, some offences involving both organised and white-collar crime, and others clearly lying in the illegitimate sphere.

This does not mean that the elements of power, class or status so long associated with the concept are unimportant, but suggests that analyses of, for example, who suffers and who benefits can be assisted by focusing on the activities as well as considering issues of power and status. Victims are harmed by a host of corporate and organisational activities irrespective of the status of offenders, although at the same time, victimisation reflects different kinds of structural relationships. The 'entrepreneurial' activities of legitimate, semi-legitimate or illegitimate 'entrepreneurs' have much in common, as do the activities of legitimate and illegitimate organisations and corporations – with their legitimacy affecting both the activities of offenders and how they are dealt with. All of these activities pose considerable problems for control and the limitations of the criminal law and criminal justice system must be recognised. 'Exposing' the harm done is also necessary to generate the kind of victim and pressure group activity which is seen as a necessary accompaniment to criminal sanctions.

REFERENCES

Ayres, I. and Braithwaite, J. (1992) *Responsive Regulation. Transcending the Deregulation Debate* (Oxford: Oxford University Press).
Box, S. (1983) *Power, Crime and Mystification* (London: Tavistock).
Braithwaite, J. (1984) *Corporate Crime in the Pharmaceutical Industry* (London: Routledge and Kegan Paul).
Braithwaite, J. (1989) *Crime, Shame and Re-Integration* (Cambridge: Cambridge University Press).

Braithwaite, J. (1995) 'Inequality and Republican Criminology', in J. Hagan and R. Peterson (eds.), *Crime and Inequality* (Stanford: Stanford University Press).

Braithwaite, J. and Pettit, P. (1990) *Not Just Deserts: a Republican Theory of Justice* (Oxford: Clarendon Press).

Carson, W. G. (1971) 'White Collar Crime and the Enforcement of Factory Legislation', in W. G. Carson and P. Wiles (eds.), *Crime and Delinquency in Britain* (London: Martin Robertson).

Carson, W.G. (1979) 'The Conventionalisation of Early Factory Crime', *International Journal of the Sociology of Law*, 7(1), 37–60.

CBI / Crime Concern (1990) *Crime – Managing the Business Risk* (London: CBI).

Clarke, M. (1990) *Business Crime: its Nature and Control* (Cambridge: Polity Press).

Claybrook, J. (1996) 'Women in the Marketplace: Targets of Corporate Greed', in E. Szockyj and J. G. Fox (eds.), *Corporate Victimisation of Women* (Boston: Northeastern University Press).

Clinard, M. and Yeager, P. (1980) *Corporate Crime* (New York: Free Press).

Cook, D. (1989) 'Fiddling Tax and Benefits: Inculpating the Poor, Exculpating the Rich', in P. Carlen and D. Cook (eds.), *Paying for Crime* (Milton Keynes: Open University Press).

Croall, H. (1988) 'Mistakes, Accidents and Someone Else's Fault: the Trading Offender in Court', *Journal of Law and Society*, 15(3), 293–315.

Croall, H. (1989) 'Who is the White Collar Criminal?', *British Journal of Criminology*, 29(2), 157–74.

Croall, H. (1992) *White Collar Crime* (Buckingham: Open University Press).

Croall, H. (1995) 'Target Women: Women's Victimisation from White Collar Crime', in R. Dobash, R. Dobash and L. Noaks (eds.), *Gender and Crime* (Cardiff: Cardiff University Press).

Croall, H. (1998) 'Business, Crime and the Community', *International Journal of Risk, Security and Crime Prevention*, vol. 3(4), 281–92.

Doig, A. (1996) 'From Lynskey to Nolan: the Corruption of British Politics and Public Service', *Journal of Law and Society*, 23(1), 36–56.

Finley, L. (1996) 'The Pharmaceutical Industry and Women's Reproductive Health: the Perils of Ignoring Risk and Blaming Women', in E. Szockyj and J. G. Fox (eds.), *Corporate Victimisation of Women* (Boston: Northeastern University Press).

Fisse, B. and Braithwaite, J. (1993) *Corporations, Crimes and Accountability* (Cambridge: Cambridge University Press).

Gross, E. (1978) 'Organisations as Criminal Actors', in J. Braithwaite and P. Wilson (eds.), *Two Faces of Deviance: Crimes of the Powerless and the Powerful* (Brisbane: University of Queensland Press).

Hawkins, K. (1984) *Environment and Enforcement: Regulation and the Social Definition of Pollution* (Oxford: Clarendon Press).

Hawkins, K. (1990) 'Compliance Strategy, Prosecution Policy and Aunt Sally – a Comment on Pearce and Tombs', *British Journal of Criminology*, 30(4), 444–67.

Henessey, J. (1994) in *The Scotsman* 8 December.

Hobbs, D. (1995) *Bad Business: Professional Crime in Modern Britain* (Oxford: Oxford University Press).

Hodgkinson, P. (1997) 'The Sociology of Corruption – Some Themes and Issues', *Sociology*, 31(1), 17–35.

Hutter, B. (1988) *The Reasonable Arm of the Law?* (Oxford: Clarendon Press).

Jenkins, A. and Braithwaite, J. (1993) 'Profits, Pressure and Corporate Lawbreaking', *Crime, Law and Social Change*, 20, 221–32.

Levi, M. (1987) *Regulating Fraud: White Collar Crime and the Criminal Process* (London: Tavistock).

Levi, M. (1988) *The Prevention of Fraud*, Home Office Crime Prevention Unit, Paper 17 (London HMSO).

Levi, M. (1989) 'Suite Justice: Sentencing for Fraud', *Criminal Law Review*, 420–34.

Levi, M. and Nelken, D. (1996) 'The Corruption of Politics and the Politics of Corruption: an Overview', *Journal of Law and Society*, 23(1), 1–17.

Maguire, M., Morgan, R. and Reiner, R. (eds.) (1997) *The Oxford Handbook of Criminology*, 2nd edn (Oxford: Clarendon Press).

McLaughlin, E. and Murji, K. (1997) 'The Future Lasts a Long Time: Public Policework and the Managerialist Paradox', in P. Francis, P. Davies and V. Jupp (eds.), *Policing Futures: the Police, Law Enforcement and the Twenty-First Century* (London: Macmillan).

Merton, R. K. (1938) 'Social Structure and Anomie', *American Sociological Review*, 3, 672–82.

Miller, M. (1985) *Danger! Additives at Work* (London: London Food Commission).

Muncie, J. and McLaughlin, E. (eds.) (1996) *The Problem of Crime* (London: Sage).

Nelken, D. (1983) *Limits of the Legal Process* (London: Academic Press).

Nelken, D. (1997) 'White Collar Crime', in M. Maguire, R. Morgan and R. Reiner (eds.), *The Oxford Handbook of Criminology*, 2nd edn (Oxford: Clarendon Press).

Passas, N. and Nelken, D. (1993) 'The Thin Line between Legitimate and Criminal Enterprises: Subsidy Frauds in the European Community', *Crime, Law and Social Change*, 19, 223–43.

Pearce, F. (1976) *Crimes of the Powerful* (London: Pluto Press).

Pearce, F. (1992) 'The Contribution of "Left Realism" to the Study of Commercial Crime', in B. McLean and J. Lowman (eds.), *Realist Criminology: Crime Control and Policing in the 1990s* (Toronto: University of Toronto Press).

Pearce, F. and Tombs, S. (1990) 'Ideology, Hegemony and Empiricism: Compliance Theories and Regulation', *British Journal of Criminology*, 30(4), 423–43.

Pearce, F. and Tombs, S. (1997) 'Hazards, Law and Class: Contextualizing the Regulation of Corporate Crime', *Social and Legal Studies*, 6(1), 79–107.

Punch, M. (1996) *Dirty Business: Exploring Corporate Misconduct* (London: Sage).

Quinney, R. (1977) 'The Study of White Collar Crime: Toward a Re-orientation in Theory and Practice', in G. Geis and R. G. Maier (eds.), *White Collar Crime: Offences in Business, Politics and the Professions – Classic and Contemporary Views* (New York: Free Press, Collier and Macmillan).

Ruggiero, V. (1992) 'Realist Criminology: a Critique', in R. Matthews and J. Young (eds.), *Issues in Realist Criminology* (London: Sage).

Ruggiero, V. (1996) *Organised and Corporate Crime in Europe: Offers that Can't be Refused* (Aldershot: Dartmouth).

Shapiro, S. (1990) 'Collaring the Crime, not the Criminal: Re-considering the Concept of White-collar Crime', *American Sociological Review*, 55, 346–65.

Slapper, G. (1994) 'Crime without Punishment', *The Guardian*, 1 February.

Snider, L. (1996) 'Directions for Social Change and Political Action', in E. Szockyj and J. G. Fox (eds.), *Corporate Victimisation of Women* (Boston: Northeastern University Press).

Sutherland, E. (1949) *White Collar Crime* (New York: Holt, Rinehart & Winston).

Szockyj, E. and Fox, J. G. (eds.) (1996) *Corporate Victimisation of Women* (Boston: Northeastern University Press).

Tappan, P. (1977) 'Who is the Criminal?' in G. Geis and R. F. Maier (eds.), *White Collar Crime: Offences in Business, Politics and the Professions – Classic and Contemporary Views*, Revised edn (New York: Free Press, Collier and Macmillan).

Taylor, I. (1997) 'The Political Economy of Crime', in M. Maguire, R. Morgan and R. Reiner (eds.), *The Oxford Handbook of Criminology*, 2nd edn (Oxford: Clarendon Press).

Van Duyne, P. (1993) 'Organised Crime and Business Crime Enterprises in the Netherlands', *Crime, Law and Social Change*, 19(2), 103–42.

Wassell, T. (1994) in *The European*, 24 June.

Weisburd, D., Waring, E. and Wheeler, S. (1990) 'Class, Status and the Punishment of White Collar Crime', *Law and Social Enquiry*, 15(2), 223–43.

Wells, C. (1993) *Corporations and Criminal Responsibility* (Oxford: Clarendon Press).

3 Crime-Work Connections: Exploring the 'Invisibility' of Workplace Crime

Pamela Davies and Victor Jupp

INTRODUCTION

This chapter uses the organising theme of crime and work connections to develop an understanding of criminal activity and its location or siting. In particular, the chapter focuses upon one location or site of criminal activity: the workplace. Criminal acts can be seen to thrive at the junctures between the legitimate and illegitimate. What is more, they not only thrive at the boundaries between the legitimate and the illegitimate but also within and between the formal and informal settings. The workplace is seen as hiding several forms of criminal activity, often 'dressing up' activities as acceptable business practice. In other instances the activities in the workplace are approaching the illegitimate and are near illegal but are nevertheless visible practices, often excused or rationalised as 'perks of the job'. The chapter also evaluates the usefulness of the concept of work for understanding some types of crimes committed for economic gain. The crime-and-work connection also points to the ways in which crimes may be understood by those seeking to explain the behaviour and activities. It is argued that explanations of such crimes might more fully appreciate the *offender*'s perspective.

The chapter is divided into four sections. First crime-and-work connections are considered. The second section considers what can be termed 'boundary problems'. This concerns the location of crime between the legitimate and the illegitimate as well as between the formal and informal. Third, the literature related to crime-at-work is critically examined, and in doing so it is argued that there is a need for a further exploration of the workplace as a location for criminal activity especially in relation to gender and class. Fourth, the value of exploring crime *as* work is examined.

CRIME AND WORK CONNECTIONS

Definitions and Images

The study of crime has long been of interest to academics and practitioners. Similarly work and employment have attracted a great deal of attention from sociologists and academics from other related disciplines. However, connections between crime and work have only partially been examined within criminology. In part, neglect of these connections can be attributed to the focus of much contemporary criminological research. In the previous chapter Croall drew attention to the ways in which criminological research on street-level crime, on the impact of such crimes on communities and on the efficacy of crime prevention has led to the prioritising of conventional constructions and definitions of crime and the neglect of the nature and impact of business and corporate crime on individual victims and communities. This view is also shared here and is illustrated in the sections that follow. First we consider the definitions of crime, work and employment.

Most undergraduate textbooks in criminology include a chapter that debates the subjects 'What is crime?' and 'What is the extent of crime?' Apart from drawing upon the official definitions of crime as law violation, such texts usually discuss crime as typically consisting of street crimes, violent crime and crimes that are committed by young men. Yet such definitions and images are partial, and neglect a large area of deviant activity. For example, Sutherland (1949) during the mid-twentieth century stimulated the challenging of the civil–criminal distinction particularly with regard to white-collar crime (Braithwaite, 1986). In addition to the range of crimes generically covered by the term 'white-collar', crimes committed against women and children, crimes that take place away from the streets, for example in the home or at work have also been neglected and have remained relatively invisible. Others, often writing from a more radical or critical perspective, suggest that our appreciation of criminal activities and victimisation should be further extended to include war crimes, which include the murder of civilians, evidence of forcible detention under poor conditions, rape and other violations stipulated by the Geneva Convention (Chaudhary and Weller, 1993; Ruggierio, South and Taylor, 1998) and human rights issues generally (Cohen, 1993; Schwendinger and Schwendinger, 1975). Additionaly, concern has been aroused about the threat posed by new crimes such as cybercrime by ruthless computer keyboard criminals (Kettle and Bowcott, 1997). These examples serve to show not only the ambiguity and controversy surrounding the definition of crime and consequently of criminal victimisation, but also the ways in which narrow and confining definitions make crimes and atrocities that do not fall within the 'traditional' categories relatively invisible.

In addition to the problem of defining crime, there are similar competing and contrasting definitions and experiences of work. Sociologists have long recognised the importance and significance of work although their attempts at definition have been met with varying degrees of success. Leaving aside the problems associated with unemployment and non-work for a moment, consider the range of ambiguities in the use of the term 'work' in everyday language. These include the more traditional notions of full-time and paid work, salaried work, hourly paid work, shift work and also the different combinations of shared work, part-time work, unpaid work, voluntary work and work by those who have retired. Others have dwelt not only upon the problematic definitions of work, but also on different experiences of work. Work for some may be a life-defining activity, for others it might be better described as a leisure-time pursuit and for others a financial necessity. Others may engage in entrepreneurial activities which many would readily describe as marginal or outright illegal. In a similar way to which we have suggested that defining crime is inherently problematic and can only lead to a blurred view about what is legal/illegal, work is also seen to be difficult to define.

Work can be conducted in many different contexts and settings, while some of these social, environmental and spatial settings might be commonly construed as illegal for such activities. It can also be suggested that workers and employees should be viewed in this less restrictive way so that those who might more traditionally be viewed as criminals can also be seen as contributing to a market economy.

Traditional and Hidden Connections

There are various connections between crime, work, employment and unemployment. On the one hand there are traditional connections between crime and non-work that have been explored by sociologists and criminologists. Such connections and relationships include those between crime and unemployment, crime and poverty as well as economic marginalisation and crime. More recently there has been a resurgence of interest in the connections between crime and the economy generally (Field, 1990; Sutton, 1998). On the other hand there are further connections between crime, work and employment that remain largely hidden and under-explored. This is because the blurred boundaries between crime and work produce the features of invisibility outlined in Chapter 1 – no knowledge, no statistics, no politics, no panic, and so on.

Exceptionally the unemployment–crime connection has been responsible for producing much heated debate, speculation, empirical research, and conflicting and complex conclusions. The net result of the many studies on the unemployment–crime link has been investigated by Box (1987) who suggested that the overall conclusion must be that there is a relation but that the link is not straightforward nor causal. Many of these individual studies have been subjected to a number of criticisms (see, for example, Box, 1992). In respect of class, race and gender dimensions the criticisms are often well directed. For example, many studies have failed to control for the differential between ethnic minority and unemployment status and crime; similarly they have failed to separate off gender and unemployment status and crime. Therefore, generalising the results for all the population produces a distorting and inaccurate picture especially as regards women, crime and unemployment. (One exception to this is an Australian piece of research which clearly demonstrates the methodological pitfalls and inaccuracies of analyses in this area (Naffine and Gale, 1989).) It is argued here, that supporters of the unemployment-causes-crime view overlook the fact that many types and varieties of crimes are committed by those who *are* employed and such crime opportunities only present themselves as a result of being in work or employment. This suggests that criminological research and theorising on the workplace as a fertile location of crime. The workplace can refer to a specific physical location in which employee theft or drug-taking take place (see Chapters 2 and 7) or an unbounded space which facilitates cybercrime (see Chapter 5).

We now turn to a consideration of work as a location of crime.

EXPLORING CRIME AND WORK

There are several ways in which we might begin to emphasise the connections between crime and work. One approach is to build upon the work of others who have typologised these interactions. Several writers drawing upon different academic perspectives and disciplines have illustrated the nature of, and relationships between, work, employment, formality and legality in the hidden economy.

Typical of the economist's approach Smith (1986) provides examples of activities in the 'shadow economy', choosing to divide this into two broad categories – first, the 'black economy' and second, the 'non-market shadow economy'. Criminal activities appear only to feature in the 'black economy' under a sub-category entitled 'households and individuals'. This includes incomes not declared for tax and the production of illegal goods and services. A second sub-category is 'private companies'. These activities include 'off the books' business and false accounting mechanisms. Activities are named in this way entirely as a means of illustrating the range of activities in the shadow economy which need to be measured and aggregated in order to demonstrate the 'real' size of the shadow economy in financial terms.

A second way of exploring the connections between crime and work is provided in an annotation of forms of economic activity in the extensive literature review offered by Harding and Jenkins in *The Myth of the Hidden Economy* (1989). Their portrayal of the hidden economy provides some potentially useful observations and illustrations concerning forms of economic activity and their location on a map of formality/informality and work/employment. These authors suggest that an understanding of activities is best achieved by using the notion of continuums. Such an appreciation allows considerable flexibility in the categorisation of any particular activity. Criminal activities in this portrayal are illustrated as ranging on a continuum from *crime* to *fiddles* and then outright *corruption*. However, there is no further elaboration on this continuum and of what types of activities might be placed on it. Nor does the analysis appear to adequately represent the degree of formality belonging to certain types of illegal activity.

Gerald Mars (1994), writing from an anthropological perspective, provides a typology of work and its rewards in terms of a hidden economy which is similar to that of Henry (1981). The dividing lines or boundaries here are between legal and extra-legal or illegal rewards and between official/unofficial/alternative rewards. The text also suggests that the idea of *continuums* is preferable and that individual rewards are calculated by adding various computations of the legal, illegal, official and alternative rewards together. Only such combinations of receipts comprise a person's total rewards from work (Mars, 1994: 8). In respect of rewards from extra-legal or illegal activities these include 'criminal rewards' (professional crime and prostitution), 'hidden economy rewards' (pilfering, overcharging) and 'black economy' rewards (unregistered production and service organisations).

Mars' (1994) typology appears to present a fuller and more complete typology of the hidden and illicit economy than that of Smith (1986) or Harding and Jenkins (1989), but there are some similarities between Mars' and Smith's analyses. Both imply that some forms of hidden economic activity are work-related (i.e. they are a spin-off from legitimate work roles and/or that illegal work routines exist in their own right). Mars expands on his analysis of roles by analysing jobs according to four distinct groups: vulture, wolfpack, donkey and hawk jobs. These groupings begin to look more closely at the actors involved in the illegitimate activities and to some extent also focus upon the locations of the illegal and often informal routines adopted in the workplace.

A further evaluation of the elusive distinctions between work and employment is addressed by MacDonald (1994) who has more recently raised the question of different allegiances to work including the options of alternative ways of working in the face of restricted avenues for legitimate employment. MacDonald is primarily concerned about changing cultures of work and he discovered – almost as a by-product of his empirical work – differing degrees of illegality, notably 'fiddly work', that is, working whilst claiming benefits. The usage of criminal terminology is carefully avoided in his discussions, however, and crime data were not systematically elicited or scrutinised. Neither does the author give attention to the gendered nature of allegiances to work. What the study does suggest, however, is that there is material ripe for empirical research and criminological theorising.

The above account of some of the different disciplinary approaches to locating crime in work serves to illustrate some of the problematic issues surrounding definitions and boundaries, and visibile and invisibile features of crime. It is along such continuums and between fuzzy boundaries that workplace invisible crimes thrive. For example, as Nelken (1997) has pointed out, the idea of continuums for understanding white-collar crimes is useful. A whole area of research is also opening up in the area of the informal economy. This is drawing upon old, and spawning new research ideas and projects (see, for example, Shapland, 1998), and it is picking out the elusive boundaries between legitimate and illegitimate occupations and working practices.

CRIME AT WORK

As argued above, it is fruitful to focus on the workplace as a specific location of criminal activity. This section looks at examples of crime at work including the different categories of people engaged in such activities. Although the notion of the workplace is problematic the lack of attention given to the workplace as a scene of crime is difficult to justify. Gill (1994) posits four arguments for a closer attention to the workplace as a site for crime:

> First, businesses contain people, and it is important to minimize victimization of them. Second, there is growing evidence that the victimization rate for businesses is higher than for households, and that some categories of worker are, to an above-average degree, at risk of crime. Third, there is a legal requirement (in addition to a moral requirement) to protect staff. Fourth, studying how crime is prevented in the business environment – where commercial security arrangements are sometimes a substitute for the police and where physical security is much in evidence – may provide clues to preventing crime elsewhere. (Gill 1994: 1)

Others have argued that organisations are criminogenic (Box, 1992; Punch, 1996) and that crime is endemic in the workplace. Following in this line, the workplace again becomes an area for analysis and review.

In 1988 the British Crime Survey (BCS) included a chapter (Mayhew et al., 1989) on 'Crime at Work', in which replies to a series of questions were presented on a whole range of issues pertinent to the workplace as a site for criminal activity. It collected data on the extent of verbal abuse at work, work as the scene of crime, crime due to workers' jobs, women and work, occupation and risk, and characteristics of job-related offences. Indeed a whole arena for new research agendas was implied by the results. The questions have not since been repeated and the British Crime Survey remains primarily a household-based survey, focusing on crimes other than business and commercial crimes and victimisations. There appears to be little pressure to conduct a nationwide business or commercial sector victimisation survey with the same regularity and profile as the BCS. However, more specific studies have been conducted on employee theft, pilfering and fiddling, customer theft or shoplifting and to some degree fraud and forgery. These have attracted attention in the criminological literature but in comparison with the total volume of criminological research they remain under-represented.

Employee Theft, Pilfering and Fiddling

Ditton (1979) described a fiddle as, 'a theft by a service agent from his customer which is practiced in such a way as to make it interactionally and inventorily invisible'. He goes on to suggest that, 'it seems to be more realistic to see those amounts pilfered and fiddled by workers in the same way as we look at the "perks" of the executive – as an invisible part of wages' (Ditton, 1979). Mars (1974, 1994), also studied pilfering. He suggested that there was consistency in the teamwork practice of the dock workers he studied. Simply put, if consistency in legitimate teamwork is accepted, then consistency in illegitimate teamwork is also likely. The same study also drew out the idea of moral careers at work involving not only learning about a new job, but how to get on in a job and this invariably means fiddling. Moral transformations must take place which allow an employee to pass both the formal training of the job and the informal procedures which are often 'shady'. An acceptable degree of pilfering was tolerated among the dock workers but overstepping the mark – for example taking something of too large a value or being too greedy – would constitute theft.

Those crimes at work that have been exposed have, as the examples above suggest, tended to concentrate on working-class operators (Ditton, 1979; Mars, 1974; Henry, 1981; Mars and Nicod, 1981; Gill, 1994). Access to such areas of work, although not without difficulties, is perhaps easier than gaining access to conduct investigations in large intimidating corporate suites. This was a problem confronted by Braithwaite (1986) who conducted an in-depth study of corporate crime in the pharmaceutical industry. But if we consider that every legitimate occupation has opportunities for crime there would appear to be a disproportionate imbalance in the academic and business research focus. There would appear to be more concentration on those workplaces that afford more ready access and which also tend to include the lumpenproletariat of criminals who commit crimes at work rather than the 'high status' criminals in the workplace. For example, Mars' (1974) study of dock pilferage was part of a wider study of longshoremen. As an anthropologist Mars worked in the field collecting case study material through participant observation. Although access was not easy there were no corporate doors to be slammed in his face. Access should not be an excuse for criminologists ignoring middle- and upper-class professions and workplaces as sites for criminal activity. As argued in Chapter 1, imaginative combinations of research techniques and methods need to be developed in order to facilitate research on crime perpetrated with the privacy afforded by 'closed doors' or by advanced information technology.

Deconstructing Crime at Work

Gender
On the whole the study of crime and offenders, up until the 1980s, concentrated upon men and boys as the primary subject matter (Heidensohn, 1996). When focusing upon the workplace as the scene of criminal or anti-social activities and engaging with the literature in this area, the same kind of bias holds true. In this particular area of criminology women as offenders and victims in the work setting have been even more routinely marginalised and hidden from view than others. Women have not been so traditionally associated with work outside the home as men and when they have been viewed as workers they have not been considered as 'real' workers in the domestic setting (Oakley, 1974) or have been seen as contributing to a limited range of work roles. This has led to a marginalisation of women as workers generally and has contributed specifically to their relative invisibility, *vis-à-vis* men, in relation to the crime-work equation.

An exception to this can be found in the work of Madeleine Leonard (1994) who has detailed various forms of informal economic activity in Belfast. A close read of this work shows it has many implications for criminologists and in particular for the gendered study of crime at work.

Women's roles as primary perpetrators of crime generally remain hidden. In particular, the independent role of women themselves as rational white-collar criminals, as business offenders, as entrepreneurs in crime, as women who are motivated by economic greed rather than need remains unthinkable. The business of crime has been masculinised and linked to an assumed male trait of entrepreneurship. There has been patchy analysis and little theorising on the ways in which some women, who on the whole commit economic forms of crime in greater proportions to other forms of crime, may be doing so because of the attractions offered by the rewards of criminal activity (for a more detailed exploration of these issues see Davies, 1998). Where women are included in research it is as secondary rather than as primary participants and they tend to be relegated to mere assistants to their male counterparts (Mars, 1974; see also Hobbs, 1995).

There is a further factor contributing to women's relative invisibility not just as perpetrators of crime but also as victims of crime. Croall has suggested (see Chapter 2 in this volume) that some male jobs are inherently more risky and hence expose men more routinely to dangerous practices. The masculinisation and feminisation of current criminological concerns in relation to, say, health and safety crimes, is worth exploring. In particular, the gendering of risk needs further research, and professions and workplaces need to be subjected to analysis in such terms. There have been some studies conducted on crime against employees, for example a survey on social workers by Norris (1990), and research on police officers (Noaks and Christopher, 1990), but few have gendered their analysis. There is potential for such analysis across a range of locations.

That said, a number of feminist-inspired pieces of empirical research *have* been carried out on some professions. Few of these approaches have been developed, although there are some notable exceptions including survey work conducted on police officers on the subject of sexual and racial harassment and equal opportunities (see for example

Brown, 1997; Anderson et al, 1993; Commission for Racial Equality, 1996). Other work has been conducted on sexual harassment in the field of education (Herbert, 1989), and on university campuses (Carter and Jeffs, 1995; Dziech and Weiner, 1990). There is scope for further analysis of harassment in the workplace.

In criminology generally there has been an emerging emphasis on the ways in which the commission of crime and victimisation are gendered and are also structured by class, race, age and other variables. Crime and victimisation are not spread evenly across the population. If crime at work is emerging as a venue for further forms of criminal victimisation then these variables must be built into the research design. Conclusions drawn from such studies can only then be usefully employed to formulate crime and victimisation prevention measures in both the private and public sectors. Making business practices, workplace environments and working routines less invisible and more transparent is only the first step towards reducing criminal victimisations.

Class

The criticisms and complexities surrounding the study of crime at work in the 1990s cannot be divorced from Sutherland's seminal work and the definitional issues which arose surrounding white-collar crime in the 1940s. His work inspired others to debate whether class-based analyses are helpful when looking at occupational, organisational, business, corporate and professional crimes. Definitional issues in respect of these categorisations have been the principal subject of other more recent work (Croall, 1992; Sheley, 1995) whilst others have exposed the over-concentration on 'proletarian' crime and deviance and have in their own work raised the profile of 'bourgeois' criminality (Pearce, 1976; Cohen, 1977; Levi, 1981; Croall, 1992; Muncie and McLoughlin, 1996). There is still much more scope for exposing further examples of inter- and intra-class criminality and victimisation. Such issues have been the subject of criminological interest in respect to traditional crimes but this has less often been true where non-traditional crimes and offenders are concerned. Braithwaite (1986) has indirectly discussed white-collar on white-collar criminality in the context of company-against-company crimes, for example, industrial espionage and bribery, and Punch (1996) has also addressed this dimension but such a focus is the exception not the rule. In the higher echelons of the corporate business world there are also variations on the theme of fiddling. In these instances the invisibility of the crime is masked not only by the workplace, but by the 'normalisation' of illicit activities as acceptable business practice (Braithwaite, 1986). In other instances it is because there is a diffusion of victimisation or because there is no obvious victim. Whatever the reason, there is scope for research which reduces the invisibility of such crime.

By focusing attention on the location of crime in the workplace we are invited to become part of a criminology that seeks to gain a much fuller understanding of the variety, extent and diversity of criminal and anti-social activities. The broad heading crime at work can be broken down into various constituent parts including crimes at work, offenders at work and victims at work. Although there have clearly been studies conducted in these areas – and some of these date back a long time – the areas have only partially been explored. For example, there has been little attention focused on the way in which the workplace is one particular location which might be susceptible to criminal activity and actions precisely because the job requirements needed and the person specifications that are valued in the workplace, are similar to those which make a good criminal. There have been examples of research on such issues but this has been fragmented. Perhaps this continued problem of invisibility is in part due to this continued lack of attention given to the structural variables of which class and gender are but two that are worthy of further cross-examination. The problem of invisibility is also, more significantly, due to the continued lack of attention given to the ways in which such variables operate within a particular location of criminal activity and victimisation. The workplace as a location for criminal activity can be used to demonstrate the blurred boundaries between what is legal/illegal, what is work/crime. It is at these types of broad junctures that many obscured forms of crime and victimisation take place.

How and why they take place will be influenced by the ways in which the features of particular locations interact with the variables of gender and class (including *their* interactions).

CRIME AS WORK

In this section we further examine relationships between legitimate and illegitimate forms of work, between business practice and the business of crime. The crimes that are discussed here are not themselves necessarily invisible: on the contrary, often they are highly visible. The invisible features, or what we refer to here as the 'blurring problem', refers to the way in which these crimes are differentially understood by both academics and offenders themselves. As Ditton has put it, the aim is 'to illustrate the utterly confusing normality with which the criminal enterprise can sometimes be clothed' (Ditton, 1979). This type of blurring is largely an outcome of our inability to theorise appropriately, and consequently this section argues that some crimes should be examined from a less traditional and more appreciative perspective. This can involve perceiving crime as a 'normal' form of work, with its own practices, its own hours of operation and its own rewards.

Criminological research that has focused on offence categories distinguishes between 'instrumental' and 'expressive' crimes, between crime for kicks and excitement as opposed to crime for economic gain. A perspective that looks at crime-as-work might start by investigating those crimes most clearly associated with the latter. A focus on ways of making a living by illegitimate or illegal means allows us to adopt an offence and/or offender specific approach. Offences such as property or 'economic' crimes including thefts and shoplifting, frauds, some drugs offences and prostitution could be reassessed in this way. By analysing these offenders and their activities and taking account of class, gender and other variables, a much more detailed and thorough understanding of the crime problem can be achieved.

Moreover, a growing body of work can be identified that recognises the connections between some types of criminal activity – and lifestyles of offenders – which have similarities with work activities and with occupational traits. This literature can be divided between that which concentrates on working-class criminals and street offences on the one hand and white-collar or occupational and business crimes on the other. Those who are concerned with the former are writers such as Hobbs (1988, 1995), Maguire (1982), Walsh (1986), Bennett and Wright (1984), Gill and Matthews (1994) who have variously written about criminal entrepreneurship, 'doing the business', criminal careers and dishonest work in burglary and armed robbery, often from the offenders' perspective. All of these writers have predominantly specialised in working-class, male criminals and their offending patterns. However, these growing understandings of male criminal career patterns could usefully be considered in relation to women's offending patterns, particularly in relation to crimes that women commit for economic reward such as property crimes, drug dealing offences, fraud and forgery, shoplifting, welfare and social security frauds and prostitution (see Davies, 1998).

The authors mentioned above draw attention to the parallels between normal, or legitimate work routines and illegal or illegitimate trades and activities. Maguire (1982), Walsh (1986) and Bennett and Wright (1984) also point out the way in which criminals go about their burglaries and robberies, the way they prepare for, talk about and rationalise their activities. It is interesting to note the use of language that their informants use to describe their activities. Rather than inventing a new language to describe what they do, they borrow from the language (and routines) used by legitimate jobs of work. They 'learn a trade', 'serve an apprenticeship', prostitutes 'clock on and clock off' (McLeod, 1982) and might find themselves – as do Maguire's burglars – on different rungs of the employment ladder as amateurs or professionals, specialists and so on. In a similar way Foster has distinguished between 'league divisions of villainy' (Foster, 1990: 14).

Authors that are concerned with the more powerful white-collar, occupational and business criminals and their activities include Block (1991a, 1991b), Conklin (1977), Levi (1987), Braithwaite (1986) and Punch (1996). That a blurring of boundaries between the legitimate and illegitimate occurs here too is variously illustrated by these authors. Punch, for example, when discussing 'The Business of Business' writes:

> What hardly occurs to most businessmen, however, is that what they are doing is illegal, unethical, or criminal. For many of the actors in the cases we know of the deviant practices were perceived as 'normal' routine (even when concealed), and normally neutral matters. (Punch, 1996: 245)

In the same publication, *Dirty Business*, Punch makes it clear that the assumption throughout the book will be that the legitimate and illegitimate are bound together; 'the phenomenon of business deviance, and business crime, *is inseparable from the legitimate conduct of business*' (Punch, 1996: 45). Levi (1987), has also pointed out the ways in which illegal and legitimate business interests merge. He uses the illustrations of fraud, tax evasion, political corruption, terrorism and narcotics, which, he writes:

> are intimately linked via the need for secrecy and immunity from law enforcement that they require. Increasingly, this has been achieved by the use of international tax havens as conduits for money and as legally registered bases for operations. It has also been achieved through using professionals – lawyers and accountants – as intermediaries in the perpetration of crime. (Levi, 1987: 277)

Braithwaite (1986) has also drawn attention to research that makes the point about 'the corporation as pusher' and about the similarities between illegitimate and legitimate businesses in the context of drugs.

The case made here is for further criminological work which seeks to understand what is formally recognised as crime but which is viewed by the participants themselves as a normal part of everyday social functioning. Such illumination should be in terms of the participants rather than the potentially blurring preconceptions of academics and of criminal justice practitioners. Building in the arguments of preceding sections, such understandings should be located in the context of the workplace (whether in the formal or participant meaning of the word) and should be mediated by the ways in which such locations interact with gender and class.

CONCLUDING COMMENTS

Several important concluding remarks can be made about crime and work connections. First, using crime and work as a principal organising theme provides a perspective from which to conduct criminological research and formulate theory. This perspective for understanding activities which might be labelled as criminal, not only reveals certain illegal activities and behaviours that take place but it does so within certain locations. In this way it begins to illuminate how the location obscures many illegal activities. The concepts of crime and work have been shown to produce a 'double blurring' of our vision of both what crime is and what work is. It is against this context that connections between crime and work can be explored.

Second, by focusing upon crime and work connections we are able to assess precisely which connections have previously been examined, what the limitations and omissions of this body of work are. The general invisibility and lack of systematic knowledge about the nature and extent of criminal acts and victimisations in different locations is widespread. Although there have been pockets of research conducted in different work-based locations of crime, including building sites within the construction industry, shopping centres, shops, business premises for example, most criminological work focuses on street-level crime. The workplace is one example of a location which might be further explored to reveal many more nuances about the nature and extent of crime and victimisation. The ways in which forms of crime and victimisations are structured in such locations has only partially been examined, and gender in particular appears to be systematically invisible.

Third, the crime–work theme allows a further dimension to be explored, that of how crime can be considered as a form of work. This form of analysis enables us to uncover, but more importantly better *appreciate*, types of activities which can be seen to contribute to either the regular and legal economy, or/and the hidden and illegal economy. This viewing of crime – as a form of work – is not a common feature of mainstream criminological work and represents a devaluation of explanation-by-understanding and of the importance of appreciating the actors' perspective. Criminologists need to 'rationalise' in the same way as the 'criminals' themselves do in their own social, environmental, economic and political situations.

REFERENCES

Anderson, R., Brown, J. and Campbell, E. A. (1993) *Aspects of Sex Discrimination in Police Forces in England and Wales* (London: Home Office Police Research Group).

Austin, C. (1988) *The Prevention of Robbery at Building Society Branches*, Crime Prevention Unit Paper, No. 14 (London: Home Office).

Bennett, T. and Wright, R. (1984) *Burglars on Burglary: Prevention and the Offender* (Aldershot: Gower).

Block, A. (1991a) *Masters of Paradise* (New Brunswick: Transaction).

Block, A. (1991b) *The Business of Crime* (Boulder, Co: Westview Press).

Box, S. (1981) *Deviance, Reality and Society* (Holt, Rinehart & Winston).

Box, S. (1987) *Unemployment, Crime and Deprivation* (London, Sage).

Box, S. (1992) *Power, Crime and Mystification* (London: Routledge).

Braithwaite, J. (1986) *Corporate Crime in the Pharmaceutical Industry* (London: Routledge and Kegan Paul).

Brown, J, (1997) 'Equal Opportunities and the Police', in P. Francis, P. Davies and V. Jupp (eds.) *Policing Futures, the Police, Law Enforcement and the Twenty-First Century* (Basingstoke: Macmillan Press).

Cameron, M. O. (1964) *The Booster and the Snitch* (London: Free Press).

Carter, P. and Jeffs, T. (1995) *A Very Private Affair, Sexual Exploitation in Higher Education* (Nottingham: Education Now).

Chambliss, W. J. (1978) *On the Take* (Bloomington: Indiana University Press).

Chaudhary, V. and Weller, M. (1993) 'War Crimes', *The Guardian Education*, 27 April.

Cohen, A. K. (1977) 'The Concept of Criminal Organisation', *British Journal of Criminology*, 17(2), 97–111.

Cohen, A. K. (1993) 'Human Rights and Crimes of the State: the Culture of Denial', *Australian and New Zealand Journal of Criminology*, 26(2).

Commission for Racial Equality (1996) *Race and Equal Opportunities in the Police Service: a Programme for Action* (London: Commission for Racial Equality).

Conklin, J. E. (1977) *Illegal But Not Criminal* (New Jersey: Spectrum).

Croall, H. (1992) *White Collar Crime* (Buckingham: Open University Press).

Davies, P. (1998) 'Women, Crime and and Informal Economy: Female Offending and Crime for Gain', paper presented to British Criminology Conference, 15–18 July 1997, Queen's Univeristy of Belfast, and in M. Brogden (ed.), *British Criminology Conferences: Selected Proceedings*, Vol. 2.

Ditton, J. (1979) *Part-time Crime. An Ethnography of Fiddling and Pilferage* (London: Macmillan).

Dobash, R. P. and Dobash, R. E. (1979) *Violence Against Wives: the Case Against Patriarchy* (New York: Free Press).

Dziech, B. W. and Weiner, L. (1990) *The Lecherous Professor: Sexual Harrassment on Campus* (Urbana: University of Illinois).

Ekblom, P. (1987) *Preventing Robberies at Sub-Post Offices: an Evaluation of a Security Initiative*, Crime Prevention Unit Paper, No. 9.

Field, S. (1990) *Trends in Crime and Their Interpretation: a Study of Recorded Crime in Post-war England and Wales*. Home Office Research Study, No. 119 (London: HMSO).

Fineman, M. A. and Mykitiuk, R. (eds.) (1994) *The Public Nature of Private Violence: the Discovery of Domestic Abuse* (New York, London: Routledge).

Foster, J. (1990) *Villains, Crime and Community in the Inner City* (London: Routledge).

Gibbens, T. C. N. and Prince, J. (1962) *Shoplifting* (London: Institute for the Study and Treatment of Delinquency).

Gill, M. (ed.) (1994) *Crime at Work: Studies in Security and Crime Prevention* (Leicester: Perpetuity Press).

Gill, M. and Matthews, R. (1994) 'Robbers on Robbery: Offenders' Perspectives', in M. Gill (ed.) (1994) *Crime at Work: Studies in Security and Crime Prevention* (Leicester: Perpetuity Press).

Harding, P. and Jenkins, R. (1989) *The Myth of the Hidden Economy* (Milton Keynes: Open University Press).

Heidensohn, F. (1996) (2nd edn) *Women and Crime* (London: Macmillan).

Henry, S. (1981) *Can I Have it in Cash? A Study of Informal Institutions and Unorthodox Ways of Doing Things* (London: Astragal Books).

Herbert, C. M. H. (1989) *Talking of Silence: the Sexual Harrassment of Schoolgirls* (London: Falmer).

Hobbs, D. (1988) *Doing the Business* (Oxford: Clarendon Press).

Hobbs, D. (1995) *Bad Business* (Oxford: Oxford University Press).

Kettle, M. and Bowcott, O. (1997) 'Analysis: Computer Crime', *The Guardian*, 12 December.

Lamplugh, D. (1997) 'Personal Safety at Work: Issues, the Law and Practice', in *International Journal of Risk, Security and Crime Prevention*, 2(1).

Laycock, G. (1984) *Reducing Burglary: a Study of Chemists' Shops*, Crime Prevention Unit Paper, No. 1 (London: Home Office).

Leonard, M. (1994) *Informal Economic Activity in Belfast* (Aldershot: Avebury).

Levi, M. (1981) *The Phantom Capitalists* (London: Gower).

Levi, M. (1987) *Regulating Fraud: White-Collar Crime and the Criminal Process* (London, New York: Tavistock).

MacDonald, R. (1994) 'Fiddly Jobs, Undeclared Working and the Something for Nothing Society', *Work, Employment and Society*, 8(4), 5–7–530.

Maguire, M. (1982) *Burglary in a Dwelling: the Offence, the Offender and the Victim*, Cambridge Studies in Criminology (London: Heinemann).

Mars, G. (1974) 'Dock Pilferage', in P. Rock and M. MacIntosh (eds.), *Deviance and Social Control* (London: Tavistock).

Mars, G. (1994) *Cheats at Work: an Anthropology of Workplace Crime* (Aldershot: Dartmouth).

Mars, G. and Frosdick, S. (1997) 'Operationalising the Theory of Cultural Complexity: a Practical Approach to Risk Perceptions and Workplace Behaviours', *International Journal of Risk, Security and Crime Prevention* 2(1).

Mars, G. and Nicod, M. (1981) 'Hidden Rewards at Work: the Implications from a Study of British Hotels', in S. Henry (ed.), *Can I Have it in Cash? A Study of Informal Institutions and Unorthodox Ways of Doing Things* (London: Astragal Books).

Mayhew, P., Elliott, D. and Dowds, L. (1989) *The 1988 British Crime Survey*, Home Office Research Study, No. 111 (London: HMSO).

McLeod, E. (1982) *Women Working: Prostitution Now* (London: Croom Helm).

Muncie, J. and McLoughlin, E. (1996) *The Problem of Crime* (London and Buckingham: Sage in association with the Open University).

Munday, R. (1986) 'Who are the Shoplifters?', *New Society*.

Naffine, N. and Gale, F. (1989) 'Testing the Nexus: Crime, Gender and Unemployment', *British Journal of Criminology*, 29(2), 1989, 144–56.

Nelken, D. (1997) 'White Collar Crime', in M. Maguire, R. Morgan and R. Reiner (eds.), *The Oxford Handbook of Criminology*, 2nd edn. (Oxford: Clarendon).

Noaks, L. and Christopher, S. (1990) 'Why are Police Assaulted?' *Policing*, Winter, 625–38.

Norris, D. (1990) *Violence Against Social Workers* (London: Jessica Kingsley).

Oakley, A. (1974) *The Sociology of Housework* (London: Martin Robertson).

Pearce, F. (1976) *Crimes of the Powerful* (London: Pluto).

Punch, M. (1996) *Dirty Business: Exploring Corporate Misconduct Analysis and Cases* (London: Sage).

Ruggiero, V., South, N and Taylor, I. (1998) *The New European Criminology* (London: Routledge).

Schwendinger, H. and Schwendinger, J. (1975) 'Defenders of Order or Guardians of Human Rights?' in I. Taylor, P. Walton and J. Young (eds.), *Critical Criminology* (London: Routledge).

Shapland, J. (1998) 'Looking at Opportunities in the Informal Economy of Cities', in H. J. Albrecht and J. Shapland (eds.), *Informal Economies: Threats and Opportunities in the City* (Freiburg Im Breisgau: Max Planck Institute for Foreign and International Criminal Law).

Sheley, J. F. (1995) (2nd edn), *Criminology: a Contemporary Handbook* (London: Wadsworth Publishing Company).

Smith, L. J. F. (1987) *Crime in Hospitals: Diagnosis and Prevention*, Crime Prevention Unit Paper, No. 7 (London: Home Office).

Smith, S. (1986) *Britain's Shadow Economy* (Oxford: Clarendon Press).

Sutherland, E. W. (1949) *White Collar Crime* (New York: Holt, Rinehart & Winston).

Sutton, M. (1998) *Handling Stolen Goods and Theft: a Market Reduction Approach*, Home Office Research and Statistics Directorate Research Findings, No. 69 (London: HMSO).

Walsh, D. (1986) *Heavy Business: Commercial Burglary and Robbery* (London: Routledge and Kegan Paul).

Part II
Types of Crimes and their Victims

4 Health and Safety Crimes: (In)visibility and the Problems of 'Knowing'

Steve Tombs

INTRODUCTION

In 1983, Steven Box described a 'collective ignorance' regarding the extent and nature of corporate crime (Box, 1983: 16). Since then, whilst some varieties of corporate crime have undoubtedly been hoisted onto social, political and legal agendas, most notably some forms of 'economic' crimes, the category of corporate crime upon which this chapter focuses – health and safety crimes by employers resulting in occupational deaths – remains largely absent from such agendas. The chapter begins with an attempt to determine the numbers of occupationally caused deaths, and the numbers of these deaths associated with crimes by employers. Each of these tasks is beset by enormous difficulties, yet it is still safe to conclude that the scale of unlawful workplace deaths vastly outweighs the numbers of recorded homicides. This blunt conclusion prompts a series of considerations, which form the second, and main part of the chapter, which examines why there remains little or no recognition of the scale of safety crimes. Here, the chapter addresses a number of mechanisms through which the discourses of law and order, and the collective ignorance regarding corporate crime in general, and safety and health crimes in particular, are created and maintained, namely: ideologies of business; media representations of crime, law and order; the nature of victimisation; causal complexity; official forms of data classification; methodological problems; and, finally, the organisation and objects of inquiry of academic disciplines.

COUNTING DEATHS AT WORK

Published, confirmed figures for fatal injuries at work, for the period April 1994 to March 1995 reveal that a total of 376 fatal injuries were reported under the Reporting of Injuries, Diseases and Dangerous Occurrences Regulations (RIDDOR, 1985), to all enforcement authorities. This figure is a 'record low' (Health and Safety Commission, henceforth HSC, 1996a: 79) for the recorded fatal injury rate. Yet despite the Health and Safety Executive (henceforth, HSE) claim that data on fatal injuries is 'virtually complete' (HSC, 1996b: 1), this data is actually far from complete. Many more people are killed by working than is indicated in this 'headline' figure.

First, it does not include deaths or injuries arising out of the supply or use of flammable gas, despite the fact that these are reportable to HSE as occupational incidents; for 1994/95, there were 36 fatalities reportable under RIDDOR (the lowest number on record). Second, this figure excludes fatal injuries that occur in the course of sea fishing and those arising out of transport and communications work under the Merchant Shipping legislation (HSC, 1996b: 102). In 1994 (a calendar year) these contexts accounted for 26 deaths and 1 death respectively (Marine Accident Investigation Branch, Department of Transport, personal communication, 4 September 1997). Third, and perhaps most significantly, fatal injury data recorded by HSC/E excludes all deaths which arise whilst driving in the course of employment. A recent series of RoSPA publications have, on the basis of conservative assumptions, attempted to estimate road traffic deaths involving people at work (Bibbings, 1996; RoSPA, 1997a, 1997b, 1998; see also *Hazards*, 1995, 52: 6); for 1994, RoSPA calculated 877 deaths (Bibbings, 1996: 21). The omission of such data from the fatal injury statistics is a glaring (and perhaps curious) one.

If all these data are taken together, 1316 deaths from fatal injuries at work can be identified. However, this figure does not exhaust the numbers of those killed as a result of work activity per annum; to this must be added deaths arising from occupationally caused fatal illness. Here existent data is much less useful (HSC, 1996a: 86). The most reliable source is maintained by HSE, based upon copies of death certificates that are forwarded to them. These cover a small number of occupational diseases, namely asbestosis, mesothelioma, pneumoconiosis, byssinosis and some forms of occupationally caused alveolitis; in other words, these are illnesses with the clearest possible occupational causes, most of them in fact related to exposure to asbestos. For several reasons, doctors and coroners are unlikely to record accurately occupational causes on death certificates (Slapper and Tombs, 1999), so that even within the specified categories of diseases, this data only includes a small proportion of relevant deaths (HSC, 1996b: 68). Moreover, such categories themselves are only a small proportion of workplace-caused fatal illness (*Hazards*, 1995, 51: 11).[1] Yet notwithstanding the gross underestimation entailed in the levels of occupational deaths recorded, data for 1994/95 records 1409 deaths caused by asbestos exposure (meso-thelioma and asbestos-caused lung cancer) in workplaces and 293 deaths due to occupationally caused lung disease other than asbestosis (that is, pneumoconiosis, byssinosis and some forms of occupationally caused alveolitis) (HSC, 1996b: 158). That is, a total of 1702 deaths have been unequivocally recorded as occupationally caused. Adding to this figure the number of deaths from fatal injuries (1316) gives a total of 3018 occupationally caused deaths in one year.

As some indication of the scale of these deaths, comparison might be made with annual homicide totals. Homicides retain a significant place within popular definitions of violence and within social constructions of problems of crime, law and order, even if the actual number of such deaths is relatively small. In 1994, the year most directly comparable with the HSE data, the number of homicides – that is, recorded deaths by murder, manslaughter or infanticide – in England, Wales and Scotland was 834 (in the ten years between 1985 and 1994, the number of homicides ranged between 700 and 850 per annum) (personal communication, Crime and Criminal Justice Unit, Home Office, and Scottish Office Statistical Bulletin, 1995). Thus the combined figure of 3018 recorded occupational fatalities is almost four times the number of recorded homicides.

Contra the claims of Box (1983) and Reiman (1979), such data represents the relative scale of the 'social problems' of deaths at work and homicide, rather than equating simply to a 'crime, law and order' problem.[2] In order to address any distortions inherent in social definitions of the latter, it is necessary to know what proportion of deaths at work are related to crimes on the part of managements or employers, since all the homicides are, by definition, the result of crimes.

HEALTH AND SAFETY CRIMES AT WORK?

Determining what proportion of workplace deaths are attributable to employers' health and safety crimes is, given the paucity of available data, a difficult exercise, and one in which assumptions certainly must be made. However, these assumptions can be made in a way which, contra Nelken (1994), and Shapiro (1983), need not descend into mere moralising (Levi, 1994: 300).

One means of calculating what proportion of deaths are the result of criminal offences by employers might be to resort to prosecution or other enforcement data. However, the reluctance of the HSE to resort to formal enforcement action is well documented (Bergman, 1991, 1993; Slapper, 1993; Pearce and Tombs, 1990, 1991), and this reluctance is becoming increasingly more marked (HSC, 1996b: 38; HSC, 1997; Tombs, 1996). But there is some available evidence which allows some comment to be made on the scale of criminal activity and omission involved in the causation of workplace deaths.

First, there exists a series of special investigations into groups of fatalities undertaken by HSE in the 1980s, representing an invaluable source of data given that many fatalities, and the vast majority of non-fatal injuries, are never subject to any detailed investigation (Bergman, 1994). Of particular significance is that the findings from these separate investigations proved remarkably consistent. It was found that managements bear primary responsibility for the 'accidents' under investigation in 73 per cent (HSE, 1985a), 78 per cent (HSE, 1985b), 83 per cent (HSE, 1985c), between 68 and 75 per cent (HSE, 1987), 70 per cent (HSE, 1988), two out of three (HSE, 1983), and three out of five (HSE, 1986) cases. While these investigations sought to determine underlying causes rather than allocate 'blame' or legal responsibility, their conclusions are of some use in clarifying the location and level of responsibility entailed in their incidence, even if they clearly cannot be taken as legal judgements (Bergman, 1994). Further, we can set these conclusions against the relevant legal test of responsibility, which is that managements must do 'all that is reasonably practicable' to eliminate a risk or prevent an accident/injury. This standard of reasonable practicability – long criticised by some for explicitly allowing an element of economic cost-benefit analysis (Moore, 1991) – is the minimal duty of care that is required by health and safety legislation in the UK, and sits at the heart of the Health and Safety at Work (HASAW) Act. On best available evidence, in the majority of 'accidental' injuries examined by HSE, most of them producing fatalities, managements were in contravention of the General Duties (Sections 2 and 3) of the HASAW Act 1974, a criminal statute, whether or not the HSE choose to enforce it as such through legal proceedings (Bergman, 1991; Tombs, 1989).

A second body of relevant data is to be found in the form of the now considerable stock of detailed material within reports which resulted from commissions of inquiry into a whole series of disasters that occurred in the UK (mostly in the latter half of the 1980s). Slapper has provided a useful catalogue of these (Slapper, 1993: 424; see also Harrison, 1992; Wells, 1993), and has rightly noted that in each case 'the relevant companies have been inculpated by the evidence (and with some official enquiry report) in contributing in some significant way to the cause of death' (Slapper, 1993: 424). Indeed, such was the weight of evidence relating to corporate misconduct that the combination of these disasters and official reports led to the re-emergence of arguments for corporate manslaughter in the UK (Tombs, 1995; Slapper, 1993), arguments eventually taken up (albeit inadequately) in the form of proposals by the Law Commission (Law Commission, 1996; Cahill, 1997), and (it seems) by the Labour government (*The Guardian*, 3 October, 1997).

Finally, there exists a series of Accident Investigation Reports, again produced by HSE, consisting of one-off, but highly detailed, examinations of particular incidents, which usually had resulted in one or a small number of fatalities. Again, in each case, despite there rarely following any prosecution (let alone for manslaughter or unlawful killing), these reports usually provide more than enough evidence to point to clear contraventions of the General Duties of the HASAW Act (Tombs, 1989).

Each of these bodies of evidence points to the clear conclusion that in the majority of cases of workplace fatalities there is at least a criminal case to answer. Unfortunately, there is no comparable evidence that can be brought to bear on the causation of occupational (fatal) illness as exists for occupational injuries. However, given that the evidence on management responsibility for occupational fatalities points to consistent and basic managerial 'failings', there is absolutely no reason to believe that occupational health is likely to be managed any more effectively. Further, there is much less scope in the context of health, rather than safety, for responsibility (organisational and legal) for fatalities to be blurred through charges of worker carelessness, apathy, stupidity, non-compliance, so that claims of collusion in the context of ill-health are even less likely to be grounded in reality than they are in the case of safety (Tombs, 1991). Matters of occupational safety are often related to physical hazards, which are (potentially at least) more 'obvious'; health hazards, by contrast, often operate 'silently', cumulatively and gradually. While occupational health is not occupational safety, the differences mean that it is reasonable to expect greater numbers of deaths from occupational ill-health to be attributable to managements than fatal accidents.

It should now be clear that there are enormous problems in determining how many people die as a result of being at work, and even greater problems determining how many of these deaths are the result of criminal activity or omission on the part of employers. Yet the scale of deaths caused by working activity is both enormous and largely obscured. Even a highly conservative estimate for workplace deaths arrived at a figure almost four times greater than numbers of homicides; at least two out of three workplace fatalities appear to occur as a result of criminals acts or omissions on the part of employers; and employers are more rather than less likely to bear responsibility for deaths from occupationally caused illness. It is absolutely clear that *deaths from safety and health crimes far outnumber deaths from homicide*. Yet while the former do not impinge upon popular representations of the crime, law and order problem, the latter are a key element of these.[3]

CRIME, LAW AND ORDER: (IN)VISIBILITY AND THE PROBLEMS OF KNOWING

It is not intended that formal political and legal constructions of crime, law and order be discussed in this chapter. For the record, however, it is clear that both formal politics and the law play crucial roles in the production and maintenance of dominant definitions of crime, law and order. At the political level, this is the case in terms of particular policies – such as resourcing for various enforcement agencies – and in the subject matter of the formal politics of crime, law and order. The political rhetoric of crime, law and order also largely excludes corporate crimes, and certainly safety and health crimes. Cries of 'zero tolerance', 'three strikes and you're out', mandatory sentences, being 'tough on crime and tough on the causes of crime', 'short sharp shocks', and protecting and furthering the rights of victims have all been deployed in the context of street or traditional crimes, even though they are perfectly applicable to corporate offending (see, for example, Etzioni, 1993; Geis, 1996; Lofquist, 1993). The collective ignorance is reinforced.[4]

Moving from formal politics to law and legal regulation, we find that at every stage of the legal process, law tends to operate quite differently with respect to corporate crimes than in the context of 'conventional' and more 'visible' crimes. An examination of the very framing of the substance and parameters of legal regulation, its enforcement, the ways in which potential offences and offenders are investigated, the prosecution of offences, and the use of sanctions following successful prosecution, all point towards the conclusion that safety and health crimes are relatively decriminalised.[5]

These claims regarding politics and law cannot, of course, be made in a static, once-and-for-all sense; the politics of crime, law and order, and the operation of each stage of the legal process noted above, are both dynamic and complex processes. Indeed, while there are trends towards criminalising safety and health offences in the UK, there are simultaneous, and more significant, counter-pressures towards deregulation and decriminalisation in the sphere of workplace safety and health (Tombs, 1996).

Ideologies of Business

One key contributing factor to the collective ignorance regarding corporate crime, or health and safety crimes at work, is that this requires speaking of business organisations as potential offenders. There are important obstacles to such speaking.

Business organisations are legitimate organisations. They perform socially useful and socially necessary functions. They create necessary goods and services, employment, taxation revenues, shareholder dividends, and so on. This is not to say that business activity could not be organised differently from current capitalist forms – it clearly could be – but it is to accept that the business *per se* is not criminal. However, the effect of this point is one that is vastly exaggerated and has consequences in terms of the 'knowing' of health and safety crimes. First, the legitimacy of business organisations is often represented as standing in contradistinction to those objects of 'traditional' crime concerns; most of those who end up being processed through the criminal justice system are treated as some form of burden upon society in a way that business organisations are not. This is intimately related to a second point. Where business organisations engage in criminal activity, then this is represented and/or interpreted (not least by many academics; Pearce and Tombs, 1990, 1991) as side-effects of their core, legitimate activities, a clear contrast with representation of many forms of conventional criminality, within which various manifestations of pathology remain predominant. In fact, there are good reasons – both empirical and theoretical – for accepting that criminality is endemic to business activity within corporate capitalism (Pearce and Tombs, 1998). Alongside the notion that crime is a side-effect of legitimate business activity stands a third, and closely related, claim: namely that where business organisations are involved in criminality, then this is mostly trivial, consisting of illegalities which are *mala prohibita* rather than *male in se*. Again, this argument is difficult to sustain either empirically or theoretically (Pearce and Tombs, 1990, 1991; Wells, 1993); yet again it retains a popular and academic predominance.

Of course, it should be noted that these ideological distinctions between business organisations and traditional criminals, and in particular the legitimacy that attaches to business organisations, are far from static. Indeed, for eighteen years Britain has witnessed a generalised and often very conscious construction of a pro-business ideology, one of a very particular form within which the concept of free enterprise has been resurrected in the context of a struggle to reassert neo-liberal hegemony (Pearce and Tombs, 1998). An element of this is of course a particular version of law and order from which business offences are largely excluded (Brake and Hale, 1992: 134). Here, the key phrase is not simply 'enterprise' but '*free* enterprise' – that is, business activity increasingly free from regulation. It is no coincidence, then, that the reassertion of this ideology has been accompanied by very conscious efforts at deregulation (Tombs, 1996). Such has been the effect of this ideological and material assault on regulation that the Labour government elected in 1997 has, far from seeking to challenge it, sought to positively embrace it, in order to establish its pro-business credentials.

The Mass Media

Images of crime, law and order within the mass media both reflect and in turn reinforce dominant social constructions of what constitutes the crime problem in contemporary Britain, within which 'traditional' or at least 'visible' street crimes are central.[6]

An examination of the treatment of crime, law and order in the broadcast media makes the relative invisibility of corporate crimes in general, and safety and health crimes in particular, immediately clear. A survey of fictional treatments of crime issues across any of the terrestrial or satellite TV channels reveals a preoccupation with 'cops and robbers', that is, with various aspects of (albeit fictionalised) street crimes. This is not to imply that there are not occasional treatments of corporate crimes but they are extremely rare and when they do exist they tend to be based on financial crimes.

One reason for this bias in fictional broadcasting may be the claim that many forms of corporate crime do not make for very interesting television, particularly where the crimes involved are based upon acts of omission: for example not testing certain hazardous substances, not acting upon information about the obvious and serious risks of ferry turnaround times, not meeting standards of maintenance on industrial plant, may not make gripping television. However, traditional crime is just as intrinsically uninteresting, only made worthy of drama through fictionalisation, so that, for example, televisual images of policework bear little or no relation to the ways in which most police officers spend most of their time.

Turning to non-fictional programming, there is perhaps more extensive coverage of corporate crime within the overall diet of crime, law and order issues. There are certainly treatments of corporate crime, and even safety and health crimes, amongst the British documentary 'classics', but there is a relative imbalance in their profile. This relative imbalance is also reproduced through daily newspaper coverage of crime, law and order issues, where conventional versions of crime, law and order predominate. To claim that corporate crime is not covered in daily newspapers would be inaccurate. But a cursory examination of recent crime, law and order reporting in a number of national newspapers suggests a number of clear, if at this stage highly provisional, conclusions.[7]

First, the sheer volume of coverage of conventional crimes vastly outweighs that of corporate crimes. Second, where corporate crime is treated in mainstream print media, such coverage is less rather than more prominent than treatments of conventional crime. Corporate crime is less likely to be reported within the mass circulation tabloids than it is in the broadsheets; and within broadsheets, corporate crime reporting has a lesser profile than that of conventional crimes, being located in specialist sections rather than in earlier news and features pages. Third, corporate crime is also treated in more specialist rather than popular contexts. Amongst the broadsheets, corporate crime receives by far the greatest volume of coverage in the *Financial Times*; but this is a publication which has a specialist rather than general readership, and stands tenth out of eleventh in overall circulation tables for daily newspapers.

Further, while specialist sections of broadsheets do cover aspects of corporate crime, they tend to do so in a way that does not treat these as crime, law and order issues. There are various ways in which this latter effect is produced, and indeed these are common both to print media and the broadcast media considered above. First, representations of corporate crimes tend not to treat them as *corporate* crimes. Most notably, corporate crimes are considered via personalities, and it is the dominance of individual, 'respectable' figures that renders them newsworthy. Relatedly, such crimes are considered newsworthy for their very abnormality. In other words, they may become individualised, which at the same time has the effect, in many instances, of obscuring their causes, their normality, their routineness. Moreover, to focus upon the individuals involved in such crimes is to obscure the corporations, structures and systems within which, and on behalf of which, they are likely to have offended.

If the corporate origins and nature of corporate crimes are often obscured in their reporting, then so is the fact that they are *crimes*. The term scandal, one frequently used to refer to corporate crimes (Tumber, 1993), is no doubt a highly critical one, but one which carries with it implications of (im)morality rather than legal offence. Moreover, where crimes are treated as scandals (or exposés, and so on), this again serves to emphasise their novelty or rarity. In these ways, the normality of corporate crimes, and their location within (and commission on behalf of) a particular organisational form – the corporation – is again obscured.

The term 'scandal' is an instance of the more general way in which particular forms of language are central to the production and reproduction of crime, law and order issues. Language carries with it particular connotations of causation (and thereby appropriate modes of prevention and regulation) and effects (seriousness). Wells (1993) has noted the potency of different forms of language attaching to different types of criminal activity:

> The word 'fraud' is an anaesthetising generic term for a number of offences including theft. If we do not call a white-collar thief a thief then we should not be surprised that it sounds a little odd to talk of a corporation stealing (or wounding or killing). The idea is difficult to contemplate because our image of the thief is of an individual physically taking the property of another. There is a conflict between the images, reinforced by the choice of language, of different types of offence and offender and the possible categories into which they could legally be placed. (Wells, 1993: 10)

Thus, she continues, 'the deployment of words such as "accident" rather than "violence" to describe the outcome of corporate risk-taking will undoubtedly influence the construction which is placed upon it' (Wells, 1993: 13).

Indeed the language of 'accidents' is one which focuses upon specific events, abstracting them from a more comprehensible context (Scheppele, 1991). It evokes discrete, isolated and random events, and carries with it connotations of the unforeseeable, unknowable and unpreventable, despite the fact that, as we have noted above, any examination of a range of incidents reveals common, systematic, foreseeable and eminently preventable causes and consistent locations of responsibility. Similarly, both the languages of accident and illness invoke events or phenomena in which victims are implicated, via their carelessness, apathy or lifestyles (bad eating, lack of exercise, alcohol or tobacco use, and so on; Tombs, 1991).

Finally, the term 'accident' carries with it implications regarding intentionality, or the lack of it, which are crucial in the context of safety and health crimes. Thus Goldman (1994) notes that what she calls 'accidentality terms':

provide us with an account of the mental element – intention, will, desire, deliberation, purpose, etc. – in some event. When describing some incident or process as an 'accident', or having 'occurred/been done accidentally' rather than 'deliberately' or 'intentionally', we conflate information not just about causation, and perhaps (if pertinent) degrees of culpability and fault to be imputed, but also about the element of consciousness that intruded into the event. (Goldman, 1994: 51–2)

There is no doubt that some of this language is the result of conscious corporate manipulation, both generally and in relation to specific events (Wells, 1993: 40). This is hardly surprising given the privileged access to, and indeed the ownership of, all forms of mass media by large corporate interests. Moreover, as Wells notes, and as is particularly the case given issues of victimisation relating to safety and health crimes in particular, the further removed the harms they cause are from the public experience, then the easier is such manipulation (Wells, 1993: 40). However, the use of particular forms of language need not be understood simply, or perhaps even largely, as the result of conscious manipulation, since 'The social construction of behaviour and events results from a complex interaction between a number of factors, including cultural predispositions, media representations, and legal rules, decisions, and pronouncements' (Wells, 1993: 13).

VICTIMISATION AND CAUSAL LOGISTICS

The Nature of Victimisation

It has been noted that victimology has become a key growth area in criminology and law (Gordon and Pantazis, 1997). A key element of victimology is the uncovering of unrecorded crime. But if self-reporting and victim-based studies can uncover significant levels of unrecorded ill-health and injury (Stevens, 1992; Davies and Teasdale, 1994), these are unlikely to reveal much about unrecorded safety and health crimes. There are a variety of reasons which lead to this conclusion.

First, many victims of health and safety crimes are unlikely to be aware of their status as victims (as is the case with corporate crimes more generally; see Croall, 1989). Most of us remain unlikely to think of our workplace as a causal site when suffering some form of illness, and even less likely to consider unhealthy conditions in terms of illegality on the part of our employer. Equally, in the event of accidents – be these major or minor – ideologies of the accident-prone worker are so prevalent that workers often routinely place blame upon themselves, as a result of their carelessness or bad luck (Tombs, 1991). Where representations of self-blaming or collusion are resisted, victims of safety and health crimes may still be unaware of the legal status of what they have experienced – that is, they may have a sense that they are victim of an injustice, or a wrong, but not a criminal offence on the part of an employer.

Second, where victims of health and safety crimes are aware of their status as victims, actually acting upon this awareness is often extremely difficult (again, this is the case with corporate crimes more generally; Croall, 1989). An informed understanding of the extent of these difficulties may actually act as a disincentive against reporting or acting (Green, 1990: 25). Yet even where victims might seek redress, independently (via civil law, for example) or through an enforcement agency, then difficulties of locating an offender or offenders, and the distance in time and space between victim and offender(s), are likely to prove overwhelming obstacles. Thus, if workers are aware that a skin rash, breathing problems, nausea, headaches and so on are likely to have a primary cause in working conditions, the burden of proof rests with them. And proof in such instances must make reference to scientific discourses to which they may not have access.

Somewhat differently, even an awareness that a particular condition can be caused by workplace exposures – for example, the well-known diseases associated with asbestos fibres – raises enormous difficulties in locating exposures to a particular workplace or employer, at a particular time. The fact that many industrial diseases take long periods to develop – sometimes as much as forty or fifty years – makes pursuing (let alone proving) a case against a particular employer very difficult. This is compounded where a worker has been employed by different companies over the course of a working life (HSC, 1996a: 63). Moreover, given the apparent increasingly complex organisation and fragmentation of businesses, as well as the enhanced prevalence of contracting out and 'self-employment', problems of locating causality and lines of accountability and responsibility are likely to be exacerbated.

In fact, there is a real sense in which those individuals and groups most likely to be victims of safety crimes are those who are least able to recognise their status, or act upon this recognition. Thus victims of safety and health crimes are much more likely to work in smaller rather than larger workplaces, or to be self-employed or on short- or fixed-term contracts, to be non-unionised, and receiving relatively low levels of pay. In other words, safety and health crimes remain relatively invisible partly because patterns of victimisation exacerbate what have been called, in another context, structures of vulnerability (Nichols, 1986). In this way, victimisation processes with respect to safety and health crimes may not be dissimilar to those of other forms of crime, particularly violent crime, of which safety and health crimes are a subset (see Maguire, 1994: 270).

Causal Complexity

There are, then, substantial technical and legal (not to mention political) difficulties associated with recognising, explaining and acting upon occupationally caused ill-health. A related issue, then, in the relative invisibility of health and safety crimes is that of causal complexity. In the context of victimisation, I touched upon issues around the complex nature between offender and victims. However, in the context of corporate crimes in general, and safety and health crimes in particular, the issue of complexity is also of relevance with respect to the nature of both offences and offenders.

Thus it is frequently noted that one key reason for a collective ignorance around corporate crime is the complexity that much of this criminality involves. Certainly much corporate crime involves complex planning, most notably in the commission of financial crimes. This complexity is partly a consequence of the transnational nature of some corporate crimes, which also renders effective regulation problematic. Thus Levi (1993) notes that 'almost all serious securities frauds involve extraterritorial informational needs on the part of national agencies' (Levi, 1993: 79); for example, 80 per cent of cases investigated in London 'have some cross-border aspects' (Levi, 1993: 80). Similarly, Braithwaite (1993) has stated of transnational pharmaceutical industry crime that:

> the offenses that we are discussing are complex to start with, before one adds the problem of international jurisdictional tangles. There is the complexity of the books – paper trails through the finances and the raw scientific data that are difficult to follow. Then there is the scientific complexity of cutting-edge technology . . . Then there is organisational complexity. (Braithwaite, 1993: 14)

However, while there is no doubt that many forms of corporate crimes are complex in their causation, it would be unwise to exaggerate this aspect of corporate offending. It is frequently the case that corporate crime arises from very simple acts of commission or omission – the failure to adequately test or label substances, the failure to train or inform employees, the failure to meet basic standards of environmentally protective engineering standards – and so on. In fact, there are two other issues that are of greater relevance here than causal complexity *per se*, but which can be confused with complexity. One is the carefully constructed and legally protected corporate veil behind which corporate structures, decision-making, lines of accountability and responsibility remain largely hidden from public scrutiny, a veil which serves, often deliberately, to confound legal challenge. As Braithwaite (1984) wryly observes, 'When Corporations want clearly defined accountability, they can generally get it. Diffused accountability . . . is in considerable measure the result of a desire to protect individuals within the organisation by presenting a confused picture to the outside world' (Braithwaite, 1984: 324).

Second, and relatedly, is the problem of intentionality. Thus when dealing with corporate crime we are dealing with corporations (and all the obscurity thereby entailed) rather than individuals, and relatedly with a body to which traditional notions of intention sit rather uneasily. These issues present themselves as problems because of the individualising nature of bourgeois law.

Yet neither of these issues presents insuperable technical legal problems. For example, while in Britain the charge of corporate manslaughter remains a highly difficult one to pursue successfully, there are no insuperable problems intrinsic to law to the effective criminalisation of such offences, as Bergman (1991, 1994), Slapper (1993) and Wells (1993) have demonstrated; what is commonly lacking is political will, itself related to particular representations of law and order and what constitutes real crime. Thus while English law does not provide for the aggregation of the actions of different controlling officers (Moran, 1992, Slapper, 1993), this is possible in other jurisdictions (Slapper, 1993), not least within US federal law (Wells, 1993: 118–20). Such initiatives indicate that the corporate veil can be pierced and the issue of intention resolved.

METHODOLOGICAL OBSTACLES TO KNOWING

A further set of factors relating to our relative ignorance of corporate crime in general, and safety and health crimes in particular, are of a methodological nature.

One type of methodological problem relates to the nature of official data which are collected and available. Reference to *the* crime statistics usually means the annual publications by the Home and Scottish Offices which include details of notifiable offences recorded by the police (Reiner, 1996: 186). These official statistics overwhelmingly focus upon conventional crimes. Thus, most corporate crimes 'do not feature in official crime statistics which serve as the basis for debates about the "crime problem"' (Nelken, 1994: 355; Green, 1990: 27).

What of official health and safety statistics? It has been argued in earlier sections of this chapter that establishing the number of deaths caused by work, let alone the numbers of deaths at work resulting from safety crimes, is far from straightforward. In fact, a more meaningful measure of corporate violence would have been major injuries at work; but there are insuperable problems in the use of official data on such injuries. Notwithstanding the legal requirement to do so, the vast majority of such injuries – fractures, loss of limbs and sight, serious burns and periods of unconsciousness – remain unreported (HSC, 1996b: 49–61; Stevens, 1992). There is almost a complete lack of utilisable data regarding the scale and distribution of ill-health caused by working. Moreover, for both safety and ill-health, the bases upon which such data are collected and classified have been subject to so many changes since 1974 that longitudinal analysis is almost impossible (Tombs, 1990, 1992; Nichols, 1991). As was demonstrated in the earlier sections of this chapter, one consequence of the paucity of available data, itself a result of legal and political processes, is that we must make a series of assumptions before we can arrive at any form of utilisable figure, and then engage in social scientific work in order to begin to make estimates about the numbers of crimes involved in these fatalities. No matter how careful one's assumptions, and no matter how rigorous the social scientific work on data and available evidence, the very fact of manipulating data opens one up to the charge of producing overly subjective and 'non-scientific' work, a charge particularly likely when researching issues which are both marginalised but also some potential threat to powerful interests (Kramer, 1989: 152). Finally, if the interest is in causation rather than outcome – that is, not the illness, injury or death *per se* but whether or not it was criminally produced – then there are enormous methodological problems in classifying the date and location of many offences, as well as problems in identifying offenders (Bergman, 1994: 11–12).

Put simply, if we want to know something about safety crime, we will not be able to learn this from health and safety statistics, nor from safety crime (i.e. enforcement action) data itself. None of this is to deny the problems with, and inadequacies of, crime statistics for so-called traditional crimes. Yet there is no doubt that one of the key means of defining or representing the seriousness or otherwise of certain forms of criminal activities is through reference to quantitative data, so that 'numbers' remain predominant as a 'descriptive medium' (Maguire, 1994: 236). If a key aspect of talking about crime, law and order is talking numbers, then it is almost impossible to include occupational deaths in any such conversation. The result is relative silence with respect to the latter.

In addition to these particular concerns relating to the inadequacies of official corporate crime data is a series of more general methodological problems encountered in attempting to examine the nature of health and safety crime. Access to offenders is problematic for researchers of conventional crime; yet in comparison with offenders or potential offenders in the context of corporate crime, conventional crime researchers are dealing with the relatively powerless which, whether we like it or not, renders such work immediately more feasible than dealing with, and seeking to focus upon, the relatively powerful (Reed, 1989: 79, cited in Punch, 1996: 4). Of course, while methodological issues such as gaining access from the 'outside', the role of gatekeepers, the co-operation of the researched and so on are common across social research, the extent to which they may, or do, prove problematic varies context by context. *In general*, there are good reasons to expect it to be more difficult to research the relatively powerful, where such research involves access to the powerful themselves. Where access *is* successfully negotiated, the possibilities of deliberate obfuscation on the part of the researched is greater where one is dealing with individuals who are often well-educated, possessing highly developed social skills, socialised into particular business ideologies and corporate cultures, and so on. Moreover, researching corporate crime often requires access to data that the offenders themselves possess, and jealously guard, be these internal financial or other forms of records, minutes, memoranda regarding safety standards or knowledge of health hazards, or knowledge of conversations. Nor do ethnographic approaches offer a more productive avenue for such research (Punch, 1996: 43).

One of the consequences of these methodological problems is a tendency to rely upon whistle-blowers and investigative journalists, so raising issues of 'accuracy, frequency, or representativeness' (Nelken, 1994: 356). Equally, material relating to corporate crime that is made available on a case-specific basis, as is often the case, raises the problematic issue of representativeness and our (in)ability to generalise (Punch, 1996).

CONCLUSIONS: ACADEMICS, (IN)VISIBILITY, AND THE PROBLEMS OF KNOWING

None of the various mechanisms noted above whereby corporate crimes are rendered relatively invisible, and particular versions of crime, law and order are produced and maintained, is remarkable in isolation. What is crucial, however, is their mutually reinforcing nature, so that in their combination they have powerful effects in terms of reproducing social constructions and also erecting obstacles to knowing about corporate crimes in general, and safety and health crimes in particular. In the face of obstacles to knowing, one group who may be approached are academics. This group possesses the economic, social and intellectual capacities/resources to bring to the empirical and analytical fore hitherto neglected social problems. Our record in terms of corporate crime is not, however, particularly impressive.

Punch has noted that there are two places within academic institutions where one might expect to find corporate crime representing an object of study, namely those places where businesses are studied, and those where crime is studied (Punch, 1996: 41). Neither is actually the site of much energy being devoted to knowing about corporate crime in general or safety and health crimes in particular.

It is hardly surprising that pro-business ideologies pervade business schools. Moreover, when the law is encountered within business curricula it is as something to be known, of course, but also to be negotiated or controlled; the law is classically part of the 'external environment' which provides a possible source of interference with business activities, the end and only goal of which must be to maximise profitability (Pearce and Tombs, 1997). Within such a value system, one which most students and academics embrace, addressing issues of corporate crime is hardly likely to be welcomed or taken seriously. To be sure, within some curricula there

are 'small enclaves' which address ethics and social responsibility (Punch, 1996); but these are frequently seen as soft,
and indeed are marginal within the overall curriculum, in
marked contrast to the real areas of business teaching (and
research), namely those of finance, marketing and strategy.
In these areas, business schools teach the 'how to do' of
business, and do so in a way which is characterised by
theoretical poverty and an 'unreflective empiricism' (Punch,
1996: 42). Any considerations of criminality or ethics are
overwhelmed by the main agendas within business schools.

If we turn to the work of socio-legal scholars and criminologists, we also find aspects of the economic, political
and social organisation of academic study which have mili-
tated against a focus upon corporate crimes in general,
and safety and health crimes in particular.

First, the work of academic criminologists remains partly
trapped by popular definitions of the crime problem, even
if there are understandable reasons for this (see, for example,
Garland, 1994: 28–31). Levi provides a particular illustra-
tion of this:

> The conceptual issue of what acts count as violence does
> not cause too many difficulties for criminologists because
> they usually ignore it. Almost all of the literature on ex-
> plaining violent crime focuses exclusively on violence as
> conventionally defined. (Levi, 1994: 322)

Criminologists still tend to focus relatively little on corporate crime (Punch, 1996: 41).

Second, it remains the case that the majority of academic
work on corporate crime remains American. This is not
problematic in the sense that much of this work raises
empirical, conceptual, methodological and theoretical issues
of more general, that is cross-national, relevance. But it
also has to be said that much of this work is context-specific
– and understandably so, given that its reference points
will include systems of law and enforcement which are specific
to US state and federal levels.

Third, within existent work on corporate crime there
remains a tendency to focus upon economic crimes, rather
than upon, for example, safety and health crimes. Kramer
(1989) notes that 'Most of the literature on white-collar

and corporate crime – and the public perception of these crimes – tends to focus on the economic effects of these acts' (Kramer, 1989: 149); thus he argues for the need to include physical harms (Kramer, 1989: 149).

It seems that researching safety and health at work in the context of criminology raises the issue of partisanship in social research. Certainly once one is drawn to a study of health and safety at work, then one is drawn – eventually if not immediately – into the proposal of reforms. Moreover, the logic of such reforms is also likely to be of the kind that will challenge the parameters set by capitalist relations of production (Szasz, 1984). This creates a peculiar terrain upon which social scientists, if they are to study the regulation of health and safety at work, must tread. They are led to studying something about which it is very difficult to be neutral, and about which being partisan has potentially real consequences. There is no need here to re-enter arguments regarding the nature of social scientific enterprise and its relationships to 'objectivity' and partisanship. My own view is that there is no necessary contradiction (though there may be contingent tensions) between adherence to criteria of good scholarship, or methodological rigour on the one hand, and political engagement on the other. Indeed, given the politicised nature of inquiries into safety at work, it is far preferable that academic interventions into this sphere are openly represented also as political interventions.

These points are particularly significant following almost two decades of Conservative government during which the terrain of acceptable academic discourse has been shifted to the right, where even critical work has upon it a greater burden of suggesting immediate and feasible reform rather than concluding in fundamental and societal critique. Indeed, the UK has been the site of considerable reordering of relationships between academic research and sources of funding. These have largely tended to render a critical, partisan social science in general, and criminology in particular, less rather than more likely. Changes in the funding and the organisation of research have resulted in a greater emphasis upon utility rather than critique, towards research which is 'more focused and market driven' (Partington, 1997:

23), and towards more rather than less monitoring from 'stakeholders' (Hillyard and Sim, 1997). Government-funded research has become more proactive, with the greater scarcity of funding being just one of the factors that allows for a much closer specification of terms and conditions of contract research (Hillyard and Sim, 1997: 56–7). The definitions of both feasible reform and utility are increasingly open to influence by those who provide funding for research. Indeed, the availability of funding affects not simply the use of the outcomes of research but the types of research that does (and does not) get done, with changing commitments of the Economic and Social Research Council (ESRC) in general, and the nature and aims of its Governance and Regulation theme in particular, being paradigmatic (Hillyard and Sim, 1997: 54–6).

Each of the these phenomena is likely to make it less rather than more likely that a partisan criminology of safety and health at work will be developed within Britain. This emerging political economy of research will influence what work is done, where it is done, how it is done, who funds it, by whom it is done, for what it is done, and what ends up being done with it. This new political economy does not bode well for a critical academic assault upon collective social ignorance of corporate crime in general, and of safety and health crime in particular.

Almost ten years ago, Ronald Kramer urged, and sketched the outlines of, a social movement against corporate crime, within which academic criminologists would play a key part (Kramer, 1989). His exigence demands reiteration. Academics have a responsibility to bring to the fore hitherto neglected social problems, to describe them, explain their incidence, frequency, costs, causation, and their amelioration. We are a privileged group, possessing the economic, social and technical resources to meet challenges posed by, and the social problems associated with, differential 'knowing'. That is, after all, our job.

NOTES

1. For example, the HSC/E notes that 'the existing routine sources of information on occupational cancer greatly underestimates its scale . . . the best available estimate is that 4 per cent of cancer deaths have occupational causes, with a range of acceptable figures from 2 to 8 per cent, which would correspond to between 3000 and 12 000 deaths per year in Britain today' (HSC, 1996b: 84).

2. And workplace deaths and injuries certainly *are* a *social* problem. For example, recent HSE studies which have considered the costs of occupational accidents and ill-health at the level of the British economy as a whole have put these at £4–£9 billion per year, or 2–3 per cent of Gross Domestic Product, equivalent to 5–10 per cent of all UK trading companies' gross trading profits in 1990 (Davies and Teasdale, 1994; see also HSE, 1993). Moreover, it is important to note that these estimates exclude what were termed either 'unpreventable' accidents (Davies and Teasdale, 1994: 73, HSE, 1993: 4) or those which did not exceed a minimum level of loss (HSE, 1993; Cutler and James, 1996: 757), potentially excluding accidents with the potential to cause serious injuries, if not fatalities (Cutler and James, 1996: 759). As Woolfson and Beck have recently noted, 'most of the costs of accidents do not fall upon employers. The primary costs are borne by insurance, injured employees' families, and, to a large degree, the welfare state' (Woolfson and Beck, 1997: 15).

3. The issues highlighted in this section are addressed in detail elsewhere (Tombs, forthcoming).

4. The argument intimated here is not meant to imply that corporate crimes can be treated homogeneously. Indeed, a key exception to this formal political focus on street crime to the exclusion of corporate crime is to be found in the cases of some forms of corporate crimes, namely financial crimes, and in particular serious frauds. There are, of course, very good reasons why financial crimes, of all forms of corporate crimes, have attracted particular political attention (see Levi, 1993; Snider, 1991; Tombs, 1995). Further, if corporate crime cannot be treated homogeneously, then it is also clear that it would be inaccurate to treat 'traditional' crime in a similar fashion. The argument here is one of a general relative contrast.

5. There is now a body of work which examines these aspects of the legal process in relation to safety and health offences in British workplaces, most notably the following: Bergman, 1991, 1993, 1994; Carson, 1971; Hawkins, 1990, 1991; Moore, 1991; Pearce and Tombs, 1990, 1991; Sanders, 1985; Slapper, 1993; Tombs, 1995; Wells, 1993; Whyte and Tombs, 1998; Woolfson and Beck, 1997. A more detailed discussion of this truncated section can be found in Pearce and Tombs, 1998 and Slapper and Tombs, 1998.

6. It is instructive that a recent text examining 'The Media Politics of Criminal Justice' contains one half-page consideration of 'white-collar crimes', and at least one other one-line reference to these crimes amongst its almost 300 pages (Schlesinger and Tumber, 1994).

7. These points regarding the coverage of corporate crime within the print media are based upon a preliminary analysis of crime, law and order reporting in *The Sun* and the *News of the World*, *The Mirror* and *Sunday Mirror*, *The Guardian* and *The Observer*, the *Daily* and *Sunday Telegraph*, and the *Financial Times* over a six-week period. Material gathered from these sources is in the process of being subjected to a detailed content analysis of the relative coverage of corporate and conventional crime, undertaken by the author and Dave Whyte.

REFERENCES

Bergman, D. (1991) *Deaths at Work. Accidents or Corporate Crime* (London: Workers' Educational Association).

Bergman, D. (1993) *Disasters: Where the Law Fails. A New Agenda for Dealing with Corporate Violence* (London: Herald Families Association).

Bergman, D. (1994) *The Perfect Crime? How Companies can get away with Manslaughter in the Workplace* (Birmingham: West Midlands Health and Safety Advice Centre).

Bibbings, R. (1996) *Managing Occupational Road Risk. Discussion Paper* (Birmingham: RoSPA).

Box, S. (1983) *Power, Crime and Mystification* (London: Tavistock).

Braithwaite, J. (1984) *Corporate Crime in the Pharmaceutical Industry* (London: Routledge and Kegan Paul).

Braithwaite, J. (1993) 'Transnational Regulation of the Pharmaceutical Industry', in G. Geis and P. Jesilow (eds.), *White Collar Crime*, 12–30 (New York: Atherton Press).

Brake, M. and Hale, C. (1992) *Public Order and Private Lives* (London: Routledge).

Cahill, S. (1997) 'Killing for Company', *Company Secretary*, March, 24–6.

Carson, W. G. (1971) 'White Collar Crime and the Enforcement of Factory Legislation', in W. G. Carson and P. Wiles (eds.), *The Sociology of Crime and Delinquency in Britain*, Volume 1 (Oxford: Martin Robertson), 220–36.

Croall, H. (1989) 'Who is the White-Collar Criminal?', *British Journal of Criminology*, 29(2), 157–75.

Cutler, T. and James, P. (1996) 'Does Safety Pay? A Critical Account of the Health and Safety Executive Document: "The Costs of Accidents"', *Work, Employment & Society*, 10(4), 755–65.

Davies, N.V. and Teasdale, P. (1994) *The Costs to the British Economy of Work Accidents and Work-Related Ill-Health* (London: HSE Books).

Etzioni, A. (1993) 'The US Sentencing Commission on Corporate Crime: a Critique', in G. Geis and P. Jesliow (eds.), *White-Collar Crime*, 147–56 (New York: Atherton Press).

Garland, D. (1994) 'Of Crimes and Criminals: the Development of Criminology in Britain', in M. Maguire, R. Morgan and R. Reiner (eds.), *The Oxford Handbook of Criminology* (Oxford: Clarendon), 17–68.

Geis, G. (1996) 'A Base on Balls for White-Collar Criminals', in D. Shichor and D. K. Sechrest (eds.), *Three Strikes and You're Out. Vengeance as Public Policy* (Thousand Oaks, CA: Sage), 244–64.

Goldman, L. (1994) 'Accident and Absolute Liability in Anthropology', in J. Gibbons (ed.), *Language and the Law* (London: Longman), 51–99.

Gordon, D. and Pantazis, C. (1997) 'Beyond Victimisation: Towards a Theory of Social Harm', paper presented at XXV Conference of the European Group for the Study of Deviance and Social Control, Kazimierz n. Wisla, Poland, 11–14 September.

Green, G. S. (1990) *Occupational Crime* (Chicago: Nelson Hall).

Harrison, K. (1992) 'Manslaughter by Breach of Employment Contract', *Industrial Law Journal*, 21(1) 31–43.

Hawkins, K. (1990) 'Compliance Strategy, Prosecution Policy and Aunt Sally: a Comment on Pearce and Tombs', *British Journal of Criminology*, 30(4), 444–66.

Hawkins, K. (1991) 'Enforcing Regulation: More of the Same from Pearce and Tombs', *British Journal of Criminology*, 31(4), 427–30.

Health and Safety Commission (1996a) *Annual Report 1995/96* (Sudbury: HSE Books).

Health and Safety Commission (1996b) *Health and Safety Statistics, 1995/96* (Sudbury: HSE Books).

Health and Safety Commission (1997) *HSC Plan of Work for 1997/9* (London: HSE).

Health and Safety Executive (1983) *Annual Report of the Chief Inspector of Factories, 1982* (London: HMSO).

Health and Safety Executive (1985a) *Deadly Maintenance: Plant and Machinery. A Study of Fatal Accidents at Work* (London: HMSO).

Health and Safety Executive (1985b) *A Guide to the Control of Industrial Major Accident Hazards Regulations 1984. HS(R) 21* (London: HMSO).

Health and Safety Executive (1985c) *Measuring the Effectiveness of HSE Field Activities. HSE Occasional Paper 11* (London: HMSO).

Health and Safety Executive (1986) *Agricultural Blackspot* (London: HMSO).

Health and Safety Executive (1987) *Dangerous Maintenance: a Study of Maintenance Accidents in the Chemical Industry and How to Prevent Them* (London: HMSO).

Health and Safety Executive (1988) *Blackspot Construction* (London: HMSO).

Health and Safety Executive (1993) *The Costs of Accidents at Work* (London: HSE Books).

Hillyard, P. and Sim, J. (1997) 'The Political Economy of Socio-Legal Research', in P. Thomas (ed.), *Socio-Legal Studies* (Aldershot: Dartmouth), 45–75.

Kramer, R. C. (1989) 'Criminologists and the Social Movement Against Corporate Crime', *Social Justice*, 16(2), 145–64.

Law Commission (1996) *Legislating the Criminal Code: Involuntary Manslaughter* (London: HMSO).

Levi, M. (1993) 'White-Collar Crime: the British Scene', in G. Geis and P. Jesilow (eds.), *White Collar Crime* (New York: Atherton Press), 71–82.

Levi, M. (1994) 'Violent Crime', in M. Maguire, R. Morgan and R. Reiner (eds.), *The Oxford Handbook of Criminology* (Oxford: Clarendon Press), 295–353.

Lofquist, W. S. (1993) 'Organisational Probation and the US Sentencing Commission', in G. Geis and, P. Jesilow (eds.), *White Collar Crime* (New York: Atherton Press), 157–69.

Maguire, M. (1994) 'Crime Statistics, Patterns, and Trends: Changing Perceptions and their Implications', in M. Maguire, R. Morgan and R. Reiner (eds.), *The Oxford Handbook of Criminology* (Oxford: Clarendon Press), 233–91.

Moore, R. (1991) *The Price of Safety: the Market, Workers' Rights and the Law* (London: Institute of Employment Rights).

Moran, L. J. (1992) 'Corporate Criminal Capacity: Nostalgia for Representation', *Social & Legal Studies*, 1(3), 371–91.

Nelken, D. (1994) 'White-Collar Crime', in M. Maguire, R. Morgan and R. Reiner (eds.), *The Oxford Handbook of Criminology* (Oxford: Clarendon Press), 355–92.

Nichols, T. (1986) 'Industrial Injuries in British Manufacturing in the 1980s: a Commentary on Wright's Article', *Sociological Review*, 34(2), 290–306.

Nichols, T. (1991) 'Industrial Injuries in British Manufacturing Industry and Cyclical Effects: Continuities and Discontinuities in Industrial Injury Research', *Sociological Review*, 39(1), 131–9.

Partington, M. (1997) 'Socio-Legal Research in Britain: Shaping the Funding Environment', in P. Thomas (ed.), *Socio-Legal Studies* (Aldershot: Dartmouth), 23–44.

Pearce, F. and Tombs, S. (1990) 'Ideology, Hegemony and Empiricism: Compliance Theories of Regulation', *British Journal of Criminology*, 30(4), 423–43.

Pearce, F. and Tombs, S. (1991) 'Policing Corporate "Skid Rows". A Reply to Keith Hawkins', *British Journal of Criminology*, 31(4), 415–26.

Pearce, F. and Tombs, S. (1997) 'Hazards, Law and Class: Contextualising the Regulation of Corporate Crime', *Social & Legal Studies*, 6(1), 107–36.

Pearce, F. and Tombs, S. (1998) *Toxic Capitalism: Corporate Crime and the Chemical Industry* (Aldershot: Ashgate).

Punch, M. (1996) *Dirty Business* (London: Sage).

Reed, M. (1989) *The Sociology of Management* (New York: Harvester Wheatsheaf).

Reiman, J. H. (1979) *The Rich Get Richer and the Poor Get Prison* (New York: John Wiley & Sons).

Reiner, R. (1996) 'The Case of the Missing Crimes', in R. Levitas and W. Guy (eds.), *Interpreting Official Statistics* (London: Routledge), 185–205.

Royal Society for the Prevention of Accidents (1997a) *Managing Occupational Road Risk. Campaign Update 12th March* (Birmingham: RoSPA).

Royal Society for the Prevention of Accidents (1997b) *Managing Occupational Road Risk. Campaign Update 12th April* (Birmingham: RoSPA).

Royal Society for the Prevention of Accidents (1998) *Managing Occupational Road Risk* (Birmingham: RoSPA).

Sanders, A. (1985) 'Class Bias in Prosecutions', *The Howard Journal*, 24(3), August, 176–99.

Scheppele, K. L. (1991) 'Law Without Accidents', in P. Bordieu and J. S. Coleman (eds.), *Social Theory for a Changing Society* (Boulder: Westview), 267–93.

Schlesinger, P. and Tumber, H. (1994) *Reporting Crime. The Media Politics of Criminal Justice* (Oxford: Clarendon).

Scottish Office Statistical Bulletin (1995) *Homicide in Scotland, 1984–1994* (Edinburgh: Scottish Office Central Statistics Office).

Shapiro, S. P. (1983) 'The New Moral Entrepreneurs: Corporate Crime Crusaders', *Contemporary Sociology*, 12, 304–7.

Slapper, G. (1993) 'Corporate Manslaughter: an Examination of the Determinants of Prosecutorial Policy', *Social & Legal Studies*, 2, 423–43.

Slapper, G. and Tombs, S. (1999) *Corporate Crime* (London: Longman).

Snider, L. (1991) 'The Regulatory Dance: Understanding Reform Processes in Corporate Crime', *International Journal of the Sociology of Law*, 19, 209–36.

Stevens, G. (1992) 'Workplace Injury: a View from HSE's Trailer to the 1990 Labour Force Survey', *Employment Gazette*, December, 621–38.

Szasz, A. (1984) 'Industrial Resistance to Occupational Safety and Health Legislation 1971–1981', *Social Problems*, 32(2) 103–16.

Tombs, S. (1989) 'Deviant Workplaces and Dumb Managements? Understanding and Preventing Accidents in the Chemical Industry', *Industrial Crisis Quarterly*, 3, Autumn, 191–211.

Tombs, S. (1990) 'Industrial Injuries in British Manufacturing Industry', *Sociological Review*, 38(2), 324–43.

Tombs, S. (1991) 'Injury and Ill-Health in the Chemical Industry: de-centring the Accident-Prone Victim', *Industrial Crisis Quarterly*, 5, January, 59–75.

Tombs, S. (1992) 'Safety, Statistics and Business Cycles: a Response to Nichols', *Sociological Review*, 40(1), 132–45.

Tombs, S. (1995) 'Law, Resistance and Reform: "Regulating" Safety Crimes in the UK', *Social & Legal Studies*, 4(3), 343–66.

Tombs, S. (1996) 'Injury, Death and the Deregulation Fetish: the Politics of Occupational Safety Regulation in UK Manufacturing', *International Journal of Health Services*, 26(2), 327–47.

Tombs, S. (forthcoming) 'Official Statistics and Hidden Crime: Researching Safety Crime', in V. Jupp, P. Francis and P. Davies (eds.), *Criminology in the Field: the Practice of Criminological Research*.

Tumber, H. (1993) '"Selling Scandal": Business and the Media', *Media, Culture and Society*, 15, 345–61.

Wells, C. (1993) *Corporations and Criminal Responsibility* (Oxford: Clarendon Press).

Whyte, D. and Tombs, S. (1998) 'Capital Fights Back: Risk, Regulation and Profit in the UK Offshore Oil Industry', *Studies in Political Economy*, 57 (September), 73–101.

Woolfson, C. and Beck, M. (1997) *From Self-Regulation to Deregulation: the Politics of Health and Safety in Britain*, Mimeo, Universities of Glasgow and St Andrews.

5 Cybercrimes: New Wine, No Bottles?[1]

David Wall

INTRODUCTION

Over the past two decades, the concept of cyberspace has developed from science fiction into a socially constructed reality (Benedikt, 1991; Gibson, 1984). It is now: 'a place without physical walls or even physical dimensions', where 'interaction occurs as if it happened in the real world and in real-time, but constitutes only a "virtual reality"'(Byassee, 1995: 199; Tribe, 1991: 15). The inhabitants of cyberspace are a virtual community of 'social aggregations that emerge from the Net[2] when enough people carry on public discussions long enough, with sufficient human feeling, to form webs of personal relationships in cyberspace' (Rheingold, 1994: 5). Only time will tell whether or not this virtual community will become Saradar and Ravetz's 'new civilisation which emerges through our human-computer interface and mediation' (1996: 1). What is certain is that the Internet creates considerably more opportunities for individuals to come into contact and to interact with others socially, economically and politically. Furthermore, as the 'intellectual land grab' (Boyle, 1996: 125) takes place for cyberspace, the emerging political economy of information capital will cause interests to become established and new distinctions to emerge between acceptable and deviant behaviour. Not only do new risk communities now accompany the old, but many previously acceptable activities have become relabelled as undesirable and now sit next to those behaviours which have been traditionally accepted as undesirable.

This chapter will explore the deviant behaviour that is becoming known as 'cybercrime'. The term cybercrime is mainly used here as a heuristic device and signifies the point(s) at which conventional understandings of crime are challenged. It is distinguished from 'high-tech' crimes, which relate to the theft of computer parts (Grundy and Wood, 1996), but is not so easily distinguished from computer crimes, of which hacking (pre-Internet, see later) was one. The first part of this chapter will consider the social impact of cyberspace, which is the site where cybercrimes can take place. The second part will outline the contours of cybercrimes by focusing upon four particular areas of undesirable behaviour which are causing concern: cyber-trespass, cyber-theft, cyber-obscenity and cyber-violence. The third part will look at who the victims of cybercrimes are and the fourth part will consider the issues which relate to the governance of this behaviour.

THE SOCIAL[3] IMPACT OF CYBERSPACE

Love it or loathe it, the Internet is here to stay. Not since the commercialisation of the radio in the 1920s has there been such a rapid growth in the usage of information technology (Walker, 1997: 9). At its current rate of growth it is estimated that there will probably be more than 500 million global netizens by the turn of the century (Mandel, 1993). In the United Kingdom, the numbers are much less, but the increase in usage is nevertheless striking. The House of Lords Select Committee on Science and Technology report estimated that in 1995/6, over a quarter of all households in the United Kingdom had personal computers and that the Internet Service Providers had in the region of 300 000 customers (1995–6: paras 1.1, 1.6). Today, the numbers are about double that figure.

Developed from a United States Department of Defence initiative to create a communications system that would survive a thermonuclear attack, the Internet has developed far beyond its original military and academic goals. During the past decade the Internet has developed into an exciting new public domain, which, by virtue of its ability to bypass geo-political, economic and social boundaries, is potentially free of conventional politics, social order and regulation. It has created a quantum leap in communications that is surpassing the introduction of the telephone, radio and television. What is significantly different this time is that the communications are two-way and can reach a potentially infinite number of people across a wide range of jurisdictions almost without restriction. So, the Internet, and particularly the cyberspace it creates, is not just a case of 'old wine in new bottles', or even 'new wine in new bottles'; for the most part it is more an example of 'new wine in no bottles'![4] Thus, cyberspace is reformulating the debate over modernity 'in ways that are not so mediated by literary and epistemological considerations, as was the case during the 1980s' (Escobar, 1996: 113).

One of the most obvious impacts of the colonisation of cyberspace has been the way that it has accelerated some of the qualities that have come to characterise high modernity, particularly the 'discontinuities' highlighted by Giddens (1990: 6) which separate modern and traditional social orders. According to Giddens, the social orders which bind time and space have become *disembedded* and *distanciated*; 'lifted out of local contexts of interaction and restructured across indefinite spans of time-space' (Giddens, 1990: 14; Bottoms and Wiles, 1996). The social impact of cyberspace upon the individual is only starting to be recognised. For the first time in history, individuals are free to develop social relations that are commensurate with their own interests or lifestyles and are potentially more meaningful than they could otherwise be. Individuals can now work in three dimensions instead of two, meaning that it is possible, for example, to do office work without office politics, and to work where abilities can be maximised, rather than where they are physically situated. However, whilst this form of social relationship has the advantage of avoiding the pitfalls of destructive *gemeinschaft*, it does, nevertheless, have a dark side in that it encourages the social deskilling[5] of the individual. A major concern is that over time, our terrestrial social life will tend to become both specialised and compartmentalised. As access to the Internet becomes more widely available through falling prices and public access policies, major divisions in society will come to be based upon access to information as much as upon socio-economic grounds. Those who do not engage with the technology will become excluded and the knowledge gap, or information exclusion, will put a new spin on our understanding of social exclusion.

In addition to engendering social and behavioural change, cyberspace has reconfigured many socially understood meanings which help to shape our behaviour. Unlike the terrestrial world, cyberspace is a virtual environment in which economic value is attached to ideas rather than physical property (Barlow, 1994). Consequently, as the numbers of intellectual property laws increase to establish ownership over these ideas, they are not only becoming commodified, but the process is, in effect, creating a new political economy of information capital (see Boyle, 1996). Because of this characteristic, these ideas or properties, and their value, are constantly faced with the threat of being appropriated, damaged or distorted.

So, perhaps the most important change from the point of view of this discussion is that cyberspace has now become an important quasi-industrial environment for capitalist production and it is also the site where intellectual, as opposed to physical, products are manufactured, traded, purchased and consumed. We have now an emphasis upon intellectual properties in the form of images and likenesses, copyrightable, trademarkable and patentable materials. These intellectual properties have immense value, due to the fact that the costs of reproduction are minimal. But these qualities also make them more vulnerable to appropriation.[6] As the nature of more familiar forms of property is changing, then so are the legitimate means by which goods are obtained. Money is rapidly becoming an electronic medium, cyber-cash can now be withdrawn from the many cyber-banks that are springing up, to be spent in any one of a number of cyber-shopping malls. In these ways, and others, cyberspace lays bare our conventional understanding of ownership and control. It also blurs the traditional boundaries between criminal and civil activities and also public and private law. Perhaps more importantly, it challenges many of the principles upon which our conventional understandings of crime and policing are based. Consequently, a number of important questions emerge as to what exactly are cybercrimes and to what extent do they differ from other activities that we currently recognise as crime?

THE CONTOURS OF CYBERCRIME

Traditional criminal activities, broadly speaking, display some fairly characteristic and commonly understood features (Gottfredson and Hirschi, 1990; Braithwaite, 1992). First, they tend to take place in real time as their time frame is determined by physical circumstances, such as speed and mode of transport. Second, they also tend to take place within defined geographical and social boundaries within which the actions they describe are governed by a body of substantive law that is germane to the area enclosed by the boundary (see Johnson and Post, 1996). Furthermore, the place where the criminal behaviour takes place is usually the same as where its impact is felt. Third, serious frauds and many white-collar crimes notwithstanding, the debate over traditional crimes is mainly located within working-class subcultures. Fourth, there are a set of consensual or core values about what does, or what does not, constitute a crime. Finally, traditional criminology has tended to be offender- rather than victim- or offence-based.

In contrast, cybercrimes differ from our understanding of traditional criminal activity in a number of distinctive ways. First, they do not respect time, space or place in that they have no easily definable boundaries, can span jurisdictions and they are instantaneous (Johnson and Post, 1996; Betts and Anthes, 1995: 16). Second, they are contentious in so far as there does not yet exist a core set of values about them which informs general opinion. At one level the culture of law enforcement is still informed by terrestrial conceptions of law; at another level few test cases have yet to go through the criminal courts to change legal cultures (Wall, 1997).[7] Third, they require considerable technical knowledge to be enacted, knowledge which is typically gained from further or higher education: although this is rapidly changing. Fourth, as the following arguments will demonstrate, there is no one set of consensual or core values about what does or what does not constitute a cybercrime. Furthermore, there is often some confusion as to whether what are regarded by some as cybercrimes, are in fact criminal activities (see later discussion). Finally, discussion of cybercrimes tends to be largely offence-, and to a lesser extent victim-based. Any discussion of the offenders tends to be in individual terms.

In short, cybercrimes possess qualities which turn many existing conceptions of traditional crime on their head; however, it will be demonstrated later that these descriptions of criminal activity serve to outline the respective polar positions. In practice, most of the (cyber) criminal activities discussed later in this chapter fall somewhere between the two. Some types of cybercrime resemble traditional crimes more than others, others resemble white-collar crimes whilst the remainder represent completely new forms of deviant behaviour.

There have been a number of attempts to classify cybercrimes. Some (Young, 1995: 1; Wasik, 1991) have focused upon the offender and have typologised them. Others have concentrated upon specific behaviours: the cybercrimes themselves (Schlozberg, 1983; Duff and Gardiner, 1996: 213). The main problem with these classifications is that they tend to have been established before the full commercial exploitation of the Internet and some even before the sophisticated development of the graphics user-interface, which has facilitated the commercialisation of the Internet. In the USA the FBI's National Computer Crime Squad identified a number of crime categories which it currently investigates.[8] They are: intrusions of the Public Switched Network (the telephone company); major computer network intrusions; network integrity violations; privacy violations; industrial espionage; pirated computer software; and other crimes where the computer is a major factor in committing the criminal offence. Although the National Computer Crime Squad's charter limits its investigations to violations of the *Federal Computer Fraud and Abuse Act* (1986)[9] the coverage, according to Fraser (1996), is still rather broad and imprecise, referring to location rather than activities.

One of the more useful attempts to understand cybercrimes was undertaken by the United Nations, which concluded in its *Manual on the Prevention and Control of Computer-Related Crime* (United Nations, 1995) that whilst there is a consensus amongst experts that cybercrime exists because 'the computer has also created a host of potentially new misuses or abuses that may, or should, be criminal as well' (United Nations, 1995: para 22), it nevertheless accepts that authors cannot agree as to what cybercrime actually is, arguing that definitions have tended to be functional, relating to the study for which they were written (United Nations, 1995: para 21).[10] The United Nations were not alone in reaching this conclusion as the Council of Europe's Committee on Crime Problems also avoided a formal definition of cybercrime, choosing instead to discuss the functional characteristics of specific activities. The committee wisely left individual countries to adapt the functional classification to their particular legal systems and historical traditions (United Nations, 1995: para 23). The United Nations manual did, however, discuss the role of criminal law, arguing that since it recognises the concepts of unlawful or fraudulent intent and also of claim of right, then any criminal laws relating to cybercrime would need to distinguish between accidental misuse of a computer system, negligent misuse of a computer system and intended, unauthorised access to or misuse of a computer system, amounting to computer abuse. It also argued that annoying behaviour must be distinguished from criminal behaviour in law (United Nations, 1995: para 24): points that were reflected in the European Commission Select Committee's recent Green Paper on the protection of minors (1996) (see later).

Beyond the problem of the specifics of definition, is the added difficulty of locating cybercrimes within an appropriate body of literature. Attempts to liken cybercrimes to white-collar crimes, state Duff and Gardiner (1996: 213), can be misleading as most forms of hacking cannot be seen as white-collar crime although the literature on white-collar crimes does inform the debate over cybercrimes. Much of the problem here is that the main body of literature on white-collar crime pre-dates the recent and rapid expansion of the Internet, and the term 'white-collar crime' has, to some extent, also become a residual category into which many non-traditional crimes have been placed. However, whilst it is clearly wrong to attempt to define cybercrimes as white-collar crimes, it is nevertheless possible to draw upon the literature on white-collar crimes to inform the debate over the nature of cybercrimes.

David Wall

A transposition of Nelken's (1997: 896) analysis of the problematic nature of white-collar crimes is particularly useful to our understanding of the nature of cybercrimes. Firstly, cybercrime is a contested concept. Not only is the nature of the subject matter in discussions of cybercrimes frequently unclear, but there is often doubt as to whether or not the behaviours actually count as crime in a formal-legal sense. This confusion arises from the fact that the definition of the severity of the offence has often been evaluated by the victims (see next section). Secondly, there is a problem of causality in that normal frameworks of criminological explanation don't really fit. There is often confusion between the 'how' and the 'why' (Levi, 1985). Furthermore, the search for causality is confused by the problem of what it is that actually needs to be explained, especially as it is often hard to distinguish between criminal behaviour and that which is deemed as normal business practice. On the one hand lies the problem of explaining cybercrime in terms used for traditional crimes, whilst on the other hand is the problem of either over-explaining or rationalising accounts so that they resemble normal business behaviour (Nelken, 1997: 907). Like white-collar crimes, the behaviour which constitutes cybercrimes is often indistinguishable from normal legal behaviour. Thirdly, there is the ambivalence of responses to cybercrimes, and these responses are important in the subsequent shaping of this behaviour. A good example of this ambivalence can be seen in the cases of the hackers Matthew Bevan, Richard Pryce and also Ehud Tannenbaum. Operating as 'Kuji' and 'Datastream Cowboy', Bevan and Pryce achieved what Campbell has described as 'a notoriety out of all proportion to their actions', when they haphazardly penetrated US Air Force and defence contractors' computers (Campbell, 1997: 2). Since 1994 this penetration had been portrayed as the work of foreign agents and was claimed to be 'the greatest electronic danger yet to hit the US Air Force on its home turf' (ibid.). At one point in the investigation, Bevan and Pryce were allegedly accused by US military sources as being 'a greater threat to world peace than Adolf Hitler' (Gunner, 1998: 5). In 1996, the Senate Armed Services Committee were told that 'Datastream Cowboy' had caused more harm than the KGB

and was the 'No 1 threat to US security' (Ungoed-Thomas,
1998: 1). The truth was subsequently found to be less dramatic, as the public portrayal of the two Britons as major
threats to US national security was largely hype. Pryce's
version of events is somewhat different to that depicted by
the US military. 'We embarrassed them by showing how
lax their security was and that's why they made out we
had been a huge security threat' (Ungoed-Thomas, 1998:
1).[11] Campbell believes that the inside story of the Bevan
and Pryce cases shows that the forensic work was too poor
to have stood up in court (ibid.).[12] In a similar case, the
hacking abilities of Ehud Tannenbaum, also known as 'The
Analyser', were reviled by the US, but applauded by many
Israelis (Sharrock, 1998: 2).

Such ambiguity encourages the redefinition of legal
behaviour as illegal and helps to obscure the dissonance
between social and legal definitions of crime, especially
regarding the location of the boundary between cybercrimes
and the risk-taking that characterises normal business practice. So, instead of making hard and fast classifications that
will become quickly outdated with techno-social change, the
following discussion will identify and focus upon generic
groups of offences which are raising concerns as we enter
the twenty-first century. The purpose of this exercise is,
therefore, to outline the contours of cybercrimes and illustrate the range of activities, rather than define hard and
fast categories. The four groups are cyber-trespass, cyber-
theft, cyber-obscenity and cyber-violence.

Cyber-trespass

Cyber-trespass includes acts which involve the crossing of
established boundaries into space which has already been
claimed. Crucial to the development of the Internet[13] was
the computer hacker, who possessed a high level of
specialised knowledge, along with a belief in freedom of
access to all information. Initially the hackers were applauded
as a celebration of the genius of youth and the pioneering
spirit of America (Chandler, 1996: 229), but they have subsequently become demonised (Chandler, 1996; Duff and
Gardiner, 1996; Ross, 1990: para 4; Sterling, 1994). Their

skills and beliefs are now widely regarded as a major threat to the interests of those who are attempting to effect monopoly control over cyberspace: namely commerce and the state (see above). It is because of this ideological baggage that the term 'cyber-trespasser' is preferred to the term 'hacker'. Furthermore, when the range of behaviours within this group is examined it is found that they clearly represent a spectrum of qualitatively different types of trespass; with intellectually motivated acts of trespass at one end and politically or criminally motivated trespass at the other. In its mildest form, cyber-trespass is little more than an intellectual challenge resulting in a harmless trespass, at its worst it is full-blown information warfare (see later) (Szafranski, 1995: 56).[14] The latter has been taken so seriously by the United States Air Force that in late 1996 it created the 609th Information Warfare Squadron (Cook, 1998) (but see later discussion). In the UK, the Computer Misuse Act 1990 made hacking a criminal offence regardless of whether or not damage was done (Akdeniz, 1996b).

Four basic types of cyber-trespasser can be identified from the literature, Young (1995: 10), distinguishes between *utopians* who naively believe that they are contributing to society by demonstrating its vulnerabilities, and *cyberpunks* who are aggressively anti-establishment, and who intentionally cause harm to targets which offend them. In addition, we can also identify two further types of cyber-trespassers, the *cyberspy* and the *cyber-terrorist*. The latter two are characterised by their motivation, typically for politics, morality or money, to disrupt a prevailing order. The former two (*utopians* and *cyberpunks*) on the other hand, tend to create disruption as the result of being at a particular site. In practice, however, the practical distinction between the two groups is hard to delineate because, as stated earlier, cyber-spies and terrorists must by definition be expert hackers to be able to gain access to sites. For the most part, any significant acts of cyber-trespass will tend to lie between these extreme positions.

The differences between the different types of cyber-trespass are illustrated by the following examples. The first example is entry to a site followed by the manipulation of presentational data, such as WWW pages, so that they misrepresent the organisation that they are supposed to represent. Two poignant cases occurred in 1997 when the websites of both the Conservative and Labour parties were entered and defaced. Images were transformed and replaced and texts were changed so as to misrepresent the sites. A similar intrusion occurred the previous year at the site of the University of York's Conservative Club (Wall, 1997). More recently a number of very popular sites have fallen victim to the hacker (McCormack, 1997), of which the defacing of the Spice Girls WWW site was probably the most well known.[15] In most cases, it is hard to ascertain whether or not these actions are merely pranks, or were intended to destabilise, either commercially or politically, the organisations running the sites. Furthermore, the University of York case, in particular, revealed the evidential problem of establishing the actual identity of the perpetrator. Whilst it was possible to trace the time and place of the hacking/trespass, the account used to gain access to the computing system and even the particular machine, it was impossible to establish conclusively who had committed the act. Significantly, the manipulated data could easily have been important research findings, or important statements of policy, national party manifestos, business portfolios and so on; the list is endless. Moreover, it is probable that such acts would not necessarily be detected quickly.

The second example is entry to a site, followed by the deliberate planting of viruses, worms, Trojan horses or logic bombs to disrupt or disable a particular function. Although the outcomes are usually similar, mainly disruption, there are some subtle differences between the four. Viruses are usually created with malicious intent to erase data or damage hard drives. They are programs which can reproduce themselves within a computer by attaching themselves to software. They can be passed from computer to computer within the software they attach themselves to, either through the Internet or by disk. Worms, unlike viruses, are transmitted in much the same way, but reproduce themselves like worms. They are not designed to erase data so much as to create chaos by using up machine or network space and causing systems to crash. Trojan horses and logic bombs are mainly methods of delivering viruses or worms. Trojan horses are programs that are hidden inside apparently normal software which can, once introduced into a host system, be triggered to distort information, cause damage or even system failure. Logic bombs, once inserted in a host computer system, are designed either to go off on a specific date or after access to the system has been gained a certain number of times (Akdeniz, 1996b).[16] Perhaps the best known of these logic bombs is the Michelangelo virus which only activates on Michelangelo's birthday. Alternatively there are blackmail viruses which are designed to be neutralised by a code once a ransom has been paid. An example of this occurred during the late 1980s, when a number of organisations, all over the world, received sets of free floppy disks which purported to be AIDS training packages. In fact, the disks contained sleeping viruses which the targets themselves inadvertently activated by loading the disk. Once loaded, the viruses could only be disabled by a code that was released once the victims had sent a sum of money to a specified address in the USA (Chandler, 1996: 241).

The third and fourth examples of cyber-trespass are cyber-spying and cyber-terrorism. Cyber-spying is where entry and exit to secret sources of information is effected as discreetly as possible in order to avoid detection.[17] Cyber-terrorism, by comparison, is the wilful destruction of material following entry to a site. In its extreme form it becomes information warfare, which is defined as intruders entering state computer systems with the intention of causing damage to their contents and thus causing considerable damage to a target society (Szafranski, 1995: 56). Such is the concern about information warfare within military circles that military strategists are preparing counter-information warfare strategies. Although the term warfare is frequently used, the targets are more likely to be non-military than military institutions. Also, and often confusingly, the term is mainly used in relation to the activities of cyber-terrorists rather than struggles between different nation-states.

As is often the case with new domains, imaginative rhetoric can exaggerate their impacts: however, this observation does not understate the potential impact of attack by cyber-terrorists. Sterling has warned that: 'hackers in Amtrak computers or in air-traffic controller computers, will kill somebody someday' (Sterling 1994: 185). It is not inconceivable, for example, that cyber-terrorists might break into a nation-state's central computer system and steal national secrets. In February 1998, the vulnerability of the US military computers was further highlighted when it was discovered that hackers had entered the Pentagon's system via a way-station computer in the United Arab Emirates. The implications of the attack were played down by the Pentagon, who suggested, in contrast to previous occurrences of hacking (see earlier), that the break-ins were the result of a contest perpetrated by a small group of amateurs (Dolinar, 1998: A03). In this case what is not known is whether the hackers left themselves trap doors: 'the digital equivalent of the key under the welcome mat to use next time' (Dolinar, 1998: A03).

As vulnerable as military computers are, the potential impact of an attack to computer systems which deal with the economic fabric of the state, such as tax codes, social security payments, national insurance codes or pension details, could be possibly more serious in the long term than an attack upon military systems. The wrongful calculation of income tax, national insurance payments or alteration of criminal records could, for example, cause irreparable damage to relations between the public and a nation-state; creating a loss of public confidence in government and ultimately destabilising the society. At the time of writing, these scenarios still remain possibilities and it is perhaps of greater significance that they have not yet taken place.

Cyber-Theft

Cyber-theft refers to a range of different types of appropriation that can take place within cyberspace. At one extreme are more traditional patterns of theft, whilst at the other are those acts which will cause us to reconsider our understanding of property and therefore the act of theft. Three types or groups of cyber-theft are identified here, theft of cyber-credit, cyber-cash and cyber-piracy (the appropriation of intellectual properties).

Cyber-credit relates to the fraudulent use of appropriated credit cards to buy goods over the Internet from a cyber-shopping mall. This is to be distinguished from the general issue of the fraudulent use of credit cards on two grounds. Firstly, the offender does not actually need to have a physical credit card to shop over the Internet: only the card number, name on the card and expiry date are required. All are details that can be obtained from a discarded credit card receipt.[18] So, the thief is effectively stealing a large part of the victim's identity in cyberspace. Secondly, the policing of the offence is complicated by the fact that the act can be initiated in one jurisdiction and committed in another.

The cyber-cash concept is developing rapidly and while the developers envisage the eventual establishment of a self-contained monetary system within cyberspace, current concepts of cyber-cash are related to the use of smart cards which are loaded with electronic cash equivalents at specific banking points. Such points of access will eventually be available through the Internet. At the time of writing, six major UK banks were all represented in two trials of cyber-cash facilities (AAP Newsfeed, 1998).[19] In Leeds a pilot scheme for smart Visa cash cards was in operation during 1997 and 1998 and another by Mondex at Nottingham University. Under these schemes the user would load cash credits onto their smart card at various convenient locations. These credits, with the smart card, could then be used to buy goods in shops, in lieu of cash. Likely to be brought into operation throughout the UK, this same cyber-cash system will eventually be used to purchase goods and services over the Internet with appropriate readers. Whilst the security potential of cyber-cash is considerably greater than conventional cash, especially when transactions are accompanied by a personal identification number, it is highly likely that the illegal reproduction of cyber-cash credits will quickly become a challenge for offenders.

Cyber-piracy is the appropriation of the new forms of intellectual property that have been created within, and given value by, the inhabitants of cyberspace. It is becoming an increasingly challenging type of cyber-theft. It will be remembered from earlier that one of the distinguishing characteristics of cyberspace was the fact that monetary values are attached to ideas rather than objects. In parallel to the growth in the Internet has been an increase in the number and complexity of intellectual property laws relating to trademarks, copyright, patents and in the USA privacy and publicity (Boyle, 1996; Madow, 1993; Wall, 1996; Vagg, 1995). Thus the intersection of the medium of cyberspace and more restrictive intellectual property laws has become quite a potent combination, especially during a time when, as Baudrillard observes, economic activity has come to be the outcome rather than the cause of cultural values and norms (Vagg, 1995: 87; Baudrillard, 1988). Importantly, the fact that productive ideas can now be effected without the need for expensive physical production, means that the monetary value of those ideas is further increased. Therefore, these various forms of intellectual property, especially trademarks, domain names and character merchandising, are becoming its real estate, or so to speak. So the terrain of cyberspace becomes marked by the struggle for control over this 'intellectual' real estate. This development also raises concerns about the proliferation of intellectual property laws, particularly with regard to the increase in monopoly control, but also, for example, unjust enrichment (Boyle, 1996; Wall, forthcoming). More specifically, the establishment of monopoly control in law, even if not in practice, means the ability to determine where the boundaries lie between desirable and undesirable behaviours.

There are two emerging, but related, strands of this type of piracy. The first exists at the peripheries of cyberspace. It is the counterfeiting of products such as toiletries, designer labels and character merchandising, which is becoming a rapidly expanding business. Perhaps the most common example of the act of appropriation of intellectual properties is the (physical) production of counterfeit products which are, typically, direct copies of the original being made and sold through the cyber-shopping malls. There is some confusion here between intellectual and physical property, but other examples of counterfeiting are emerging which are purely within the confines of cyberspace. For example, where pictures of a famous pop star are appropriated from Internet images or scanned from physical sources. They are then repackaged in a glossy and professional format with some explanatory text and sold, via a cyber-shopping mall, to customers who purchase them in good faith. To frustrate detection, the mall may be on a server in the USA and the proceeds paid into an Australian bank account. The whole operation would take little more than a couple of weeks, by which time the deception is detected, the proceeds have been removed from the bank account and the perpetrators gone.

In many ways, the above examples of cyber-theft are fairly predictable in that, although the medium is quite different and detection of the offence is thwarted by the nature of cyberspace, they nevertheless follow the *actus reus* and *mens rea* of many traditional thefts. The second variant of cyber-piracy/theft (of intellectual properties) is quite different and finds the boundaries between criminal and civil extremely blurred. It is where owners' interests in their properties, for example, in images, trademarks, texts or general character merchandising, are threatened by theft or release into the public domain of the Internet. This threat takes the form of 'dilution', a term used in intellectual property law to describe the reduction in value through unrestricted use and also to justify the continuation of legal control,[20] even though the appropriation may not necessarily be motivated by the prospect of financial gain, such as for artistic or moral reasons.[21] Of the many possible examples that could be given, three culturally different, yet significant, examples of the appropriation of popular iconography through the WWW spring to mind which illustrate the point: they are Elvis Presley, the Tellytubbies and the pop-group, Oasis.

The posthumous ownership of Elvis Presley's intellectual properties (trademarks, image and likeness etc.) was established during the 1980s under US law by five landmark cases and, in some states, legislation, for example, the Tennessee Celebrity Rights Act 1984 (see Wall, 1996). Elvis Presley Enterprises, who are charged by Elvis' descendants to vigorously and aggressively police the Elvis image, have been described as the 'Darth Vader of merchandising' (Gwynne, 1997: 48). They see the appropriation of the intellectual property known as Elvis as an offence which is against the law. An interesting point here is that although these acts fall under US civil law, the transporting of counterfeit goods across state boundaries is a federal matter. In 1987 (on the tenth anniversary of the death of Elvis) the FBI in Memphis arrested a number of Elvis merchandisers. During the late 1980s and early 1990s the estate of Elvis Presley established fairly secure legal controls over his intellectual properties. However, this control was tested by the fact that as the WWW developed, the image of Elvis Presley became the focus of a number of websites and the Elvis image became further developed away from its original form – to the point that if he suddenly came back from the dead, it is possible that he would have some difficulty in laying claim to it all (Wall, 1996). In fear of diluting the image and the subsequent fall in its intellectual property value, lawyers working on behalf of Elvis Presley Enterprises have identified risk groups, which could threaten the intellectual property value. Within the context of this discussion these are the WWW site owners, who have been perceived as infringing the rights of Elvis Presley Enterprises and who have been sent sternly phrased cease and desist letters (Wall, 1996). One such offender was identified as Andrea Berman, owner of the Unofficial Elvis home page,[22] who had created a 'Cyber tour' of Graceland, which as the name suggests, contained copyrighted pictures, audio clips and information about Elvis and the Graceland mansion. She was sent a cease and desist letter which stated that 'EPE will have no choice but to exercise its rights under the law to their fullest extent'[23] and in fear of punitive action she immediately signed an affidavit, subsequently regretting that she had not sought legal advice beforehand.[24]

A similar situation developed in 1997, when a set of four technicolour aliens and their friendly vacuum cleaner became very popular with infant TV viewers; the Tellytubbies also became popular with students. Furthermore, and much to the consternation of the programme's producers, Tinky-Winky became a gay icon due to the fact that he sported a large purple plastic shopping bag. This growing interest subsequently led to many Tellytubby related sites appearing on the WWW which contained a variety of materials that were mainly taken from promotional materials. The

BBC, who owned the rights to the Tellytubbies, felt that these sites were misrepresenting the original aims of the children's television programme. The BBC's lawyers responded by sending stern cease and desist letters to the site owners. When word of these actions got around the various WWW sites, most were discontinued. A policing function was achieved without recourse to the formal legal process.

Also in 1997, the pop group Oasis and its management, Ignition, sent an e-mail message to hundreds of unofficial fan WWW sites asking them to remove photographs, sound clips and text containing lyrics from their sites. The message accused WWW site owners of 'stealing from the band they claim to support' and warned them that failure to remove any pictures, lyrics or sound clips by a specified date would lead to legal action. Whilst most of the unofficial sites are run by dedicated fans and make no money, Ignition argued that bootleggers can use them as a source of pictures and music and sell them, as posters, CDs or in other forms. Uhlig observes that this may be one of the first examples of a pop group to try to censor its fans' 'out-pourings' over the Internet. In response, the fans apparently see the Ignition's statement more as an attempt by the record company to suppress information that it does not want made public; however, the irony of Oasis' own record of flouting conventions was not lost on them (Uhlig, 1997).

The point of these examples is that they demonstrate the extent to which owners of the intellectual properties feel that appropriation threatens their interests, threats which they took very seriously indeed. In many ways these defensive actions are quite normal and common business practices, but are notable for two reasons. Firstly, as described earlier, the Internet has complicated the issue by providing a new medium for the transmission of intellectual products. Secondly, as also stated earlier, in a new environment such as cyberspace, these policing activities are serving to define, or redefine, the boundaries between the legal and the illegal, rather than vice versa, especially where corporate interests intersect with those of the state, for example, the Customs and Excise through the VAT and tax evasion in the UK, which counterfeiting and piracy involve. So they are not only identifying risks to their product, but are also labelling the main risk groups. In this way, the outcome is little different to the actions of the state police against those they perceive as criminals. This risk assessment function becomes very important as the pluralisation of policing continues to increase. Interestingly, the legality of some of these policing actions against the so-called appropriators is contestable, as the use of the intellectual properties may possibly be covered by the provision of various defences in the intellectual property laws of most jurisdictions. Such defences may be based upon educational, transformative or fair use. Rarely, for example, are the appropriated properties used on the Internet in a commercial sense; rather they tend to be the centre of a parody, or as a news item which is accompanied by discussion.[25] Furthermore, in some cases there may be a public interest in the public availability of the property. In the extreme, there is the irony that the cease and desist actions themselves could amount to acts of harassment or even stalking.

Cyber-obscenity

In 1995 research published as 'The Carnegie Mellon Survey' (Rimm, 1995) suggested that as much as half of all Internet use may be related to the consumption of pornography, mostly in relation to the usenet discussion groups. It purported to identify '917,410 images, descriptions, short stories, and animations downloaded 8.5 million times by consumers in over 2000 cities in forty countries, provinces, and territories' (Rimm, 1995: 1849). The debate which followed this publication was a major contributor to the development of a panic over the use of the Internet. However, the methodology by which this estimate was calculated was subsequently found to be flawed, as it concentrated upon newsgroups and bulletin boards (see Wallace and Mangan, 1996). The true figure was subsequently estimated to be in the region of less than 1 per cent. However, whilst the panic has subsequently subsided, it nevertheless made a lasting impact upon the direction of the debate over Internet regulation. It was, for example, instrumental in the debate leading up to the initial passage of the Communications Decency Act 1996 (47 USC s.223) in the US (see later) which, although partially overturned in 1997,[26] laid the precedent for legislative intervention.

Overall, the debate over the regulation of obscene materials on the WWW has tended to lack focus and has been characterised by emotive rhetoric. This was largely because of the fact that pornography is defined by the obscenity laws of individual legal jurisdictions, which can vary. In Britain, for example, individuals regularly consume images that might be classed as obscene in many middle-Eastern countries. And yet, what individuals class as obscene in the United Kingdom may be acceptable to the citizens of many Scandinavian countries. In seeking to clarify this issue in relation to pornography, the European Commission's *Green Paper on the Protection of Minors and Human Dignity in Audio-Visual and Information Services* made the important distinction between situations where children might gain access to sites with pornographic content and illegal, obscene, acts which are subject to penal sanctions.[27] Of course, whilst the former are not necessary illegal, they may nevertheless still be deemed as harmful for children's development (European Commission Select Committee, 1996: ch. 1). The usefulness of such a distinction is that it identifies the point at which self-regulation may cease and state intervention might start, particularly where specific moral and political agendas drive public opinions.

The discussion over cyber-pornography is dealt with more fully elsewhere (see Akdeniz, 1996a; 1997a), but for the purposes of this discussion, the moral panic over pornography which arose then subsided during the early to mid-1990s was an important driving factor in the wider debate which has called for a policing policy for the virtual community. Moreover, the pornography issue highlights the fact that future criminologies of cyberspace will have to reflect its unbounded nature and will have to accommodate a set of dynamics which both undermine conventional understandings of causality and cut across the traditional treatment of crime.

Cyber-violence

Cyber-violence refers to the violent impact of the cyber activities of another upon an individual or social grouping. Whilst such activities do not have to have a direct physical manifestation, the victim nevertheless feels the violence of the act and can bear long-term psychological scars as a consequence. The activities referred to here range from cyber-stalking to hate-speech and bomb-talk.

Cyber-stalking can take a number of different forms. It can range from the persistent tracking and harassment of an individual by another, for example by the persistent sending of e-mails, through to the sending of obscene messages or even death threats. The problem lies in deciding where to draw the line between the genuine threat and the nuisance. The flexibility of this borderline was apparent in the renowned Jake Baker case.[28] During the mid-1990s, Baker was prosecuted after publishing fantasy rape-torture and snuff stories on the 'alt.sex.stories' newsgroup. In one story called 'Doe', Baker named the victim as one of his fellow students (Wallace and Mangan, 1996: 63). Baker had not stalked the girl in the real sense of surreptitiously following the victim; in fact he had not even contacted her. Moreover, it was later suggested that the girl's real name was only used because one of the syllables in it rhymed with the popular name for the male phallus. Yet, he had caused her and the others who had read the story considerable worry. Although it was about violence, the Baker case eventually became one in which the central issue became his right of freedom of speech.

A second form of cyber-violence is cyber-hate, or hate-speech. If cyber-stalking violates the individual, then cyber-hate violates social or ethnic groupings. The Internet is the site of some very disturbing hate-speech. Perhaps one of the most dramatic examples of hate-speech on the WWW is Holocaust denial, which, as the name implies, attempts to rewrite history by denying that the persecution of the Jewish people by the Nazis ever took place.[29] A number of WWW sites are devoted to the issue of holocaust denial (see Greenberg, 1997: 673).

Bomb-talk is another, worrying, form of cyber-violence in so far as it provides the technologies by which to carry out the ideas circulated by hate-speech. It exists at the extreme of a spectrum of 'Tech-Talk' whereby subversive technological ideas are circulated over the Internet via bulletin boards, user groups and IRC. At one end of the spectrum is the free circulation of sophisticated technologies which are designed to circumnavigate existing infrastructural frameworks.[30] For example, Pryce, the hacker mentioned earlier, stated that he used bulletin boards to get software and also access to hardware.

'I used to get software off the bulletin boards and from one of them I got a "bluebox", which could recreate the various frequencies to get free phone calls,' he said. 'I would phone South America and this software would make noises which would make the operator think I had hung up. I could then make calls anywhere in the world for free.' (Ungoed-Thomas, 1998: 1)

At the other end of the spectrum is bomb-talk which ranges from circulation of instructions as to how to make a bomb or other weaponry to the deliberate targeting of groups with a view to committing an act (see Wallace and Mangan, 1996: 153). Perhaps the most vivid example of the latter was the alleged use of the Internet by members of various militias in the planning of the Oklahoma bombing.

The policing of both of these latter examples of cyber-violence is frustrated by the fact that in some jurisdictions, for example the United States and Canada, whilst the intent behind hate-speech might contravene criminal codes, the fact that they are speech gives them protection under the United States Constitution and Canadian Charter of Rights[31] which guarantee freedoms of expression.

The four generic areas of cybercrimes illustrated above provide a useful categorisation of offences whilst also creating space to include the broad range of activities that can occur within them. Such categorisation is arguably more useful than lumping activities, such as fraud, hacking, espionage and theft of intellectual property, under the banner of economic crimes as is the case in the recent European Union report on legal aspects of computer-related crime

(Seiber, 1998).[32] Especially problematic with this approach is the observation that some of the acts mentioned do not necessarily involve a financial motive. Furthermore, the examples cited earlier demonstrate the contested nature of the acts, the problems of identifying causality and also the ambivalent responses that are made towards the 'offences'. The examples also demonstrate the inadvisability of attempting tight definitions of cybercrimes, particularly as the focus has been upon the offence rather than the offender or the offended (victim). The following section will draw upon the previous discussion to make some observations about the victims of cybercrimes.

VICTIMS OF CYBERCRIMES

Other than the fact that the great majority of the victims are members of the virtual community, experience of victimisation varies and is hard to collectivise. It will be some time before a comprehensive sociology of cyber-victimisation can develop, especially as most of the discussion of cybercrimes has tended to focus upon the deviant act rather than either the deviant group or the victims. Furthermore, it is also too early to attempt an assessment of the extent of cyber-victimisation; indeed there are some very good reasons as to why this might never be possible. Each of the above categories denotes a particular victim group; however, this group does not necessarily contain an internal coherence. The literature on white-collar victimisation (Zedner, 1997: 593; Box, 1983: 17) illuminates our understanding of cyber-victimisation and suggests that it is likely that cyber-victims will vary considerably in terms of their status, level of victimisation and group collectivity. They will range from individuals to corporate bodies to whole societies and the (cyber) harms done to them will traverse from the actual to the felt. In some cases there is no primary victim, as many victims of cybercrimes are secondary, or indirect, for example, as with cyber-piracy or cyber-spying/terrorism. In other cases, such as cyber-stalking or the theft of cyber-cash, the victimisation is felt directly by the individual. Furthermore, as is the case with reporting behaviour for white-collar crimes, it is likely that many victims of cybercrimes may be unwilling to acknowledge that they have been a victim, especially those in the business sector who may fear adverse publicity and negative economic consequences (Steele, 1997: 500). Or it may simply take victims some time to realise that they have been victimised. Alternatively, where the victimisation has been imputed by a third party upon the basis of an ideological, political, moral, or commercial assessment of risk, the victim or victim group may simply be unaware that they have been victimised, or even believe that they have not, as can be the case with the various forms of pornography and hate-speech.

THE GOVERNANCE OF CYBERCRIMES

Two important and very practical concerns exist with regard to the debate over the criminalisation of cybercrimes. Firstly, much of the rhetoric regarding the extent of cybercrimes has not only been 'overblown', but has subsequently led to considerable funding for state security and policing organisations. The two may not in fact be mutually exclusive as this increased funding, in turn, raises the concern that those organisations will then seek to justify that increased expenditure by creating new 'security markets' for their services. But Campbell believes that the 'oversold threats' regarding the threat of breaches of security that were made during the investigation of the hackers Bevan and Pryce (see earlier), helped win funding from Congress for the cyber-investigators, funding which led to the development of new military and intelligence 'infowar' units (see earlier), which have subsequently sold their security services to private corporations (Campbell, 1997: 2). Secondly, another problem arising from overblown rhetoric is the great danger that deviant cyber-behaviours become the subject of formal regulation before they are fully understood. A graphic example of this process emerged following the previously mentioned panic over obscenity during the mid-1990s. A solution, in the form of the now partly repealed (US) Communications Decency Act 1996, was sought before the problem had been properly identified (Wallace and Mangan, 1996: 174, Akdeniz; 1997c: 1003).

The panic over pornography also gripped the debate over Internet regulation in the United Kingdom. In August 1996, for example, the Club and Vice Unit of the Metropolitan Police issued a stern letter to Internet Service Providers to demand that they ban 133 newsgroups (Walker, 1997: 28).[33] At this time it was not unknown for senior police officers to make dramatic pronouncements to the effect that the Internet was little more than a library of pornography (Uhlig, 1996). Interestingly, such views were in contrast to the views of Chief Constable David Blakey who emphasised that 'it is not necessarily for the police to patrol the super-high-way looking for violations' (Blakey, 1996: 18). Like many previously new situations, most of the issues highlighted above will resolve themselves in practice, especially forms of regulation and remedy. However, the point made earlier remains very pertinent, namely that the unique properties of cyberspace challenge many of our conventional under-standings of crime and control. Moreover, the traditional referents – class, ethnicity, gender – are not necessarily relevant anymore. And where formal procedures are under-taken, there has to be a respect for due process in the pursuit of justice.

At the time of writing, there remain three distinct char-acteristics of cyberspace that we are continually going to have to come to terms with. The first is the aforemen-tioned fact that the robustness of the Internet is going to frustrate attempts at direct governance by removing the possibility of the ultimate sanction: disconnection. The second characteristic is the problem of deciding in which particu-lar jurisdiction cyberspace lies. Can it, for example, exist independently of the real world which is organised into its geographical jurisdictions? In practice, the conflict (of laws) is not so much a problem for law as a practical problem for the administration of law, as the following two examples demonstrate. Within the USA, the few legal cases, mostly prosecutions involving child pornography, that have reached the courts have been the subject of forum shopping, which not only provides a way around the problem, but, as recent practice in the USA has demonstrated, can also work to the advantage rather than disadvantage of the prosecution. In *United States of America v. Robert A. Thomas and Carleen Thomas*,[34] a case involving the misuse of bulletin boards, the prosecutors not only had a choice of forum but they also chose for the trial, the Sixth Circuit which covers an area of the USA, mostly Tennessee, where they felt the population would feel most offended by the subject matter of the prosecution. However, such advantage would not be found as easily in inter-jurisdictional offences such as when, in the mid-1990s, a police lieutenant from Jefferson County, Kentucky, USA broke a major child-pornography ring in the United Kingdom, without leaving his state. Lieutenant Baker received an 'e-mailed' pointer from a source in Switzerland which led him to an Internet site based at Birmingham University in the United Kingdom. After three months of investigation, Baker contacted Interpol, the Metropolitan Police and the West Midlands Police, who arrested the distributors (Sussman, 1995).[35] Whilst it is arguable that one could see this as an example of cross-border police co-operation, it is as likely that the decision to pass the case to the British was also prompted by the complexities of obtaining extradition orders.

The third characteristic is the shift of power that cyberspace creates. The traditional exercise of power has been to restrict physical, economic or mental access to an environment whether it be by coercive means, mobilising the agenda or through the use of ideological apparatus (Lukes, 1974). In cyberspace, information is not only the source of power, but also facilitates access.

Of particular interest to observers will be whether or not these characteristics effect a check upon the general encroachment of the nanny state and the control culture that has developed within it. Inherent to this control culture is the rather pessimistic, Hobbesian, view of human nature which asserts that anarchy will prevail in the absence of regulation by the nation-state. Therefore, it is widely assumed that without regulation, netizens cannot be trusted to behave in an orderly manner. This lack of trust became quite clear during the 'libraries of porn' debates that followed the publication of the Carnegie–Mellon findings (see earlier). And yet, with the exception of very extreme behaviours, the experience of cyberspace does not bear out the pessimists' predictions. Steele, for example, puts forward the commonly held view that 'The lack of a legal barrier has led to a rapidly growing sub-culture which preys upon the inhabitants of cyberspace' (1997: 500). However, two points emerge in response to such views. Firstly, why then are there not more cybercrimes and why, for the most part, does the system clearly seem to police itself? Second, we must be somewhat wary, but not be too dismissive, of reports which show that the number of incidents of cybercrimes have proliferated (see above), especially when those reports originate from people who are currently engaged in the growing cybercrime industry.

Views upon the regulation of cybercrimes are therefore split between the pessimists, who wish to impose stringent regulations, and the optimists who believe that individuals can regulate themselves effectively: part of the long-standing liberal tradition. In 1919 (US) Judge Oliver Wendell Holmes argued in the case of *Abrams v United States* that 'the ultimate good desired is better reached by free trade in ideas' on the basis that 'the best test of truth is the power of the thought to get itself accepted in the competition of the market'.[36] Simply put, Wallace and Mangan hope that 'truth and beauty [will] drown out violence and smut' (Wallace and Mangan, 1996: 81; Walker and Akdeniz, 1998). Interestingly, in order to demonstrate the futility of over-regulation, Wallace and Mangan cite the example of the failure of sixteenth-century French censorship policy and observe that even the sanction of death failed to staunch the distribution of books (1996).

There is considerable evidence to favour a more liberal and optimistic approach. Indeed, a system of multi-tiered governance is rapidly developing within cyberspace which is largely based upon self-regulation by netizens of cyberspace, but which also has various higher tiers of governance to accommodate situations to which self-regulation does not apply or is not applied (Akdeniz, 1997a; Walker, 1997: 28; Wall, 1997: 222; Wall, 1998). Where self-regulation either fails or is inappropriate, then the regulating functions are split between three further groups. First are the Internet Service Providers who have created regulatory organisations such as the Internet Watch Foundation to overview the use of the Internet and to bring to the attention of ISPs illegal materials (Akdeniz, 1997a). Second are the state-funded non-police organisations such as Customs and Excise in the United Kingdom who seek to investigate VAT or tax frauds or the Postal Service Investigators in the USA who investigate misuse of the postal service. Third are the state-funded police organisations such as the regular (Home Office) funded police in the United Kingdom and any specialised units which they may have created to deal with specific problems. In the USA the FBI has created a computer crimes unit for the simple purpose of dealing with a wide range of Internet and computer-related crimes (Wall, 1997: 224).

Not only is wholesale external regulation virtually impossible to effect, but it is also highly impracticable as a form of general governance. It is more appropriate to control or remedy the more extreme and specific forms of behaviour, such as child pornography. In any form of regulation, there is always a dilemma between the need to punish past behaviour and the need to protect individuals from the future behaviour of others. Over the past two centuries, these legally based models have arguably failed with regard to traditional crimes; it is therefore likely that they will continue to fail as models for dealing with new types of offending behaviour. The application of the laws of the Internet is clearly more problematic than the more terrestrial laws. Self-regulation is a far more feasible basis for a system of governance and it is also a more preferable way of protecting the future than external regulation which for the most part is driven by an agenda which seeks to punish the past. Interestingly, the recent EC report on legal aspects of computer-related crime (Seiber, 1998) takes this approach, but it also argues that for self-regulation to be effective there also needs to be in place an infrastructure of international agreements over the boundaries of acceptable and non-acceptable activities. Yet, any framework of non-legal remedies, such as the regulation in technology, education and industry and also in procedural law should preserve, and not interfere with, fundamental civil liberties. Consequently, a criminology of cyberspace will have to explore normative perceptions of deviance in addition to their impacts.

CONCLUSIONS: TO BOLDLY GO . . .

It is no coincidence that the debate over the control of cyberspace, the aforementioned intellectual land grab, has corresponded with the increased potential for the commercial and political exploitation of the Internet. Consequently, it is of little surprise that initiatives to introduce control have come from two directions: sovereign states, whose interests have become threatened; and commerce, who wish to gain monopoly over areas currently in the public domain of cyberspace. Thus, groups with access to cyberspace have increasingly come to be evaluated in terms of either their potential threat to established commercial or political interests, or in terms of their potential opposition to those new interests. Consequently, we see the labelling of specific groups, for example the hackers, according to their perceived level of risk. It is against this backdrop that the behaviours of these groups are increasingly becoming defined, or redefined as cybercrimes. Such definitions are largely normative and at this early stage there is the very real problem of evaluating their true impact. We need to be able to distinguish between real and the virtually real behaviours: we need to be able to identify those which are actually a threat to society and those which, for various reasons, we are told are a threat.

It is fairly early on in the life and times of cyberspace to start predicting its impacts with any degree of certainty, especially as the power-play has only just started to develop. It is very likely that some behaviours will work themselves out and will either cease to be popular or it may be the case that developments in technology will simply eradicate them: much in the same way that British Telecom's 1471 last-caller service almost eliminated the obscene phone call.[37] However, at the end of the day we shall be left with a series of new types of 'criminal' behaviour, which in some cases will cause us to rethink and augment our existing understandings of crimes and deviant behaviours. Understandings, which are largely based upon our social experiences of traditionally bounded space. This shall be one of the challenges for criminology during the twenty-first century.

NOTES

1. This chapter builds upon and develops themes that were first raised in Wall (1997). My thanks go to the editors and also Yaman Akdeniz and Clive Walker at the University of Leeds.
2. The term Internet is also frequently referred to as the information super-highway. It is the medium which facilitates the World Wide Web, newsgroups, file transfer protocol (FTP), gophers, Internet Relay Chat (IRC), e-mail and other methods of communication.
3. The term 'social' is being used quite broadly, given the recent debates over the death of the social (Rose, 1996: 327).
4. Paraphrasing John Perry Barlow's 'Selling Wine Without Bottles: the Economy of Mind on the Global Net' <http://www.eff.org/pub/ Publications/John Perry Barlow/HTML/idea economy article.html>
5. Extending Braverman's (1976) hypothesis to the construction of social life.
6. For a discussion of the policing and maintenance of intellectual property see Wall (1996).
7. Although a number of cases involving child pornography are currently in the process of going through the courts.
8. See the FBI pages at <http://www.fbi.gov>, more specifically see <http://www.fbi.gov/congress/compcrm/compcrm.htm>
9. Pub. L. No. 99-474, 100 Stat. 1213 (1986) with the amending 18 U.S.C. § 1030.
10. Rather confusingly, the UN have tended to use the term 'computer crime' to include many of the activities referred to in this chapter as cybercrimes.
11. In March 1997 Pryce admitted 12 offences under the Computer Misuse Act 1990 which makes hacking/trespass a criminal act; however, conspiracy charges against both Bevan and Pryce were dropped in November 1997 (Ungoed-Thomas, 1998: 2).
12. Perhaps the greatest irony of Bevan's case is that he is now employed as a security consultant by the types of institutions into whose systems he once used to hack, in order to test their online security systems.
13. For further discussion of the 'demonisation' of the hacker see Chandler (1996); Duff and Gardiner (1996); Ross (1990: para 4); Sterling (1994).
14. For further details of Information Warfare see United States Air Force Fact Sheet 95-20; also see Szafranski, (1995). Also see the executive summary of the Information Warfare Tutorial at <http:/ /144.99.192.240/usacs/iw/tutorial/exesum.htm>.
15. At the time of writing (April 1998) a number of examples of hacked web sites could be found at <http://www.2600.com>.
16. Sometimes referred to as sleeping viruses or time-bombs.
17. An example of computer spying was illustrated in the case of the Hanover Group (Hafner and Markoff, 1991; Young, 1995: 11).
18. See 'Credit Card Fraud Technique' at <http://www.echotech.com/ ccfraud.htm>.

19. The concept of cyber-cash is differentiated here from the company called CyberCash which offers web and electronic credit card, cheque, and cash products (Electronic Commerce Briefing, 1998).
20. The dilution argument is highly contested (Madow, 1993).
21. For example, in the UK the authors of the Jet report, in direct contrast to those who had commissioned it, felt that its publication was in the public interest, which puts a slightly different spin on this argument. See Akdeniz (1997a).
22. <http://sunsite.unc.edu/elvis/elvishom.html>.
23. Letter to Berman dated 10/11/94.
24. Interview with Berman (see Wall, 1996).
25. See, for example, the decision in the Scientology case cited in Wallace and Mangan (1996).
26. *ACLU et al. v. Reno* (1997), 117 S. Ct. 2329.
27. In November 1997 this resulted in an EU action plan, *Communication from the Commission to the European Parliament, the Council, the Economic and Social Committee and the Committee of the Regions Action Plan on promoting safe use of the Internet*, November 1997.
28. *United States v Alkhabaz* (1997); U.S. App. LEXIS 9060; (1996) 104 F.3d 1492; (1995) 48 F.3d 1220 and U.S. App. Lexis 11244.
29. See *R. v. Zundel* 95 D.L.R. (4th) 202 (1992) and (Can.Sup. Ct. Aug. 27, 1992, unreported).
30. See Mann and Sutton (1998) for a very useful description of the use of news groups for the distribution of information about the technologies used for committing offences.
31. In the USA by the First Amendment to the US Constitution and in Canada the Canadian Charter of Rights s. 2.
32. This chapter was written after the EC report was published and it therefore does not fully engage with it.
33. Also reported at <http://www.ukvbc.net/censorship>.
34. 74 F.3d 701; 1996 U.S. App. Lexis 1069; 1996 Fed App. 0032P (6th Cir.).
35. See *R v Fellows* and *R v Arnold*, ibid.
36. *Abrams v. United States* (1919), 250 U.S. 616, 63 L. Ed. 1173, 40 S. Ct. 17 (Holmes, J., dissenting).
37. Although there are an increasing number of ways to prevent the transmission of the sender's number, especially with mobile phones.

REFERENCES

AAP Newsfeed (1998) 'Nationwide General News; Finance Wire', *AAP Newsfeed*, 18 March.
Akdeniz, Y. (1996a) 'Computer Pornography: a Comparative Study of US and UK Obscenity Laws and Child Pornography Laws in Relation to the Internet', *International Review of Law, Computers and Technology*, 10(2), 235–61.

Akdeniz, Y. (1996b) 'Section 3 of the Computer Misuse Act 1990: an Antidote for Computer Viruses', *Web Journal of Contemporary Legal Issues*, 3.

Akdeniz, Y. (1997a) 'Governance of Pornography and Child Pornography on the Global Internet: a Multi-Layered Approach', in L. Edwards and C. Wealde (eds.), *Law and the Internet: Regulating Cyberspace* (Oxford: Hart Publishing), 222–41.

Akdeniz, Y. (1997b) 'Copyright and the Internet', *New Law Journal*, 147, 965–6.

Akdeniz, Y. (1997c) 'The Battle for the Communications Decency Act 1996 is Over', *New Law Journal*, 147, 1003.

Barlow, J. P. (1994) 'The Economy of Ideas: a Framework for Rethinking Patents and Copyrights in the Digital Age (Everything you Know about Intellectual Property is Wrong)', *Wired*, 2(3), 84.

Baudrillard, J. (1988) 'Consumer Society', in M. Poster, *Jean Baudrillard: Selected Writings* (Oxford: Blackwell), 29–56.

Benedikt, M. (ed.) (1991) *Cyberspace: the First Steps* (Cambridge, Mass.: MIT Press).

Betts, M. and Anthes, G. H. (1995) 'On-line Boundaries Unclear: Internet Tramples Legal Jurisdictions', *Computerworld*, 5 June, 16.

Blakey, D. (1996) 'Policing Cyberspace', *Policing Today*, 2(1), 19–21.

Bottoms, A. and Wiles, P. (1996) 'Understanding Crime Prevention in Late Modern Societies', in T. Bennett (ed.), *Preventing Crime and Disorder: Targeting Strategies and Responsibilities* (Cambridge: University of Cambridge, Institute of Criminology).

Box, S. (1983) *Power, Crime and Mystification* (London: Routledge).

Boyle, J. (1996) *Shamans, Software and Spleens: Law and the Construction of the Information Society* (Cambridge, Mass.: Harvard University Press).

Braithwaite, J. (1992) *Crime, Shame and Reintegration* (Cambridge: Cambridge University Press).

Braverman, H. (1976) *Labour and Monopoly Capital* (New York: Monthly Review Press).

Byassee, W. S. (1995) 'Jurisdiction of Cyberspace: Applying Real World Precedent to the Virtual Community', *Wake Forest Law Review*, 30, 197–220.

Campbell, D. (1997) 'More Naked Gun than Top Gun', *The Guardian* (OnLine), 27 November, 2.

Chandler, A. (1996) 'The Changing Definition and Image of Hackers in Popular Discourse', *International Journal of the Sociology of Law*, 24, 229–51.

Cohen, S. (1980) *Folk Devils and Moral Panics* (Oxford: Basil Blackwell).

Cook, N. (1998) 'The Big Question: Can Saddam be Beaten by Bombing Alone?', *Jane's Defence Weekly*, 29(8), 19.

Dolinar, L. (1998) 'Hackers hit Pentagon System/Organised Attack Highlights Flaws', *Newsday*, 26 February, A03.

Duff, L. and Gardiner, S. (1996) 'Computer Crime in the Global Village: Strategies for Control and Regulation – in Defence of the Hacker', *International Journal of the Sociology of Law*, 24, 211–28.

Electronic Commerce Briefing (1998) 'CyberCash still Chasing the Money', *Electronic Commerce Briefing*, no. 506, 1 March.

Escobar, A. (1996) 'Welcome to Cyberia: Notes on the Anthropology of Cyberculture', in Z. Saradar and J. R. Ravetz (eds.), *Cyberfutures: Culture and Politics on the Information Superhighway* (London: Pluto Press).

European Commission Select Committee (1996) *Green Paper on the Protection of Minors and Human Dignity in Audio-Visual and Information Services* (Brussels-Luxembourg).

Fraser, B. T. (1996) 'Computer Crime Research Resources', School of Library and Information Studies, Florida State University, <http://mailer.fsu.edu/~btf1553/ccrr/search1.htm>.

Gibson, W. (1984) *Neuromancer* (London: HarperCollins).

Giddens, A. (1990) *The Consequences of Modernity* (London: Polity Press).

Gottfredson, G. and Hirschi, T. (1990) *A General Theory of Crime* (Stanford: Stanford University Press).

Greenberg, S. (1997) 'Threats, Harassment and Hate On-line: Recent Developments', *The Boston Public Interest Law Journal*, 6, 673.

Grundy, M. and Wood, B. (eds.) (1996) *A Growth Industry: the Theft of Computer Hardware and Component Parts* (Manchester: Henry Fielding Centre, University of Manchester, Association of Chief Police Officers).

Gunner, E. (1998) 'Rogue Hacker Turned Legit Code-Cracker', *Computer Weekly*, 7 May, 5.

Gwynne, S. C. (1997) 'Love Me Legal Tender', *Time Magazine*, 11 August, 46–9.

Hafner, K. and Markoff, J. (1991) *Cyberpunk: Outlaws and Hackers on the Computer Frontier* (New York: Simon & Schuster).

The Herald (1996) 'Inquiry into Pornography on Tory Students' Internet Page', *The (Glasgow) Herald*, 19 August, 6.

House of Lords Select Committee on Science and Technology (1995–6) *Information Society*, HL 77 (London: HMSO).

Johnson, D. and Post, D. G. (1996) 'Law and Borders: the Rise of Law in Cyberspace', <http://www.law.syr.edu/Course.Materials/Chon/borders.html>.

Kumar, K. (1978) *Prophecy and Progress: the Sociology of Post-Industrial Society* (Harmondsworth: Penguin).

Levi, A. (1985) 'A Criminological and Sociological Approach to Theories of and Research into Economic Crime', in D. Magnuson (ed.), *Economic Crime-Programs for Future Research Report No. 18* (Stockholm: National Council for Crime Prevention, Sweden), 32–72.

Lukes, S. (1974) *Power: A Radical View* (London: Macmillan).

Madow, M. (1993) 'Private Ownership of Public Image: Popular Culture and Publicity Rights', *California Law Review*, 81, 125–240.

Mandel, T. F. (1993) *Surfing the Wild Internet* (SCAN: Business Intelligence Program, SRI International, Menlo Park, No. 2109, March.

Mann, D. and Sutton, M. (1998) '>>Netcrime: More Change in the Organisation of Thieving', *British Journal of Criminology*, 38, 210–29.

McCormack, M. (1997) 'Net Closing on High Profile Hackers', *Electronic Telegraph*, 23 September, Issue 851.

Nelken, D. (1997) 'White-Collar Crime', in M. Maguire, R. Morgan and R. Reiner (eds.), (1997) *The Oxford Handbook of Criminology*, 2nd edn (Oxford: Oxford University Press), 891–925.

Rheingold, H. (1994) *The Virtual Community: Homesteading the Electronic Frontier* (New York: Harper Perennial).

Rimm, M. (1995) 'Marketing Pornography on the Information Super-highway: a Survey of 917,410 Images, Descriptions, Short Stories, and Animations Downloaded 8.5 Million Times by Consumers in over 2000 Cities in Forty Countries, Provinces, and Territories', *Georgetown Law Journal*, 83(5), 1849–1934.

Rose, N. (1996) 'The Death of the Social: Re-figuring the Territory of Government', *Economy and Society*, 25, 327–56.

Ross, A. (1990), 'Hacking Away at the Counter-culture', *Postmodern Culture*, 1/1: <http://jefferson.village.virginia.edu/pmc/issue.990/contents.990.html>.

Saradar, Z. and Ravetz, J. R. (1996) 'Reaping the Technological Whirl-wind', in Z. Saradar and J. R. Ravetz (eds.), *Cyberfutures: Culture and Politics on the Information Super-highway* (London: Pluto Press).

Schlozberg, S. (1983) *Computers and Penal Legislation* (Oslo: Norwegian Research Centre for Computers and Law).

Seiber, U. (1998) *Legal Aspects of Computer Related Crime in the Information Society*, Legal Advisory Board for the Information Market, <http://www2.echo.lu/legal/en/comcrime/sieber.html>.

Sharrock, D. (1998) 'The Hacker Who Turned Himself In', *The Guardian*, 26 March, Online, 2–3.

Steele, H. L. (1997) 'The Web that Binds Us All: the Future Legal Environment of the Internet', *Houston Journal of International Law*, 19, 495–517.

Sterling, B. (1994) *The Hacker Crackdown* (London: Penguin Books).

Sussman, V. (1995) 'Policing Cyberspace', US News 38; World Rep., 23 Jan. 1995, at 54, Lexis, News Library, Usnews file, 1995 WL 3113171.

Szafranski, Col. R. (1995) 'A Theory of Information Warfare: Preparing for 2020', *Air Chronicles*, 1, 56–65. <http://www.cdsar.af.mil/apj/szfran.html>.

Tribe, L. H. (1991) 'The Constitution in Cyberspace: Law and Liberty Beyond the Electronic Frontier', *The Humanist*, 26 March, 15.

Uhlig, R. (1996) '"Safety Net" on Internet will Catch Child Porn', *Electronic Telegraph*, 23 September, no. 488.

Uhlig, R. (1997) 'Oasis Threatens Fans over Internet Piracy', *Electronic Telegraph*, Friday, 16 May, Issue 721.

Ungoed-Thomas, J. (1998) 'The Schoolboy Spy', *Sunday Times*, 29 March, 5, 1–2.

United Nations (1995), *International Review of Criminal Policy No. 43 and 44 – United Nations Manual on the Prevention and Control of Computer-Related Crime*, <http://www.ifs.univie.ac.at/~pr2gq1/rev4344.html#crime>.

Vagg, J. (1995) 'The Policing of Signs: Trademark Infringement and Law Enforcement', *European Journal on Criminal Policy and Research*, 3(2), 75–92.

Walker, C. P. (1997) 'Cyber-Contempt: Fair Trials and the Internet', in E. Barendt (ed.), *The Year Book of Media and Entertainment Law* (Oxford: Clarendon Press), 3–29.

Walker, C. P. and Akdeniz, Y. (1998) 'Virtual(e-) Democracy', *Public Law*, Autumn.

Wall, D. S. (1996), 'Reconstructing the Soul of Elvis: the Social Development and Legal Maintenance of Elvis Presley as Intellectual Property', *International Journal of the Sociology of Law*, 24, 117–43.

Wall, D. S. (1997) 'Policing the Virtual Community: the Internet, Cyber-Crimes and the Policing of Cyberspace', in P. Francis, P. Davies and V. Jupp (eds.), *Policing Futures, the Police, Law Enforcement and the Twenty-First Century* (London: Macmillan), 208–36.

Wall, D. S. (1998) 'Catching Cyber-Criminals: Policing the Internet', *International Review of Law Computers and Technology*, 12(2).

Wall, D. S. (forthcoming) *Policing the Soul of Elvis* (London: Pluto Press).

Wallace, J. and Mangan, M. (1996) *Sex, Laws and Cyberspace* (New York: Henry Holt).

Wasik, M. (1991), *Crime and the Computer* (Oxford: Clarendon Press).

Young, L. F. (1995), 'United States Computer Crime Laws, Criminals and Deterrence', *International Yearbook of Law, Computers and Technology*, 9, 1–16.

Zedner, L. (1997) 'Victims', in M. Maguire, R. Morgan and R. Reiner (eds.), *The Oxford Handbook of Criminology*, 2nd edn (Oxford: Oxford University Press), 577–611.

Part III
Regulation and Control

6 Regulating Fraud Revisited

Michael Levi

INTRODUCTION

In the United Kingdom, as in the United States and other advanced industrial nations, neither the nature of offender/ victim relationships nor the social class composition of 'white-collar criminals' – convicted or unconvicted – are simple: those involved in obtaining money by deception and corruption include members of the inner and outer circles of 'the upperworld' and 'the underworld', and comparatively junior employees. Even upmarket-sounding crimes such as insider dealing may be committed by the company chairman or the company typist. Attempts to sidestep the traditional ambiguities surrounding the 'white-collar crime' label, such as Weisburd et al.'s (1991) 'crimes of the middle classes', arguably ought to exclude the majority of credit card and cheque fraudsters, plus those gang members who have black-mailed corporate staff into fraud: but whether they imply social status or deception as core criteria, Weisburd's and other Yale studies include plastic fraudsters alongside other federal offences. Consequently, the social composition of the category of 'fraudsters' is much wider than for other 'criminals for gain', even if one restricts oneself to con-victed offenders, but *a fortiori* if one extends – with greater definitional difficulties than in other areas where there is a 'dark figure' – one's analysis to unprosecuted persons. Whatever definitional subtleties one engages in, the vast majority of frauds reported to the police and recorded by them are as follows: first, cheque and credit card frauds committed by 'blue-collar' criminals; second, embezzlements by modest-status staff, such as thefts of incoming or outgo-ing company cheques and their conversion into cash; and third, deceptions by businesspeople obtaining money in

143

advance for goods or loans that never materialise, or goods on credit for which they never intended to pay. In short, involvement in sophisticated financial swindles is far from being the preserve of a social élite, although, with the exception of extortion, it is by definition outside the range of the routine criminal *lumpenproletariat* who constitute the majority of prisoners (Levi, 1987; Croall, 1992, Chapter 2 in this volume; Levi and Pithouse, forthcoming).

However, the traditional focus upon offenders in the white-collar literature tends to generate a particular 'take' on the crimes: a focus on social reaction to the *victims* is illuminating. If we look at frauds not so much by the number of each type reported but by the amount of money lost and the amount of money at risk in financial markets, we can better appreciate why institutions such as the Serious Fraud Office (SFO) – created as a key measure by the Criminal Justice Act 1987 – or the parallel institutions in other countries exist. Special white-collar crime investigative bodies exist for the following reasons. First, the 'new classes' of victim – for example, shareholders in privatised utilities and collectors of early retirement/redundancy pay – constitute a political risk that calls for a response. Second, Britain was and is concerned about its reputation in the global marketplace, given its dependence upon income from 'invisibles' to the balance of payments. Also, because almost one in five of Londoners in employment works in financial services (though numbers are declining due to 'down-sizing'), financial services are strategically important in a country in which injuries at work have been reduced substantially by closing down many risky environments in the process of deindustrialisation. Britain is the most dependent of advanced industrial countries on its financial services industry. Third, though the importance of this fluctuates over time and space, there are fears that 'organised crime' may infiltrate 'commerce', whether by fraud or by integration of the proceeds of crime in the money-laundering process (Levi, 1981; Simon and Swart, 1984; Poveda, 1994; Levi, 1997).

In the United States (Cullen et al., 1987) and Italy, and to a lesser extent elsewhere, there has also been a populist movement for 'equal punishment' of social and political élites engaged in crime, though – whether due to a desire not to 'rock the boat' or as a consequence of more direct political pressure from above – this has only intermittently filtered through to the prosecution process (see Levi and Nelken, 1996), even in the US (Calavita and Pontell, 1994; Zimring and Hawkins, 1993). In countries where corruption has become a major political and economic problem, anti-corruption agencies have been established: a process that will be encouraged by the 1997 OECD Convention which seeks to criminalise companies and their senior executives who commit bribery overseas. This is partly in response to US complaints about its competitive disadvantage resulting from its own 1977 legislation (for analysis of this, see Rossbacher and Young, 1997; Pickholz, 1997). The latter is too substantial a topic to review here. Instead, this chapter seeks to review some key themes in the policing and prosecution of fraud, and examines the nature and impact of changes wrought during the decade since the publication of *Regulating Fraud* (Levi, 1987).

FRAUD INVESTIGATION AND PROSECUTION IN ENGLAND AND WALES: A BRIEF HISTORY

The focus by government and leading City figures on the legitimacy and opacity of financial markets coincided with increased concern about the ability of the criminal process to deal with major fraud. Before 1985, the traditional method of dealing with any fraud was that some of the (then) 588 British police Fraud Squad officers or the Department of Trade and Industry (DTI) or the revenue department (or any combination of those bodies) would carry out an investigation (perhaps over several years), prepare a report for (in less serious cases) their in-house lawyers or for (in major police and DTI cases) the Director of Public Prosecutions (DPP). After the investigation was concluded, someone in the Office of the DPP would decide if there was a better than 50 per cent chance of producing a conviction and, if it seemed that there was, would pass it on to outside counsel to draft charges. Sometimes, counsel would observe that most of the police effort had been wasted and that the police should really have focused on issues they did not examine properly: then the case would either be dropped or the police would be told to go away and do some further investigation, though this might be difficult, since the police had no official access to bank account information prior to a suspect being charged and sometimes such information would be needed to justify the institution of proceedings in the first place. To try to short-circuit the inefficiencies in this process, the DPP established in 1985 the Fraud Investigation Group, which was intended to work in an interdisciplinary way to provide early consultation for the police and other agencies to avoid wasteful investigation (see Levi, 1987).

With regard to the courts, during the early 1980s serious problems had arisen in a number of lengthy trials. Some defendants were acquitted at the direction of judges who accepted their arguments that the conduct complained of was normal market practice and that the accused were therefore not dishonest; while some others involved jury verdicts that were regarded as 'perverse' by police and prosecutors. These were far from being the only difficulties encountered in prosecuting cases. In fairness to the accused, one judge ordered a retrial in a multi-defendant case that had lasted over 100 days and cost over £1 million in legal fees, after a newspaper reported that some of the accused had been convicted previously: in the retrial they were all acquitted. In another fraud trial, a retrial was ordered after 137 days when someone believed to be connected with defendants approached jurors: after this retrial the principals were convicted. The political perception was that 'the system' was not working, that is, was not delivering convictions reliably or quickly enough (Levi, 1983, 1988).

The Conservative government's response was to set up a committee under one of the most senior judges, Lord Roskill, which focused initially on the (in)adequacy of trial by jury, but developed into a broad-ranging review of the investigation, prosecution and trial processes (Fraud Trials Committee, 1986). It concluded that what was needed was a new, unified body that could both investigate and prosecute 'serious or complex' fraud. The Cabinet, after heavy internal debate about costs, agreed to establish a new body

– the Serious Fraud Office (SFO) – under a Director who, like the Director of Public Prosecutions who heads the Crown Prosecution Service (CPS) and who retains by statute the duty of deciding whether or not to prosecute corruption cases, would be supervised by the Attorney General. (In the mid-1990s, both Directors are appointed on five-year contracts, making them – like chief police officers – potentially more susceptible than persons on permanent contracts to political influence if they wish to remain in post, though I have no evidence of direct influence in prosecution or non-prosecution decisions: indirect 'second-guessing' is more difficult to determine, and the SFO, like other public bodies, is dependent on political support for its resource levels.) Roskill had intended that this new body should take over revenue and DTI prosecutions, but as a consequence of political in-fighting, those agencies retained their own prosecution departments, possibly on the logic that for them (as for the other regulatory agencies discussed by Tombs, Chapter 4 in this volume), prosecution was used strategically as part of a more general regulatory function, rather than being a core activity that routinely followed the determination that crime had been committed.

The Serious Fraud Office was established by the Criminal Justice Act 1987, and by 1997 had a staff of 130, two-fifths of whom are lawyers and law clerks, one-fifth accountants, and the remainder administrators and support staff. Its brief is to deal with 'serious' and/or 'complex' fraud, loosely defined as frauds involving at least £1 million 'at risk' and/ or of considerable public interest and/or where the details are 'complex'. (The minimum cost has fluctuated between £1 million and £5 million, but costs of fraud often are a term of art.) Following a Treasury review which decided that it should continue to exist and expand its role, it has increased its own caseload from 60 to an expected (in 1998) 100 cases per year, the remaining fraud cases being dealt with by the Crown Prosecution Service, which has far fewer resources and has decentralised its headquarters Fraud Divisions since 1996. During the first two years of the SFO's life, no data were collected on the value of frauds it investigated, but in 1990 their aggregate value was £1.3 billion, while subsequently, it has fluctuated to a maximum of £6 billion 'at risk', not necessarily stolen. In 1996–97, the estimated value of alleged frauds in its caseload was £3 billion at the beginning and £2 billion at the end, the difference being accounted for by the completion of two cases: the Bank of Credit and Commerce International, and the Maxwell pensions fund fraud cases.

The establishment in 1988 of a unified investigative and prosecutorial body to deal with serious fraud raised some difficulties of principle, since following the creation of the Crown Prosecution Service under the Prosecution of Offences Act 1985, England had recently shifted towards greater independence of prosecutors from the police, at least in theory. (The Scottish tradition was always more independent.) Some of the few constitutional concerns expressed at the time were allayed by the argument that serious fraud posed unique investigative problems, and also that the considerable powers of investigation needed were, firstly, possessed by other governmental bodies; secondly would be exercised only by non-police staff of the Serious Fraud Office, that is by lawyers and accountants; and thirdly, admissions made under compulsion could not be introduced directly in evidence. It was also felt that white-collar defendants could look after themselves competently under questioning and were likely to be well-represented by their lawyers. Nevertheless, the curious consequence was that the key interviews of witnesses and suspects, who are required to answer questions on pain of imprisonment, were carried out by relatively inexperienced lawyers and accountants and not by the police who have far greater experience in interviewing. One might crassly have represented this as illustrating the belief that élite professionals would be less likely than the police to abuse citizens' rights, though allegations by a few SFO defendants would not support this sublime Establishment self-confidence (see Levi, 1993; Widlake, 1996).

THE POWERS OF FRAUD INVESTIGATIVE AGENCIES

The Department of Trade and Industry, financial services regulators – to be subsumed after 1998 under the Financial

Services Authority – who have responsibility for deciding whether or not those who conduct banking and investment business are 'fit and proper' and for disciplining rule-breakers, the Serious Fraud Office, HM Customs & Excise, and the Inland Revenue are all involved in the exercise of substantial state power. (The fact that such powers seldom lead to prosecution does not mean that they are not employed or are not salient to those against whom they are exercised.)

Under section 2 of the Criminal Justice Act 1987, when authorised by the Director, and without the need to go to court for a Production Order from a circuit judge, legal and accountancy staff at the SFO are given major powers. Anyone believed to be connected with a serious fraud case can be required – instantly if the SFO wishes – to produce documents and/or to answer questions, even if answers to the questions might incriminate them. Such answers cannot automatically be admitted in evidence, but they can be introduced if the suspect or witness subsequently gives evidence in court inconsistent with what they said under compulsion. Five people have been imprisoned and another fined for refusing to answer section 2 questions (to the end of 1997). Lying to the SFO is also a criminal offence. The use of these powers has increased four-fold in the decade since the SFO was established, partly reflecting the heavy involvement in major corporate manipulations of professional people with obligations of confidentiality who seek the protection of compulsion under law to allow them to talk – what the SFO refers to as 'willing recipients' – and partly reflecting increased flexing of regulatory muscles. In 1988–99, 233 notices were issued; in 1989–90, 574; in 1990–91, 765. There were fluctuations in subsequent years rising again to 690 in 1995–96 and a record 908 in 1996–97, plus a further 144 issued on behalf of investigations by other countries. Of the 908 given section 2 notices in 1996–97, 415 were banks. Over half (554) were orders to produce only documents, without answering questions.

These SFO powers are not unique: since the Middle Ages, bankruptcy examiners have had the power to require answers from bankrupts which can be used in evidence against them, and these powers have been exercisable against directors of insolvent companies since the nineteenth century. When the Department of Trade and Industry (DTI) appoints inspectors under the Companies Act 1989 (and under previous legislation) to investigate allegations of corporate misconduct, answers are both compellable and admissible in subsequent criminal trials. The impact of such involuntary confessions on trial outcomes is a matter of dispute, but they were used substantially in the Guinness case in 1990 and the Blue Arrow case in 1992: a point not lost upon the European Court of Human Rights in *Saunders and the UK* [ECHR Reports of Judgements and Decisions, 1996 Part 6 No. 24: 2044–2104], which upheld Saunders' complaint that his human rights had been violated by the admission in evidence of statements made under legal compulsion, though his conviction has not been quashed by the English Court of Appeal. On the other hand, in most fraud investigations the police have no power to require answers to their questions, though with relative ease, prior to arrest or summons, they can obtain Production Orders from circuit judges for documents required in their investigations.

THE PROSECUTION AND TRIAL OF FRAUD

The Serious Fraud Office has proven to be an important political institution, the first agency in Britain to have a bureaucratic interest in prosecuting fraud. Its title gives a sense of power and prestige: the announcement by the Attorney-General that 'the Serious Fraud Office is investigating company X' triggers the perception that this case is being taken seriously. Although many trial verdicts result from judicial and jury decisions that may be unforeseeable, and even capricious, the SFO has taken a severe media and political battering during the 1990s – accompanied by labels such as 'Serious Farce Office' and 'Seriously Flawed Office'. This is for two reasons: first, the fact that several high-profile prosecutions – the later Guinness trials, brokers UBS Phillips & Drew and merchant bankers County NatWest, ex-boxer George Walker, Roger Levitt, and the Maxwell brothers – did not end in conviction or, in Levitt's case, an alleged £37 million fraud resulted in a derisory 240 hours' (legal maximum) community service sentence following a controversial plea bargain; and secondly, the fact that some of the prosecutions above were proceeded with at all, offending the sentiments of some business and media people who considered that there had been an over-reach of the criminal law to cover what was either tolerated behaviour or behaviour that could be 'more appropriately' dealt with by regulators (Levi, 1993; Levi and Pithouse, forthcoming). Nevertheless, despite not being the high-prestige body that was initially envisaged, SFO morale is high compared with the Crown Prosecution Service, which deals with most other fraud prosecutions.

It has been alleged by some defendants and media commentators that the SFO is too prosecutorially aggressive or, in the alternative, that it is too timid in taking on those whose prosecution might embarrass the government (such as the Al Fayed brothers who purchased Harrods with the government's blessing). It is important to note that corporate criminal liability is notoriously difficult to prove in England, even more so than in the United States (Wells, 1993). Judges have hitherto rejected almost all such charges in manslaughter and serious fraud cases without giving the jury a chance to impose 'popular justice'. English criminal lawyers have had to learn how to conduct team investigations, and despite a flurry of legislation, there remain problems in obtaining admissible or even informative evidence from some overseas jurisdictions favoured by fraudsters. Nor have the courts found it easy in practice to force the defence to produce more than cursory pre-trial responses to the prosecution case statements in the preparatory hearings intended to narrow down the issues and make jury decisions easier (Levi, 1993). The SFO has taken on – albeit largely by referral from the government – major allegations which are being pursued more vigorously to trial than happened before it was established, but despite its overall conviction record of about three-quarters of persons tried, convictions of the principals in the most spectacular cases have seldom been easy.

Controversy continues about the effectiveness of the regulatory and white-collar trial processes. These led, in 1998, to a Home Office Consultation Paper about the future of fraud tribunals, though as I write, there is no government view on the principle of abandoning jury trial. Partly, this reflects acute concern about the purpose of the criminal process: it is curious that such philosophical *angst* occurs only when high-status defendants are tried! It should be understood that the Serious Fraud Office touches only a tiny portion of prosecuted frauds: of cases prosecuted by it which were concluded during 1996–97, there were 8 trials involving 14 defendants, 12 of whom were convicted. (At the high point, 1991, 45 defendants pleaded guilty to or were convicted of criminal offences, while 8 defendants were acquitted at courts.) In strictly numerical terms, therefore, the Crown Prosecution Service is the more important fraud prosecution body. But it is agreed on all sides that during the 1990s, as in all decades post-1960 and even before, that highly publicised fraud trials are taking far too long and that their results are unfair on everyone: defendants, jurors, judges and – when considered – victims and tax-payers. In Britain, unlike Canada, New Zealand, the United States and parts of Australia, the defendant cannot choose trial without jury. Trials taking between three and seventeen months lead to almost no middle-class persons in employment being willing to serve as jurors, so this destroys the concept of representative juries.

The prosecution of seven defendants for conspiring to defraud the market in 1987 during the £837 million 'rights issue' by Blue Arrow, the employment agency group, by attempting to suppress the information that the stock flotation had been less successful than it actually was led to a trial lasting 187 days. In the end, after the judge had directed the acquittals on legal grounds of two corporate and one individual defendant, the jury convicted four and acquitted one defendant: the Court of Appeal quashed the convictions on the grounds that the trial had become so unmanageable that it constituted an abuse of process. In the case of the prosecution arising out of the take-over of Distillers by Guinness in 1986, which basically involved the unofficial and unlawful taking of company funds to reward 'friends' who bought large quantities of Guinness shares, thereby making those shares more attractive as exchanges to Distillers shareholders than they would otherwise have been, the first trial lasted 118 days but did result in the conviction of four major entrepreneurs in 1990. In the second trial, however, the two accused engaged in lengthy defences which dragged out the case to the extent that after 68 days, only 10 out of 80 prosecution witnesses had given evidence. Defendant Seelig who, refusing Legal Aid because he did not want to have to make a financial contribution to his defence if he were convicted, represented himself, and allegedly became so stressed that he was suicidal, and the judge decided that the trial could not continue. The prosecution then agreed to offer no evidence against him and not to retry his co-defendant. In the light of this, the SFO abandoned the third trial – which had not yet commenced but which involved Seelig and a very high-status stockbroker in the élite firm Cazenove – leaving the future trial of American lawyer Thomas Ward as the only unfinished business: he was later acquitted by the jury. A further case – Barlow Clowes – a huge investment fraud in which thousands of investors were conned into believing that they were investing in safe, government securities rather than in speculation and private Lear jets and yachts, ended after 100 days with the conviction of two and the acquittal of two defendants. The latter case was regarded as a model of lawyer co-operation and judicial clarity, but it is hardly surprising that a surrealistic tone creeps into debates on fraud trials. In one case, ending in 1992, which was not serious or complex enough to be dealt with by the Serious Fraud Office, four out of five defendants were convicted after a jury trial lasting seventeen months. The acquittal of the Maxwell brothers of charges of a £400 million pension fund fraud after a six-month trial, despite massive pre-trial hostile publicity (Corker and Levi, 1996), led to further questioning of the competence of the SFO as well as of the jury system. On the other hand, all the defendants involved in the largest banking fraud in English history – the Bank of Credit and Commerce International – were convicted, the last of them, Abbas Gokal, for a fraud involving an alleged £800 million.

Perceptions of effectiveness – real and symbolic – appear to vary according to the latest 'results' and embody the assumptions that firstly, acquittal is only very rarely a correct verdict, and secondly, if an acquittal occurs, the SFO could not have done its job efficiently. SFO Directors' statements that their objective is to pass the scrutiny of adequacy imposed by the trial judge are regarded as weak, defensive excuses rather than statements of constitutional due process principle. This has its political effects in resources for the SFO.

POLICE ATTITUDES TO FRAUD IN THE UK

Interest in fraud among senior police officers has increased since the mid-1980s, probably due to greater attention to it by television, radio, and in the main crime and news sections of newspapers as well as in the business sections that non-specialist officers are less likely to read. Moreover, as in the United States, the prospect of well-paid post-retirement jobs for police officers makes expertise in financial crime investigation a more desirable attribute than has been the case in the past. (Indeed, increasingly, competent Fraud Squad officers are being lured out of the police by corporate investigation and consultancy firms.)

Nevertheless, outside the City of London, there is very little appreciation by chief officers of the importance of policing fraud, whether of the élite or blue-collar kind: their practical indifference extends to all crimes with corporate victims, and even to most crimes against investors (Levi and Pithouse, forthcoming). In this respect, little has changed since the mid-1980s (Levi, 1987), though the sheer volume of increased complaints and complex inquiries into real estate frauds and public sector corruption has generated larger Fraud Squads, at least temporarily. The explanation for this neglect is far from clear, but it appears to relate to some Victorian conception of prudence whereby everyone who does not take sufficient care of their own property deserves little sympathy. There are also pragmatic factors such as there being little political pressure on them to do more about fraud; the low productivity of Fraud Squad staff in relation to standard police performance indicators, fraud being more labour-intensive to investigate; and chief officers' own relatively unsophisticated appreciation of the business world and the possible impact of fraud losses on the local and national economy. The fact, however, that even crimes committed by non-élite persons against corporations are neglected by the police indicates that the police are far from being the hand-maidens of finance capital.

BRITISH FRAUD INVESTIGATION IN AN INTERNATIONAL CONTEXT

When one discusses élite fraud and its control in Britain, one must see this against the backdrop of global financial and industrial markets. Let us take, for example, the Boesky/ Guinness connection. Shapiro's (1985) excellent review of the prosecution approach of the US authorities to securities fraud suggested that most cases were marginal outsiders involved in parochial affairs, but she did not display sufficient awareness of the historically contingent nature of this judgement. Soon after her work was published, the almost accidental discovery of Dennis Levine's insider trading network led to his sacrificing American trader Ivan Boesky as part of his plea bargain; Boesky informed not only on star investment banker Mike Milken (who, unfortunately for him, had no one higher to trade in, and therefore got a formal ten years' imprisonment, reduced on appeal) – for a good account, see Rosoff, Pontell and Tillman (1997) – but also on those who had formed an illegal operation with him to support the price of the Guinness shares which were being offered in exchange for Distillers shares in the United Kingdom. This information was passed by the United States regulatory authorities to their United Kingdom counterparts in the Department of Trade and Industry, and thence to the police. It is a matter for speculation whether the British authorities would have prosecuted if they had not been concerned that competitive leaking by the Americans would have harmed the reputation of the United Kingdom financial services industry: former Guinness chief executive Ernest Saunders has maintained (personal communication) that he was a victim of the then Prime Minister's desire to show the world that Britain was tough on white-collar crime and of 'the Scottish Mafia' upset at his refusal to move the Guinness headquarters to Scotland, as allegedly promised. But whatever the reason, the consequence was the prosecution of a series of major British entrepreneurs and professionals, and the imprisonment of some high-status businesspeople. The crucial point is that without this international exchange – and the risk that overseas regulators, who have an interest in trumpeting their regulatory vigour at the expense of both intra-national and international competitors – the prosecution of some serious frauds would never have happened. We live, in a sense, in a global regulatory village, though some parts are policed more heavily than others. Competitive pressures in globalised financial services markets intensify this cross-national competition for scarce business.

The multinational convergence in prosecution arises largely because of the risks that fraud is posing to popular capitalism, to investments on securities markets and to deposits in financial institutions, as well as the fear of 'organised crime' infiltration into business. It is also happening because almost all serious securities frauds involve extra-territorial informational needs by national agencies, and these have to be provided for by national legislation and Memoranda of Understanding. Eighty per cent of cases investigated by the London police in 1991 had some cross-border aspects and, without mutual legal assistance, many investigations would fail. In 1996–97, the SFO accepted 54 requests for assistance from foreign countries for investigation in the United Kingdom, double the previous year. Yet when it is proposed that officers might have supranational powers, there is massive resistance, not least because it is hard to see how and to whom such officers are accountable (though similar problems arise in cross-border drugs investigations, conducted via Europol).

Policing powers are influenced not just by law but, inter alia, by the visibility of particular police actions and the tolerance of the courts. Coping with overseas jurisdictions, the difficulty of informal as well as formal action increases considerably, since the patterns of pressure, friendship, Masonic Lodge membership, etc. make for fewer and less powerful trade-offs and for greater uncertainty about responses in different cultures. Secrecy statutes also present legal obstacles to the conveying of information which many United Kingdom police officers find particularly irksome. Evidentiary rules present major problems: for example, for something to be admissible in the US courts, witnesses have to be given the same rights that they would have had if the evidence had been collected in America.

There are also conflicts of interest between different agencies, both nationally and internationally. The 1991–92 investigations into the Bank of Commerce and Credit International (BCCI) and into the dead financier and publisher Robert Maxwell produced considerable tensions between British and American investigators. In the BCCI case Robert Morgenthau, the District Attorney for New York, complained about lack of co-operation from the Serious Fraud Office, and in March 1992, the SFO enraged him further when it charged with fraud a former senior accountant at BCCI who had been co-operating with the New York authorities. Similar conflicts arose over other BCCI officers whom the District Attorney wanted to assist him. (Morgenthau equally complained about the dilatoriness and obstructiveness of the United States Department of Justice.) Were it not for the international rule that confiscated profits lie where they are at the time when they are frozen – rather than be repatriated to the place where the crime was committed – there would doubtless be even less co-operation beyond those with clear mutual interests, as international bounty-hunting would be encouraged: there has been a plethora of Mutual Legal Assistance Treaties to permit asset-sharing, though historically, these have been mainly in the arena of drugs rather than fraud (Levi and Osofsky, 1995).

KEY PROBLEMS IN THE CRIMINAL JUSTICE PROCESS AND FRAUD

The Roskill Committee – and much contemporary public debate in the 1980s – was concerned about people escaping justice by weaving complicated international webs around their activities. Current high-profile media debate suggests that little has changed. However, this is too simplistic. Many allegations of high-level fraud continue to be made but prosecutions do not follow when the police or prosecutors find 'insufficient evidence' for them. But some more élite frauds are prosecuted today, and very few such frauds dealt with during the early 1980s – none of which led to conviction – were as complicated as those currently dealt with by the Serious Fraud Office. Given that the SFO was established to enhance public confidence that 'serious fraud' was being dealt with properly, it is hard to resist demands that it should actively investigate a major case, even if that case is not as likely to yield a result as other less politically significant cases (or if it consumes resources that might lead to the conviction of many 'more convictable' cases). This is the dichotomy between seriousness and convictability that is observable elsewhere in the criminal process and which creates the ambience in which miscarriages of justice have arisen in non-fraud cases.

One issue which has not been addressed by the media focus on the Serious Fraud Office has been the range of frauds that are very costly but do not pose serious risks to the commercial reputation of the country or involve major public figures. With so many of the mere 755 or so (in 1996) Fraud Squad officers in Britain being tied up in dealing with major international frauds and property swindles involving professional lawyers and real estate agents, there are few resources left to deal with the frauds under £2 million which either individually or collectively may cost businesspeople, consumers, or taxpayers a great deal more, financially or emotionally. Likewise, only a tiny number of persons are prosecuted annually for tax evasion or for companies offences.

The irony is that with the enormous cost and risks of prosecuting complex frauds – defence costs in the prosecution for misleading the market in the take-over of American Blue Arrow by the British Manpower corporation were estimated at £30 million, though the prosecution 'only' cost £2 million, and the 'failed' Maxwell prosecutions cost some £25 million – there is a swell of opinion building up that American-style plea-bargaining should be adopted in England and Wales. However, even those who find such bargaining to be ethically proper accept that for plea-bargaining to work, the downside risks of conviction have to be serious.

Although the stress factor and economic costs are high, British fraudsters normally face modest prison sentences even after contested trials. The four Guinness defendants who were convicted got – after reductions by the Court of Appeal – sentences of two and a half years for former Guinness Chairman Ernest Saunders; 21 months for stockbroker Anthony Parnes; one year plus a £5 million fine for Gerald Ronson (then the fifteenth richest man in Britain); and a £3 million fine for Sir Jack Lyons, who was later stripped of his knighthood. (English law does not allow the imposition of a fine as well as community service.) Much controversy was caused when Ronson was allowed to shake hands with the Queen Mother at a charity function while on parole (Levi, 1991). They all went immediately to open prisons and received parole early. Saunders 'discovered' after the Court halved his five-year sentence that his Alzheimer's disease was in fact the result of the cocktail of drugs he had been taking in prison, and effected a superb recovery, though he never recovered his economic or social position.

In the Blue Arrow market manipulation case, the judge imposed suspended prison sentences on the four convicted and neither fined them nor disqualified them from future trading, arguing that they had suffered enough and had not carried the offence out for personal gain. In Barlow Clowes, the classic 'widows and orphans' fraud by someone not part of any respectable élite, the principal got 10 years and a co-accused 18 months. In 1997, one of the principals involved in BCCI, Abbas Gokal, was sentenced to 14 years. So there is a substantial variation in penalties, though – depending on how one chooses to define membership – there are too few members of the socio-economic élite convicted to draw any conclusions about leniency or severity of their treatment compared with others. Indeed, how could one judge the relative 'fairness' of penalties for such unlike activities? In England and Wales, during 1989, only five persons were imprisoned for more than five years for fraud, and only 59 people got more than three years:

in 1995, the numbers were five and 48 respectively, despite the burgeoning number of heavy sentences for violent and drug 'trafficking' offenders.

So unlike the United States, there is relatively little for the prosecution to bargain with, except perhaps the offer of certain non-imprisonment, which tempted Levitt to plead guilty to the minor charge of deceiving the regulators. My interviews suggest that after imprisonment, what the defendants wish to avoid most is the label of 'dishonesty': many people and corporations who currently plead not guilty to fraud would be willing to plead guilty to offences which charge merely gross recklessness. What other possibilities are under examination?

ALTERNATIVE SANCTIONS FOR WHITE-COLLAR CRIME: TOWARDS REGULATORY 'JUSTICE'?

In the mid and late 1990s, there has been a prevalent atmosphere of misery and disillusion about the criminal justice process, both generally and for fraud in particular. The furore about the appropriateness of jury trial after the acquittal of the Maxwell brothers in 1996 was only a symptom of the 'crisis of fraud'. Despite some longer sentences around the country, there is also disillusion about the lack of seriousness with which fraud is being taken by the courts, reflected for example, in the judgement of Buckley J. that since the banks had not actually lost money though they were deceived, he would not have imposed very severe sentences on the Maxwells even had they been convicted of the second set of charges, and that the latter were trivial compared with the pension fund thefts. Such populist criteria for 'just deserts' are commonplace, and underpin everything from police resources to parole decisions.

Decisions about the relative roles of regulators and criminal courts should and will remain a matter of symbolic as well as pragmatic debate: the argument is about the ethics of not criminalising white-collar criminals while other, lesser crooks go to jail, as well as being about the best way of reducing future misbehaviour. This is partly the problem addressed by Braithwaite and Pettit (1990) and by Fisse and Braithwaite (1993) in their rejection of a 'just deserts' approach to dealing with crime and corporate accountability generally. In practice, officials are less receptive to applying such a future-oriented approach to fraudsters than to 'corporate criminals' (see Tombs, Chapter 4 in this volume), but whether fraud will be dealt with by persuasive tactics or by retributive prosecution depends on many factors. These are whether the victim considers that there is any point in reporting the offence; how busy the police are and whether they are willing to record it; whether it comes to the attention of the authorities in any other way, for example via proactive audits; whether the 'offender' is a live company that has a regulatable future; how morally bad the offender is perceived to be (with organised crime connections increasing substantially the seriousness score); and how expensive and how successful a prosecution is estimated to be.

A complicated, multi-jurisdictional fraud involving people with no prior serious criminal records and untraumatised victims losing less than a million pounds is very unlikely to be treated as a high priority, but it partly depends on the caseload of police and prosecutors. With many fraud cases arising in the context of 'closed' transactions that are not part of a systematic process of offending by companies, one has to distinguish within the overall category of white-collar crime such 'unpromising' cases from those where multiple victims and multiple offenders can be 'encouraged' to change their ways. In the case of multiple victims – whether private or public sector – a review of business processes may yield preventative insights which can reduce fraud (Levi et al., 1991; Audit Commission, 1997; Levi and Handley, 1998; Levi and Pithouse, forthcoming): but multiple corporate offenders may be harder to spot, as audit firms usually argue.

How would such a forward-looking approach to fraud be implemented, if regarded as socially acceptable? Prevention mechanisms against company directors at large are much more limited than they are with persons selling financial services, who have to be vetted as 'fit and proper' persons before they can be licensed to operate: there is no bar upon anyone setting up in business, however ill-qualified

they may be by competence and/or morality, and no bar
upon their trading at the risk of others, provided that those
others are willing to offer the businesspeople and/or their
corporate vehicle credit. As some creditors of the Ostrich
Farming Company – an alleged 'scam' in which investors
were offered high rates of return on the purchase of birds
whose meat was supposedly due to rise in price, and found
that many of them owned the same bird! – understandably
stated, if one of the grounds for the DTI's wishing to wind
up the company was that one of its directors had shown
himself to be unfit in the past, why was he allowed to become
a director of the OFC at all (*The Times*, 11 May 1996)?
(Though it is an offence for bankrupts to obtain credit
without informing others of their status, in 1995, the huge
total of 88 people were convicted of this in England and
Wales, of whom one was jailed for more than a year.) People
may come out of jail after conviction for fraud and set up
a new business or become a director of an existing one
without anything to prevent them looting it. Nor, except
in rare circumstances occasioned by DTI investigations –
following which an application can be made under the
Companies Act to wind up the company 'in the public interest' – is there any means to put an end to a company
unless it fails to pay its debts, in which case an application
can be made to wind it up and/or make the directors
personally bankrupt. *After* their business has 'failed', people
can also be disqualified by criminal courts (following offences
committed 'in connection with the management of a company') under section 2 and section 5 of the Company
Directors' Disqualification Act 1986 (CDDA), and by civil
courts under sections 3, 4, 6, 8, 10, and 11 CDDA from
taking part in the management of a company *in future*, at
least without the permission of the court. (This combines
a permissive attitude to entrepreneurialism with regulation
of persistently fraudulent and incompetent people who are
a danger to others.) Altogether, between the end of 1986
and the end of 1997, 4800 directors were disqualified, two-
thirds of them for more than three years. However, the
absence of data broken down by multiple 'failed' directors
makes it difficult to demonstrate the extent to which this
is the commercial equivalent of the 'three strikes and you're

out' incapacitation equivalent of imprisonment policy in the United States.

What the *effects* of such disqualifications are is unknown: in practice, there is nothing to stop banned directors from inventing a new identity and starting a new business under a false name, though they commit a criminal offence by doing so. (At the beginning of 1998, a 'hot line' was established to encourage reporting of this offence.) Unlike those financial services jobs that require authorisation in almost all Western countries, where vetting tends to be more rigorous (including criminal record and personal indebtedness checks), one cannot be confident that their previous status would be discovered even if their *next* company subsequently went into liquidation. There are also problems about defining what constitutes a violation: for example, in the mid-1990s, there was a United States Federal investigation into whether or not former imprisoned junk-bond king Mike Milken violated his agreement not to participate in the securities industry by acting as 'consultant' in two take-over bids. At the end of 1997, the SEC obtained a court order to extend his probation for one month, and – without accepting guilt – he agreed in March 1998 to pay $47 million to the SEC to settle charges in relation to two deals including the investment by MCI of $2 billion in Murdoch's News Corporation. Also, Roger Levitt – who is disqualified from acting as a company director as well as being banned for life from the securities business – had a role in an offshore partnership to engage in boxing promotions and other non-securities activities (*Private Eye*, 5 April 1996), but those alleged business involvements were not with limited companies and were therefore not illegal *per se*. As the DTI discovered when it failed to extradite him from the United States, alleged lying to the DTI Inspectors is not covered by the United Kingdom/United States Extradition Treaty. But this ineffectiveness serves no conceivable British élite interest, so conspiracy theories are inappropriate here. In short, even where bans are in force and activities are known to the authorities, commercial incapacitation can be incomplete.

The impact of media publicity and disciplinary sanctions upon *organisations* has been revived by the 'naming and shaming' tactics developed by the Treasury during 1997 to 'encourage' life assurance firms to compensate the estimated 1.5 million people who were sold inappropriate private pensions when their company pensions were more beneficial to them. After 1998, the Financial Services Authority will be able to fine persons who are not members, unlike previous regulators, who were unable to do anything with non-members such as Robert Maxwell and Asil Nadir, at least prior to bankruptcy or liquidation. The occupational costs of 'prosecution' *per se* applies also to the impact of formal regulatory sanctions: there were major shake-outs of senior management following disciplinary action taken by regulators against some large firms, such as Invesco-Mims, which was required to appoint an internal reviewer of their systems and make changes. Much depends on how profitable the firm itself is: if the reason it has gone into crooked business is that it was not managing to break even by legitimate means, the prospects for reform are poor. But if it was committing or turning a blind eye to employee fraud to maximise corporate profits and/or personal bonuses, the theoretical prospects for reform are better, since the firm can survive without misconduct.

Whether regulatory sanctions (or formal monitoring) really deter fraudsters depends on what 'sort of people' they are. Even the most hard-nosed tycoons accused of white-collar crime dislike bad publicity, for they generally want others to think well of them. Part of the 'techniques of delinquency' of those who do offend are beliefs – prevalent among offenders generally – that their acts cause no real harm to anyone. Hence the imagery of seriousness in the media and among those whose opinions they may value is important, though the ingenious can always differentiate their contemplated or past acts as belonging to the lower range of harmful or even harmless actions. But the symbolic and practical messages that are sent out to white-collar offenders have an impact on deterrence as well as retribution: hence the controversy over the Queen Mother shaking hands with Guinness convict Gerald Ronson while on parole (Levi, 1991; Levi and Pithouse, forthcoming). I return to the moral issue because even if it were no less ineffective to deal with people outside the criminal justice process, would it be ethically right to send a few thousand shoplifters a year to jail while leaving a director who stole more than all of them put together to be disqualified? It may have been pragmatic, but was it right to deal with the systematic 'mis-selling' of private pension schemes as a regulatory matter rather than as an offence namely 'obtaining a pecuniary advantage by deception' contrary to the Theft Act 1968, at least by some salespeople. (It might be impossible to show that senior executives and/or the companies had sufficient mental awareness to found criminal culpability.)

CONCLUDING REMARKS

It seems appropriate to end this review with a quotation from Lord Justice Brett in the unreported case of *Wilson v. Clinch* (1879):

> I must confess to such an abhorrence of fraud in business that I am always most reluctant to come to the conclusion that fraud has been committed.

When white-collar crime is committed by strangers, it is relatively easy to accept and to act against, though for pragmatic reasons – getting the money back, lack of confidence in the police and courts, and/or not wishing to waste expensive management time – even frauds by strangers usually go unreported (see Levi and Pithouse, forthcoming). When 'people like us' are involved, it is harder to believe that the person was really dishonest and, though such persons are sometimes punished severely for 'letting the side down', sentencers often experience empathy at their suffering while spending perhaps years awaiting the verdict and at their Fall from Grace. At one level, this humanity – for it is generally empathy rather than a belief that the fraud was not serious (Wheeler et al., 1988) – is laudable. Is it acceptable, however, that such judicial reflection about the value of punishment tends to be restricted to the small élite of white-collar offenders who are not 'selected out' of the prosecution process, and is so seldom extended to those who have no grace from which to fall?

REFERENCES

Audit Commission (1997) *Protecting the Public Purse: 1996 Update* (London: Audit Commission).

Braithwaite, J. and Pettit, P. (1990) *Not Just Deserts* (Oxford: Oxford University Press).

Calavita, K. and Pontell, H. (1994) 'The State and White-Collar Crime: Saving the Savings and Loans', *Law and Society Review*, 28(2), 297–324.

Corker, D. and Levi, M. (1996) 'Pre-trial Publicity and its Treatment in the English Courts', *Criminal Law Review*, September, 322–32.

Cressey, D. (1953) *Other People's Money* (Glencoe: Free Press).

Croall, H. (1992) *White-Collar Crime* (Milton Keynes: Open University Press).

Cullen, F., Maakestad, W. and Cavender, G. (1987) *Corporate Crime under Attack* (Cincinatti: Anderson Publishing).

Fisse, B. and Braithwaite, J. (1993) *Corporations, Crime and Accountability* (Cambridge: Cambridge University Press).

Fraud Trials Committee (1986) *Report* (London: HMSO).

Friedrichs, D. (1996) *Trusted Criminals* (Belmont, CA: Wadsworth).

Lampe, A. (1992) 'Media Coverage of Complex Commercial Fraud', in P. Grabosky (ed.), *Complex Commercial Fraud* (Canberra: Australian Institute of Criminology).

Levi, M. (1981) *The Phantom Capitalists: the Organisation and Control of Long-firm Fraud* (Aldershot: Gower).

Levi, M. (1983) 'Blaming the Jury: Frauds on Trial', *Journal of Law and Society*, 10, 257–69.

Levi, M. (1988) *Regulating Fraud: White-Collar Crime and the Criminal Process* (London: Routledge).

Levi, M. (1988) 'The Role of the Jury in Complex Cases', in M. Findlay and P. Duff (eds.), *The Jury Under Attack* (London: Butterworths).

Levi, M. (1991) 'Sentencing White-Collar Crime in the Dark: the Case of the Guinness Four', *Howard Journal of Criminal Justice*, 28(4), 257–79.

Levi, M. (1993) *The Investigation, Prosecution and Trial of Serious Fraud*, Royal Commission on Criminal Justice Research Study, No. 14 (London: HMSO).

Levi, M. (1997) 'Evaluating the new Policing: Attacking the Money Trail of Organised Crime', *Australian and New Zealand Journal of Criminology*, 30(1), 1–25.

Levi, M., Bissell, P. and Richardson, T. (1991) *The Prevention of Cheque and Credit Card Fraud*, Crime Prevention Paper 27 (London: Home Office).

Levi, M. and Handley, J. (1998) *The Prevention of Plastic and Cheque Fraud Revisited*, Home Office Research Study, No. 182 (London: Home Office).

Levi, M. and Nelken, D. (eds.) (1996) *The Corruption of Politics and the Politics of Corruption* (Oxford: Blackwells and Special Issue of *Journal of Law and Society*).

Levi, M. and Osofsky, L. (1995) *The Investigation, Seizure and Confiscation of the Proceeds of Crime*, Crime Detection and Prevention Series, Paper 61 (London: Home Office).

Levi, M. and Pithouse, A. (forthcoming) *White-Collar Crime and its Victims: the Social and Media Construction of Business Fraud* (Oxford: Clarendon Press).

Pickholz, M. (1997) 'The United States Foreign Corrupt Practices Act as a Civil Remedy', in B. Rider (ed.), *Corruption: the Enemy Within* (The Hague: Kluwer Law International).

Poveda, T. (1994) *Rethinking White-Collar Crime* (Westport, Conn.: Praeger).

Rosoff, S., Pontell, H. and Tillman, R. (1997) *Profit without Honor* (Upper Saddle River, NJ: Prentice-Hall).

Rossbacher, H. and Young, T. (1997) 'The Foreign Corrupt Practices Act: an American Response to Corruption', in B. Rider (ed.), *Corruption: the Enemy Within* (The Hague: Kluwer Law International).

Serious Fraud Office (1997) *Annual Report, 1996–97* (London: HMSO).

Shapiro, S. (1985) 'The Road not Taken: the Elusive Path to Criminal Prosecution for White-Collar Offenders', *Law and Society Review*, 19 (2), 179–218.

Shapiro, S. (1990) 'Collaring the Crime, Not the Criminal: Liberating the Concept of White-Collar Crime', *American Sociological Review*, 55, 346–64.

Simon, D. and Swart, S. (1984) 'The Justice Department Focuses on White-Collar Crime: Promises and Pitfalls', *Crime & Delinquency*, 30, 107–19.

Titus, R., Heinzelmann, F. and Boyle, J. (1995) 'Victimization of Persons by Fraud', *Crime & Delinquency*, 41, 54–72.

Weisburd, D., Wheeler, S., Waring, E. and Bode, N. (1991) *Crimes of the Middle Classes: White-Collar Offenders in the Federal Courts* (New Haven: Yale University Press).

Wells, C. (1993) *Corporations and Criminal Responsibility* (Oxford: Clarendon Press).

Wheeler, S., Mann, K. and Sarat, A. (1988) *Sitting in Judgment* (New Haven: Yale University Press).

Widlake, B. (1996) *The Serious Fraud Office*, 2nd edn (London: Little, Brown).

Zimring, F. and Hawkins, G. (1993) 'Crime, Justice and the Savings and Loans Crisis', in M. Tonry and A. Reiss (eds.), *Beyond the Law* (Chicago: University of Chicago Press).

7 Regulating the Invisible? The Case of Workplace Illicit Drug Use

Peter Francis and Peter Wynarczyk

INTRODUCTION

Under the somewhat crude headline banner 'Tinker, Tailor, Soldier, Smackhead: Doctors on Heroin, Nurses on Pills, Executives on Coke' the homeless weekly magazine *The Big Issue* ran a two-page article in early 1998 questioning 'how serious is drug taking at work?' The general thrust of the article was that data on the size of the problem was inconclusive – 'opinions come easy but facts are harder to find' (Williams, 1998: 14) – but the underlying theme was not: that the control and regulation of illicit drugs was becoming more commonplace across industry and commerce in the United Kingdom following developments in the United States, and was something that was not going to go away. The same week as *The Big Issue* article, Granada Television's flagship current affairs programme, *World in Action*, televised an exposé of illicit drug taking within the medical profession and asked the question 'what can be done?', while two weeks previously, several broadsheet newspapers reported that the British army was testing soldiers' hair for traces of illicit drug use, although on a rather limited scale due to the financial cost of the test – two hundred pounds per scalp as opposed to ten pounds per urine test! *The Guardian* newspaper reported during October 1997 that 'the Forensic Science Service (FSS), an executive agency for the Home Office, announced it was offering its services to help identify job applicants and employees who may have taken illegal drugs. It is the latest development in a growing trend for drug testing at work – both of people applying for a job, and on a random basis for existing staff' (Campbell, 1997: 6).

168

While the content of these and similar news stories pub-lished over the recent past should come as no surprise to those with knowledge or experience of the changing nature and dynamics of work, employment and employee/employer relations at the end of the twentieth century, what *is* surprising is the paucity of *academic* debate surrounding the need for workplace regulatory testing programmes and mechanisms against illicit drug use. In particular, we would argue, there has been a neglect, especially within the British social science literature, of any exploration: of whether there is a growing problem surrounding illicit drug use and the workplace; of the consequences of such workplace use; of the effectiveness and efficacy of workplace drug testing programmes/mechanisms; of the consequences of such mechanisms and programmes for workers' rights and em-ployee/employer relations, as well as broader theoretical debates surrounding workplace testing, employment, dis-cipline and the surveillance society.[1] Indeed, it is in acknowledgement of the neglect of many of these critical issues that the current chapter has been written. The aim of the chapter is threefold: first, to highlight and explore the development and boundaries of workplace illicit drug testing on both sides of the Atlantic – mainly in the US – but where possible Canada and the UK; second, to criti-cally explore the efficacy of some of the more pertinent arguments which have been used to support the introduction of illicit drug testing within the workplace environment over the last thirty years; and third, to establish a number of issues from this review which need further critical discussion and analysis. In particular the chapter aims to problematise the evidence upon which much current regulatory testing practice has developed and to critically review broader connections between drug use and work, surveillance and regulation in late modern society. The chapter will not only allow for an understanding of the scale of the area under review, but also of some of the key themes that arise as a result, and of the unanswered questions they raise for workplace regulation and control. The chapter hopes to offer a multi-disciplinary discussion of some of the more critical issues affecting debates concerning illicit drug testing and the workplace as we enter the new millennium.

The structure of the chapter is as follows. Section one maps the development, nature and form of regulatory testing programmes against drug use in the workplace over the recent past, highlighting its emergence and development, form and content, and the associated array of possible consequences for the various professions, agencies and actors involved. Section two presents a brief review of several well-rehearsed arguments in support of workplace testing, including those suggesting that illicit drug use is a prevalent problem within the workplace; is causally related to increased workplace risk, be it either to the employees themselves or the employer or customer; and that regulation in the form of workplace testing reduces the chances of such risk. Having outlined both the parameters of, and arguments for, workplace illicit drug testing, section three goes on to problematise many of these arguments by exploring the available research material and evidence on this area. The particular emphasis of this section is directed towards unpacking the inconclusive nature of much of the literature. In doing so the section offers a preliminary review of what is actually known about workplace drug use, before questioning the argument and evidence suggesting that workplace illicit drug use is growing, already worryingly large, that it is closely related to increased levels of workplace risk, or that testing is able to lower such risk. Section four locates the development of testing programmes within broader conventional wisdom(s) about drug use and prohibition, before offering a critical challenge to these. Overall, the purpose of these two sections is to question the appropriateness and effectiveness of much workplace illicit drug regulation in the form of testing at the present time. The final section develops this critical line of thinking, by drawing out and discussing many of the key issues which the review highlights. The chapter concludes by stressing the need for caution in travelling down the path of *regulating the invisible*, suggesting that there is a danger of being sold the drug testing myth. It is our view that a better starting point would be to gain an improved understanding of the actual nature of, and relations between, illicit drugs, employee performance and the workplace.

Before proceeding to section one, we would like to note

that in this chapter we are primarily concerned with the consumption of illegal drugs, those prohibited regarding their use by law (rather than their production or sale) and its consequences for the workplace. We remain cognizant of the fact that alcohol/tobacco and other legal substances have workplace consequences but only refer to these when they provide a foil for comparison with illegal drugs (for example with regard to legalisation and current control issues within the workplace). We are also concerned to distinguish between drugs *and* work and drugs *at* work. Our focus is upon the more general issues related to the former. Drug taking outside of work can have repercussions at work; drug consumption well removed spatially and temporally from the workplace may still impact upon that environment. (It may be extremely difficult to *clinically* distinguish between on-the-job and off-the-job drug use.) We also embrace a broader and more general view of the workplace than that attached to one where it is a strictly formal, legally centred, arrangement between employee and employer. We would argue that there are other less legally defined arrangements – 'unofficial arrangements' – tailing off at one extreme into the 'twilight workplaces' of illegal activity.[2] Finally we are concerned primarily with regulation as practised through drug screening and testing programmes, either pre-employment and/or during employment. We are aware of debates surrounding workplace health and safety legislation and policy developments regarding drug use more generally, but these are not the focus of this chapter.

DRUGS, WORK AND CURRENT REGULATORY PRACTICES

There has developed since the 1960s, primarily within the US but also elsewhere, an increasing prevalence of preventative and regulatory mechanisms aimed at controlling workplace drug use. With regards to drug testing in the US, Konovsky and Cropanzano (1993) report that in 1986 approximately 25 per cent of all Fortune 500 companies had some drug screening programme in operation, while in a review of more recent estimates, the authors go on to indicate that the average number of *all* companies undertaking some form of drug testing is around 40 per cent. Similarly, Kaestner and Grossman (1995: 55) cite evidence that in 1990, 46 per cent of all firms with 250 or more employees had some form of drug testing programme, while Macdonald (1995: 703) cites evidence for 1993 from the American Management Association (AMA) News (1993) that approximately 85 per cent of major firms have some form of drug testing programme in place.

Whilst it remains the case that drug testing varies between industry type and characteristic (Macdonald and Wells, 1994: 122), size of organisation (being more likely in larger organisations – those with a substantial workforce and several work sites) (Axel, 1989), nature of work conducted (with manufacturing industries and transportation and utility sectors more likely to have screening programmes) and geographical location, Konovsky and Cropanzano (1993) maintain 'that a large proportion of the American workforce will be tested for drug use at least some time in their careers' (1993: 171). Some writers, such as Murphy et al. (1990, in Konovsky and Cropanzano, 1993), estimate that the number of employees tested could be upwards of 4 million per annum, with this figure including only employees of those 'organizations regulated by the federal government' (Konovsky and Cropanzano, 1993: 171). Williams (1998: 15) in a more recent, but speculative review suggests that the US figure is now approaching 15 million employees tested for drug use. Similar estimates can be found in the work of Macdonald and Wells (1994), Macdonald (1995), and DuPont et al. (1995). In terms of financial cost, Hoffman and Silvers (1987) and Williams (1998) both suggest that drug testing has become a multi-billion dollar a year industry within North America today.[3]

In highlighting such parameters, one point to note, however, is that as Macdonald and Wells (1994: 123) argue, this direction of change has not been solely one way, since, 'a proportion of companies in the United States have abandoned their programs'. This reduction usually, but not always, is the result of a discontinuation of testing amongst smaller size companies, and/or a questioning of the size of drug use amongst particular employee groups.

Drug testing programmes and practices within the US first appeared during the 1960s and 1970s, and grew out of a changing social and political climate of perceived increased drugs consumption amongst upper-middle-class college students and of reportedly high levels of drug use amongst American service personnel returning from the Vietnam war (Konovsky and Cropanzano, 1993: 171–4) (see also Macdonald and Wells, 1994; and Macdonald, 1995). The reported prevalence of drug use amongst these two groups led, Konovsky and Cropanzano (1993) argue, to a heightened concern over the effect of drug use on both academic and military performance, resulting in a move – especially within the American military – to some form of drug testing to correct 'behavioural problems of its personnel' (Macdonald and Wells, 1994: 122).

Several additional factors have subsequently helped rapidly to establish workplace drug testing programmes across the US during the 1980s and 1990s. The first factor surrounds the heightened concerns displayed during the 1980s of a growing epidemic of urban drug use and associated high levels of violence and property crime (see for example Goode, 1997). The second factor concerns the federal government's 'war on drugs' discourse and practice aimed at eliminating the drugs market (see Cullen et al., 1996: 30–31). Blackwell (1994) argues that the public perception of the 'drug problem' has been socially constructed through such discourse, allowing for increased public spending on police, customs, armaments, surveillance, technology and prison construction. As she argues, 'Drug war discourse has generated strong public support for a supply side "tough guy" approach to drug policy.' A third factor responsible for concretising drug testing programmes has been the development of a more reliable technology for testing and the birth of an industry capable of delivering it (Zimmer and Jacobs, 1990). Blackwell (1994) identifies a further three factors which help explain how the stage was set for the development and implementation of drug screening: a convergence of supply and demand side interventions at a national level; development of citizen groups which redefined the drug problem to include *all* drug users, not simply those causing harm, thus making zero-tolerance the norm;

and the need to maintain labour discipline in the promotion of business interest. Finally, as Macdonald and Wells (1994: 122) argue, the late 1980s also saw 'important legislative developments in the United States that opened the doors to widespread implementation of drug screening programmes'. In particular, the Drug Free Workplace Act 1988 required federal government contractors to maintain drug-free workplaces, with Executive Order 12564 requiring all federal agencies to establish drug-free workplaces (Kaestner and Grossman, 1995).

In comparison with the literature on workplace drug testing programmes and practices in the US, the development, nature, extent and cost of drug testing programmes in Canada and Europe is much less well documented. As Macdonald and Wells (1994: 123) suggest, 'few studies have been conducted on the prevalence of drug screening programmes in Canada . . . [while] . . . the extent of testing programs in Europe is largely unknown'. Four points can be made about developments beyond the US. First, it is certainly the case that the extent and level of testing is much less than that detailed for North America. Moreover, the evidence which exists is usually speculative or localised; Campbell (1997: 6), for example, has suggested that the percentage number of UK firms who test employees for drug use is, at 1997 figures, approximately 10 per cent and rising, while Williams (1998: 15) details those firms as being ones with particular health and safety concerns such as London Underground and Virgin Atlantic Airways (see *Transport and Workers Act* 1992). Similarly, in Canada Macdonald and Wells (1994: 123) suggest that in 1990 just under 4 per cent of companies employing more than fifty employees had some form of drug screening programme; although like the US and the UK, these were located within particular companies especially concerned with health and safety matters. Second, drug testing at work is a relatively recent phenomenon in Canada and Europe. Third, in part this is the result of the fact that little 'legislation mandating drug screening programmes is known to have been enacted' (Macdonald and Wells, 1994: 123) (although in the UK see *Transport and Workers Act 1992*). The fourth point is that developments within these countries have, to a large extent, closely followed those implemented within the US; either because of the exchange of ideas and practices and/ or because of the global expansion of American-owned companies across Canada and Europe – what Ritzer (1995; 1997) references in his investigation into the changing character of contemporary social life as the *McDonaldization of society*.

Most workplace drug testing programmes fall into one of several categories.[4] According to Macdonald and Wells (1994: 124–6), who detail those in operation in the US specifically, workplace testing programmes and practices include: *pre-employment testing* in which job applicants are tested for illicit drug use; *random testing* of employees usually but not always without notice or cause; *periodic testing* whereby employees are tested on a predetermined timetable; *probable-cause testing* in which employees are tested after an accident or injury; *reasonable suspicion testing* whereby employees are tested on showing signs of drug use; *post-treatment testing* in which employees are tested on completion of some form of medical treatment for drug or alcohol abuse; *transfer and promotion testing* of employees who gain transfer or promotion; and *voluntary testing* whereby employees choose to be tested. A number of these mechanisms are obviously more commonly used than others, and some are employee and company specific. That said, in general terms, they all share an official goal of preventing or reducing illicit drug use in the workplace, and consequently of enhancing employee health, safety and productivity. In addition to this primary goal, Schottenfeld (1989: 413) argues that workplace testing programmes have also been advocated as a way of achieving a number of closely related, secondary objectives, including:

> expediting identification and referral for treatment of impaired workers, fostering public trust in the business or industry using such programs, decreasing the likelihood that employees will engage in illegal activities . . . in order to support expensive drug habits or to avoid blackmail, and complying with federal regulations or orders requiring such testing.

The impact of such programmes can be both direct and indirect. The *direct* impact of workplace drug testing mechanisms and programmes are quite straightforward. There are three ideal typical consequences for those who test positive. With regards to pre-employment positive testing, the applicant will usually not be offered the post; with other forms of positive testing the employee will either be dismissed or will be provided with various forms of treatment and reha- bilitation. Actual consequences depend upon the type of employer, the nature of the work, the drug use detected, the broader company health policy in operation, and the nature of the screening programme. In contrast, *indirect* costs are more difficult to ascertain, but some have ident- ified a number of negative consequences resultant from employee drug testing programmes. These include lowered workforce morale and productivity; negative attitudes of prospective job applicants towards companies and organ- isations that test; and broader social and economic effects beyond the workplace for those who have been dismissed (Macdonald and Wells, 1994: 127).

ARGUING THE CASE FOR WORKPLACE REGULATION

The previous section detailed the emergence and develop- ment of work-based illicit drug testing programmes at both the micro organisational and larger structural level, and do not need repeating here. Similarly, the section detailed a number of aims and objectives which are usually for- warded in support of drug testing. In this section, we present three ideal typical responses most frequently recited by supporters of workplace drug testing in the US and else- where. In the following section we problematise the evidence upon which these are grounded.

Perhaps the most significant argument forwarded by sup- porters of workplace testing programmes is that drug taking is a prevalent and, therefore, major problem for the workplace environment. Four interconnecting points are usually associated with this view; first, that research evi- dence has dispelled the image of the isolated and mainly unemployed illicit substance user (see Lehman et al., 1995: 253); second, that workplace drug use is related to growing illicit drug use within wider society; third, that the drug *addict* is as much a problem for the workplace as they are to society at large. Overarching these, a fourth point suggests that if recreational and polydrug use in general society is fairly prevalent, then it is safe to suggest that many employed persons have experience of illicit substance use. Indeed, a programme televised in the UK during spring 1998 suggested that one in five full-time employees under thirty years of age had experience of an illegal drug (*Drugs Debate*, 1998). Compounding such points there has been the increasing newsworthiness of illicit substance use amongst members of particular professions such as doctors, nurses and transportation industries including rail and air transport.

A second argument forwarded in support of workplace drug testing concerns the consequences of such use. In particular, it is commonly perceived that the use of drugs poses a number of risks within the workplace environment, no matter what the work entails. Hecker and Kaplan (1989: 693) detail such consequences in terms of the possible risks drug use poses to an individual's 'own health and safety, risks to the safety of fellow employees and/or the public from drug induced impairment, and risks to the production process'. The association between drug use and increased risk for some is growing (Lehman et al., 1995: 253) – a perception certainly indicative of the views of many writers on the subject (see, for example, Bottomley, 1998 and Millard, 1991) as well as professional and industrial organisations and representatives including, in the UK, the Health and Safety Executive (see Health and Safety Executive, 1992, 1994, 1998), the Confederation of British Industry (see Confederation of British Industry, 1986) and the Institute of Personnel Management (see Institute of Personnel Management, 1986; Dickinson, 1988). An example of such views in the US can be seen in the writing of Millard (1991: 46), who argues that employees who use 'drugs not only take more sick days, but are more likely to make compensation claims against employers', while in financial terms he goes on to suggest that 'substance abuse raises the cost of insurance by $50 billion each year and costs more than $36 billion in lost productivity, medical expenses, profits and damages'.

One final argument advanced in favour of workplace drug testing is that testing programmes and mechanisms are effective in reducing employee risks and employer costs. Their effectiveness is measured by the extent to which programme objectives are achieved; usually these are in terms of reducing employee accidents, injuries and deaths at work along with increasing worker productivity and enhancing profitability. In addition to this triumvirate of responses a broader or more general reason advanced to support drug testing mechanisms in the workplace is that they may help reduce societal levels of use. With the threat of being caught at work, so this deterrence argument goes, individuals' usage of drugs outside work decreases. As a result, societal levels of drug misuse are supposed to decline also.

PROBLEMATISING THE EVIDENCE

Despite such arguments supporting the necessity of workplace drug testing a critical review of the literature raises more questions than confirmations about its worth at the present time. Whilst arguments in favour of testing appear commonsensical, research evidence presents a more inconclusive picture of the case for workplace regulation.

1. Drug Use is a Major Workplace Problem

Statistical and other data on workplace illicit drug use is at best partial and at worst unreliable. Despite the attention given to the general use of drugs in society today, as Martin et al. (1994: 3) point out, 'there have been few systematic attempts to document these behaviours empirically among employed persons', and those that do either focus upon alcohol rather than illicit drug usage (see University of Strathclyde, 1997) and/or suffer from serious conceptual and methodological weaknesses. In consequence, whilst many assert that illicit drug use is a major workplace problem, it is much more difficult to empirically demonstrate in actuality: as a result, drug use and the workplace remains invisible, and the case for testing inconclusive.

In part, this invisibility is the result of conceptual and

definitional problems surrounding what is actually meant by workplace drug use. This is because there are differing ways of defining both its nature and boundaries. Strictly speaking, workplace drug use is, as Newcomb (1994: 40) highlights, the ingestion of drugs at work during periods of explicit employment. 'Based on this definition', Newcomb continues, 'a three martini lunch or two joint break would not be considered drug use on the job' as such use is during the employees' free time, and often well away from the actual place of employment. However, as we made clear at the beginning of this chapter, some suggest that many drugs (both licit and illicit) have a long period of effect, and may therefore affect performance many hours after ingestion during formal working hours. Moreover, studies fail to identify the focus of analysis; whether it is all drug use or purely illicit drug use. While a more detailed discussion is not deemed necessary in this current context, problems defining both the nature and boundaries of workplace drug use problematises the availability, accuracy and reliability of the data on the subject, as all too often, distinctions and differences are neither considered nor discussed.

The invisibility of workplace illicit drug use is also in part the result of the difficulties of measurement. Fillimore and Caetano (1982) have documented the difficulties associated with securing reliable estimates of employee alcohol prevalence rates, and for the most part obtaining reliable documentary estimates of workplace illicit drug use is similarly if not more problematic. Means of measuring workplace illicit drug use vary greatly across employer, industry, government and country, and include prevalence surveys of sample employee populations, specific employee testing programmes, and anecdotal evidence based upon hearsay or observation, while findings range from gross average 'guesstimates' based upon a proportion of employees across a number of companies to details about individual addicted persons. Such variety in the use of 'operations and populations' to assess levels of maladaptive uses of alcohol and drugs is bound to cause uncertainty, given that estimates generally vary depending upon the population studied and the measures utilised (Martin et al., 1994: 10). Moreover, the failure historically to see the workplace as an arena for research into illicit drug use further compounds the paucity of reliable and comparable estimates and maintains what we would see as the 'invisibility' of much workplace illicit drug use over the last three decades or so.

As may be expected, given specific legislative enactment, the country with the richest data sets available on workplace drug use is that of the US; but even here, analysis and interpretation of the evidence must be undertaken with caution. As Newcomb (1994: 41) argues, even 'these estimates are based on at best guesses . . . and not any reliable assessment of drug use on the job'. Martin et al. (1994) are similarly cautious, informing the reader that 'given the range of available prevalence estimates, it is unlikely that a consensual estimate of alcohol or drug abuse can be obtained from the research literature' (1994: 10). Nevertheless, this has not stopped many attempting to do so. DuPont et al. (1995), drawing upon data derived from the Department of Health and Human Services, suggest that for any given year, approximately 7 per cent of employees in the US use an illicit substance, and that approximately two-thirds of all illicit drug users are employed full time; Lehman et al. (1995: 253) inform the reader that 'data from the 1988 US National Household Survey indicated that 70% of those reporting illicit drug use in the last month were employed' and quote the findings of a report published in 1994 by the National Research Council in the US which estimated that 'as much as 10 per cent of workers have used illicit drugs within the last year'; while Delaney (1987) has estimated that when alcohol is introduced into any calculation the proportion who use drugs at some time during their working life increases to between 12 per cent and 15 per cent, equating to some 13 million to 20 million employees across the US (see also Backer, 1987). Conscious of the problems and limitations surrounding many such estimates, in their primary analysis of national survey data in the US,[5] Martin et al. (1994) focus upon drug use rates and employment and occupational status. Rather than offering simplistic prevalence data, their analysis details particular consumption patterns of both licit and illicit workplace drug use. First, more people report alcohol abuse than they do illicit drug use and of those that do report

the latter, it is less likely to be the harder substances reported; second, more males than females report drug use;
third, drug use is mostly a youthful activity – what they
call the clear 'inverse relationship of age to substance use
and abuse' (1994: 24); fourth, there are few differences
amongst part-time and full-time employees involved in drug
use; and lastly that differential drug usage is evident across
different occupational levels (Martin et al., 1994: 23–4).

Given our discussion in section one, estimates of, and
research into, workplace drug use in the UK is generally
less expansive, especially at a national level, and certainly
no more informative of actual rates. That said, findings
from recent sweeps of the British Crime Survey (see Ramsay
and Spiller, 1997; Ramsay and Percy, 1996) provide some
comparable material.[6] Drawing upon findings from the 1994
survey, Ramsay and Percy (1996) generalise that those in
full-time employment have a lower level of drug taking
than those not employed (with the exception of the 30–59
age group); that those not employed were more susceptible to use within the last month across all age bands; and
that there was no clear pattern for those employed part
time. In the 1996 British Crime Survey, Ramsay and Spiller
(1997: 21) indicate that 'drug use is spread relatively evenly
across all social groups, manual and non-manual, inner city
and suburban, rich and poor'. As the authors of the report
go on to state, 'while low income is a modest pointer to
drug use in general . . . [the evidence] . . . shows that not
having a job is at least as important a factor, if only in the
case of the 16–29 age group' (Ramsay and Spiller, 1997:
22). In particular the authors indicate the contrast between
those aged 16–29 who are employed and those not, suggesting that as many as 45 per cent of that age group who
are unemployed reported drug use within the last year.

While far from conclusive about the size or nature of
the problem, the data derived from these two sweeps
of the British Crime Survey do provide some indications
of drug use amongst those individuals who are in both
full-time and part-time work across the UK, patterns which
are similar to those reported by Martin et al. (1994); namely
that drug use at work appears to be *comparatively rare* amongst
employees; that it is mostly a *youthful phenomenon*; that there

is *no significant difference* in response between those employed part time and those employed full time; and that there is some evidence of *difference in consumption by occupational level*. While such data must be read with caution, it seems to be the case that *illicit drug use within the workplace setting is both a relatively rare and a predominantly youthful activity*, and that other pressures may also affect use, *most notably a person's lifestyle* characteristics (Ramsay and Percy, 1996).

Such findings attempt to provide national estimates and/or patterns of usage. Localised means of measuring workplace drug use include the collation and analysis of particular company surveys of staff drug use; records of notifiable addicts receiving treatment at clinics who report their employment status; results from specific employee testing programmes and pre-employment schemes; as well as information detailed in the media. However, such methods suffer similar problems of representativeness and accuracy as outlined above. Two examples highlight such problems well. Dickinson (1988: 10) suggests that while between one-quarter and one-half of addicts attending drug clinics for treatment reported that they were employed, such figures represented the tip of an iceberg 'given that only one in ten approach services for treatment' in the first place, and we would suggest that even this latter figure is somewhat of an estimate. Similarly Newcomb (1994) details a case whereby 75 per cent of individuals telephoning a national cocaine helpline indicated that they had used drugs at work, with cocaine being the most-used drug. Yet as Newcomb goes on to argue, these estimates are certainly biased in at least two ways. First, cocaine abusers (as opposed to the general population or abusers of other drugs) are most likely to call a cocaine hotline. Second, those having problems with drugs are most likely in general to call the hotline. Such factors thus restrict somewhat the generalisability of these figures to only those who admit to having a problem with cocaine and are willing to telephone the hotline.[7]

2. Drug Use Increases Workplace Risk

In order to elucidate understanding of the relationship between increased risk and workplace illicit drug use, it is appropriate to categorise the types of risk and provide a critical discussion of each. For our purposes here, we detail these under three main headings: *employee risk*, under which we discuss research conducted into the relationship between drug use and workplace accidents, injuries and deaths; *employer risk*, under which we detail various attempts to understand the possible costs of workplace drug use to the employer; and *customer risk*, by which we refer to the impact workplace drug use may have on the delivery of a service or product to the general population.[8]

1. Employee risk

According to Martin et al. (1994: 5) there is a relatively large body of research which 'has sought to demonstrate the association of employee substance abuse patterns to the frequency of accidents and injuries both on and off the job'. The results of this research indicate that in some cases drug use *may* be related to workplace injuries and accidents both individually and collectively, although many *are not* conclusive. Both Martin et al. (1994: 5–7) and Konovsky and Cropanzano (1993: 174–6) review the literature relating employee drug use patterns to the frequency of accidents and injuries. Their discussions indicate a number of studies reporting some degree of positive association. Martin et al. (1994: 6–7) also detail research which has focused upon the relationship between illicit drug use and employee fatalities. In doing so, they highlight positive correlations found in research conducted by Lewis and Cooper (1989) and Alleyne et al. (1991).

However, Macdonald and Wells (1994: 129) argue that 'the methodology of and accuracy of conclusions drawn from many of these studies . . . have been vigorously challenged', citing criticisms that: often several drugs are combined into one category; users are simply compared with non-users; that moderate and heavy use is not distinguished; and that past and current use is never differentiated. They also repeat the claim by Konovsky and Cropanzano (1993) that a study by Normand et al. (1990) failed to find significant differences between drug positives and negatives in terms of job accidents or injuries.

In the light of such criticisms, Macdonald (1995: 705), in his review of the literature on employee risk, divides the research conducted into those that compare job injuries of drug users and non-users as determined through self-report studies; and those which compare accident rates of drug positive and drug negative employees, determined by pre-employment tests. With regard to the former, he highlights research in the US conducted by Hingson et al. (1985) and Bross et al. (1992) as indicating some degree of association between general workplace illicit drug use and employee injury and accident; while of those that compare accident rates of drug positive and drug negative employees, determined by pre-employment tests, studies by Zwerling et al. (1990) and Crouch et al. (1989) indicate some degree of positive correlation.

Macdonald concludes his review by stating that while many studies appear 'to indicate that a relationship exists between drug users and on the job injuries', since the relationship between workplace drug use and accidents and injuries has not been *empirically established*, and since few studies have explored the *role* of drugs in work injuries 'definitive conclusions cannot be drawn' (1995: 705) (also Macdonald and Wells, 1994: 130). Thus, a critical reading of the literature indicates that although correlations *may* have been established, establishing *causality* is more problematic. Indeed, Macdonald suggests that too little weight or attention is given to non-drug predictors such as job conditions, demographic variables or other lifestyle characteristics (Macdonald, 1995: 714). Indeed, in his own research, the primary purpose of which was to address these limitations, Macdonald suggests that the 'relationship only holds up for males and youngest age groups' (1995: 717), and more generally that drug use therefore may not be a major cause of employee accident or injury.

2. Employer risk
A number of studies have systematically attempted to measure the costs of workplace illicit drug use to the employer. Often

these are discussed either in terms of the economic cost analysis framework or the human capital cost of illness (DiNardo, 1994). In general terms, three areas affecting employer risk are usually identified: worker absenteeism and associated costs; the costs associated with employee turnover; and the costs associated with impaired employee performance.[9] In reviewing the literature on these three areas, the inconclusive and sometimes contradictory nature of the research is again an overriding feature.

With regard to absenteeism, Normand et al. (1990) found that marijuana use was associated with greater staff absence amongst the US postal service; while Sullivan et al. (1990) found that self-reported attendance problems were the second most frequently mentioned 'on the job' effects of an individual drug dependence (35 per cent) amongst a sample of 300 registered nurses. Bross et al. (1992) detail similar results. With regard to employer costs arising from employee turnover, Zwerling et al. (1990) suggest that workers who use illicit drugs have a higher turnover, as do Sullivan et al. (1990), White et al. (1988), Kandel and Davies (1990), Sheridan and Wrinkler (1989) and Kandel and Yamaguchi (1987). The study by Normand et al. (1990), however, did not find any such relationship. The final and perhaps the most hypothesised employer cost is that associated with poor employee performance. Walsh et al. (1991), Burt (1981), White et al. (1988) and Sullivan et al. (1990) all provide cursory evidence of lowered performance resultant from illicit drug use, although as Martin et al. (1994: 8) go on to argue, there are also a number of studies which 'have been unable to document this connection'. Indeed, as Blackwell (1994: 326) argues, 'the evidence rallied to support the extent and costs of worker impairment does not stand up to close scrutiny, nor does the presumed elevated risk of drug users to experience workplace accidents and injuries'.

Despite the inconclusive nature of much of the evidence on employer cost, the general perception prevailing within much of the literature is that workplace drug use *is* associated with increased risks, be they financial and/or productivity-related (through accidents, injury, turnover, absence and retraining). Kaestner and Grossman (1995) suggest that this speculation is unsurprising given that in the US over the last 30 years there has been a noticeable decline in productivity alongside an increased visibility of workplace drug use. In particular, they suggest that this has led to the two facts being combined to form a new 'conventional wisdom that drug use is a significant cause of declining productivity' with estimates of loss ranging from $8.6 billion to $33 billion per year; although as they go on to suggest, this causal linkage is surprising 'in light of the fact that most of the evidence on the issue is anecdotal in nature' (1995: 55). Indeed, DiNardo (1994: 58) argues we should have 'no reason to believe that current estimates of the costs of alcohol and drug use are too high, too low or about right. Both conceptually and empirically', he goes on to argue, 'the enterprise rests on very shaky foundations.'[10] Martin et al. (1994: 24) are similarly sceptical, arguing further that not all patterns of workplace drug use need be viewed in the generic category of costs. While job performance decrements are definite costs to the workplace, Martin et al. argue this does not necessarily hold for absenteeism. Instead, absenteeism may actually reduce costs in comparison to those incurred had the employee remained within the workplace environment.

3. Customer impact
There is little research evidence on the impact workplace drug use has had or can have on the broader realm of consumer and customer relations. This has not stopped the detrimental effect of workplace drug use upon customer relations being taken for granted. For example, a guide on the dangers of drug use at work published in Great Britain by the Health and Safety Executive (1998) states that successfully tackling drug taking within the workplace will enhance the public perception of that organisation. However, at the time of writing, research is needed to determine the association and effects, if any, that drug use has on the customer. Merely assuming causality is simply inadequate and problematic.

3. Workplace Illicit Drug Testing is Effective in Lowering Risk

Measuring the effectiveness of workplace drug employee testing programmes is similarly problematic. Usually, the effectiveness of any given programme is measured against its stated primary objective(s). As we indicated in sections one and two, such goals include the reduction of workplace accident, injury and death, and increased workforce productivity and performance. However, because such regulatory measures can be implemented in a variety of ways, their effectiveness partly depends upon the type of programme, its implementation, its aims and objectives and the particular risk involved. For example, if we take the suggestion that random drug testing reduces the risk of accident and injury, the starting point for any hypothesis about effectiveness would be that drug use is causally related to increased risk. However, the problem is that, as we have detailed above, there is little conclusive evidence that drug use is causally related to poor performance through accident or injury. As a result, it follows that the effectiveness of drug testing programmes in reducing possible illicit drug related consequences is also 'scientifically unproven' (Macdonald and Wells, 1994: 130–1). Indeed, as we also make clear, even those studies that do indicate drug use to be in some way related to increased risk of accident, it is not clear whether such drug use is primarily the cause.

Similar inconclusive findings can be suggested for studies into pre-employment testing programmes. Macdonald and Wells (1994) again draw attention to the serious methodological weaknesses associated with such research. That is, while some pre-employment studies have suggested lowered job performance, they neglect to analyse individual user characteristics (type of drug, nature of use and degree of addiction), and that such studies do not include the large variety of over-the-counter and prescription drugs which may also affect job performance. Moreover, many studies (as cited earlier) indicate that minimal differences exist in terms of lowered job performance between those testing positive and negative in pre-employment programmes. Finally, Macdonald and Wells (1994: 137–9) stress caution in measuring the 'outcome effects' of regulation as measured in the percentage reduction of accidents, injuries and performance problems resultant from some form of regulatory mechanism, because such programmes fail to take account of the possible and actual effect of non-drug testing factors (such as increased employee training, and superior capital equipment) in reducing risk. Indeed, such measures may account for the majority of the reduction in risk, thus problematising the effectiveness of workplace regulatory mechanisms themselves. Given this discussion, we would stress caution when reviewing the effectiveness of drug testing programmes in the workplace. First, prevalence rates remain low. Second, the causal link between illicit drug use and employee or employer risk is unsubstantiated. This point is cogently made by Macdonald and Wells (1994: 139):

> In summary, it appears that evidence is inconclusive, not only that drug use is related to work performance problems and work accidents, but also that drug screening programmes actually reduce such work performance problems. Too few empirical studies on the effectiveness of drug screening programs exist at this time to prove that programmes are effective in reducing drug use among employees, accidents and performance problems in the workplace, or drug problems in society as a whole.

CONVENTIONAL DRUG WISDOM(S) AND CHALLENGES TO IT

Despite the inconclusive nature of such research, evidence and argument, the growth of drug testing measures appears to go on unabated. This raises the question, why do workplace drug testing programmes continue to be popular on both sides of the Atlantic especially with medium and large-sized firms? We would suggest that the rapid growth of such programmes during the last 30 years or so is entangled within the growing embeddedness of a number of conventional drug wisdom(s) surrounding prohibition, increased legislative regulation, and the irrational user. In this penultimate section, we detail these wisdom(s), and offer challenges to them, arguing that theoretically there is also a need to review our thinking about regulating drug use in society at large.

For many, the drug problem remains intractable. Illegal drug production, consumption and control are areas of vital public concern. The illicit drugs market continues to grow alarmingly. According to Prinz (1997: 373) around 50–70 million people use illegal drugs, while some 20 million engage in producing them, generating a revenue of between US$100 billion and 1 trillion a year. The problem posed by illegal drugs is far more pronounced in the US than in Europe with illicit drug sales estimated somewhere between $50–100 billion and direct law enforcement expenditures in excess of $20 billion.

Whilst there appears to be a spectrum of feasible alternative law enforcement regimes (bounded by prohibition at one end and a free market at the other) prohibition has become the dominant orthodoxy (Blackwell, 1994; Goode, 1997). Within a prohibition regime drugs strategies are directed at the supply side and demand side of the market: supply side measures target producers and dealers; demand side measures target users. Supply side policies apply penalties to those who engage in illegal drug production and trafficking; a package of measures from international diplomacy, crop substitution assistance, seizure, destruction, heavy fines, and lengthy imprisonment have all been applied in order to reduce illicit drug availability. Demand side policies apply sanctions against users of illegal drugs and utilise drug education programmes in order to reduce consumption. There is a changing emphasis upon a mixture of instruments based upon repression, prevention and medical treatment (therapy, harm reduction, rehabilitation). Whereas drug trafficking and supply of all drugs continues to attract stiff penalties worldwide, there is a growing recognition especially within Europe of the need to take a less repressive stance on drug consumption (especially soft drugs) and a more medically tolerant stance on the frequent user of hard drugs. There is an increasing separation of the addicted and casual user; with the latter presented as more responsive to legal sanctions, persuasion and market forces than the former. The 'British system' of controlled availability of drugs to heavily dependent users helps remove the especially vulnerable from this illicit market whilst at the same time permitting state or market deterrents in the form of tough penalties and high prices to act as disincentives to new or casual users.

However, such orthodoxy, we would argue, raises a number of issues meriting further discussion. First, the success of supply side measures remains open to debate. They have certainly succeeded in causing an upward shift in the supply curve for all illegal drugs by imposing a significant 'tax' (punishment) burden on suppliers. The outlawing of drugs has also resulted in more noticeable price and income rather than quantity effects. Not only are street prices of illegal drugs considerably higher than their legal pharmaceutical equivalents (up to 60–100 times higher for heroin and cocaine) but illicit drug gains are substantially higher, and the drug supply environment far worse, than under a free market.[11] One consequence of this has been the promotion of a climate of increasing violence and other drug-related crimes.[12] It has also resulted in a mixture of greater emphasis, policy innovation, and faith being placed on demand side measures. A comment in the *Financial Times* (11 March 1998) highlighted the need to focus more attention on drug demand. It referred to the United Nations Commission on Narcotic Drugs meeting scheduled to be held in Vienna in the following week and its commitment to an intensified policy of drug demand reduction; this was seen as marking a significant shift away from a heavily punitive approach to one skewed towards prevention, greater awareness and understanding, and widened medical treatment and social care. Unless more action was directed at drug consumption then efforts aimed at supply side policies would continue to be 'as effective as bailing out a boat with a sieve'. It is within such a climate that workplace illicit drug testing mechanisms have been advocated, in particular as an extension to the demand side regulatory armoury. As Blackwell (1994: 320) argues, 'Advocates of drug screening in the workplace claim it is a demand-reduction measure, because working people will be forced to choose between illicit drug use and employment, and therefore should logically choose the latter.' That is, employee testing is seen not only as a tool for increased productivity within the workplace, but also as a means of regulating the broader society. Indeed, as Macdonald and Wells (1994: 139) argue, a 'major objective of drug screening is, by reducing drug use in the workplace, to reduce drug use in society as a whole'.

However, two recent critical appraisals of prohibition regimes from an economic perspective have raised serious misgivings about the merits of such a regime, both in theory and in practice. Miron and Zwiebel (1995) argue with regard to the US, that 'the social costs of drug prohibition are vastly greater than its benefits' and they suggest that 'a relatively free market in drugs is likely to be vastly superior to the current policy of prohibition'. Likewise, Stevenson (1994), drawing upon UK experience, presents what he terms 'the uneasy case for prohibition', and charts its failure and alternatives to it, concluding that legalisation is the best option. It would make drugs 'cheap, pure and legal'; criminals would be driven out of the drugs market, drug-related crime would significantly diminish, enforcement costs would fall, and drug harm would probably be reduced. The general legalisation position is underlined by Miron and Zwiebel (1995: 187) when they argue that 'most of the negative consequences associated with illegal drugs derive from the prohibition rather than the consumption of the prohibited good'.

What appears to be clear is that the current prohibition regime is one we need to move away from; this has certainly been happening with regard to both the frequent hard and soft drug user. We have already alluded to the less repressive stance on drug consumption (especially soft drugs), sometimes characterised as the 'Dutch model' since the trend to *de facto* decriminalisation is more advanced there, alongside an increased appreciation of the 'British system' of medical support for those addicted to hard drugs. There are many who find this more gradualist approach away from an overly punitive policy on the demand side attractive. It is a middle way between the inherent *ex post* costs of tough prohibition and the promised speculative *ex ante* benefits of legalisation. It is seen to avoid calls for an unjustified increase in law enforcement and repression alongside the irreversible 'big-bang' of liberalisation and the consequent increase in drug experimentation and consumption that may follow. There are some who support a more lenient position with regard to addicts and their treatment, in order to draw them away from the illegal drugs market, whilst at the same time raising drug entry costs to new and casual users. Frey (1997) presents this as the 'third way' and cites the case of the Zurich Drugs Policy Experiment which successfully applied this drug strategy option. Much current European drugs policy appears to accept both a lenient stance towards addiction and a repressive stance towards trafficking, it remains more fuzzy and unsettled in connection with potential drug consumer entrants and casual users. In contrast, those who advocate full legalisation tend to adopt what is referred to as the cigarette/alcohol model where similar government controls to those currently in place for these more socially acceptable drugs would be extended to cover presently illicit drugs. Within this framework governments will still endeavour to reduce consumption via such policies as taxation and education along with minimum age restrictions. This legal regime would also endorse some state regulation of production and distribution (sale) directed at quality, marketing and other issues. The problem of illicit drugs would be resolved by their integration into normal culture (not dissimilar to what happened to other once-illicit drugs such as tobacco, coffee and tea).

Whatever regime is followed, drugs will remain a permanent feature of our society. Paradoxically, the softening on the demand side, alongside wider drug availability, could mean, as Stevenson (1994: 66) noted, that 'drug testing for some occupational groups such as cab drivers and airline pilots might become more commonplace'. Indeed, as we have highlighted, this is *already* commonplace in the US where drug-testing by many private firms, federal government contractors, and all federal agencies, takes place as a matter of routine. This is less true of the UK and Europe; paradoxically, given our discussion of the cigarette/alcohol model above as an exemplar for drug legalisation, workplace controls on tobacco and alcohol consumption appear to be more pronounced here than illegal drug testing.[13]

An additional conventional wisdom is that drug users are irrational consumers; easily hooked, myopic in the sense of being present- rather than future-oriented, and guilty of underestimating the true costs of their habit. They are, all too often, only seen as addicts a world apart: they cannot hold down regular jobs, are unable to earn legitimate regular incomes, and incapable of living regular lives. They are seen as morally inferior, untrustworthy and threatening (Blackwell, 1994). They engage in crime in order to finance and sustain their deviant consumption pattern. In Becker's (1963) term, they are all too often regarded as *outsiders.* Such a caricature has been partly responsible for our failure to address the issue of drugs and the workplace more directly, it has often remained hidden behind the more visible facade of the socially detached heavy user. This stereotype is under attack from both theory and reality. Sociologists and economists have seriously challenged this myth and increasing evidence is being generated which suggests a different underlying reality.

Mainstream sociologists, as Blackwell (1994: 323) argues, have revealed over the recent past 'a diversity of drug-using patterns involving varying degrees of risk'. For example, much research has indicated drug use does not necessarily have disastrous effects for the user or others and that there is a high degree of recreational and polydrug use. Moreover, research has indicated a sensible approach to use amongst many. As Blackwell (1994: 323) continues, 'Research has shown that the so-called drug problem is not the homogeneous monolith it was once thought to be, but rather a heterogeneous complex of illicit *and* licit drug usage patterns representing varying degrees of social damage.' This understanding calls for sophistication in framing policies. These developments act as a complement to mainstream orthodox economics, which itself presents drug consumption as a rational activity. Frey (1997) has argued that drug use is widespread, that drug users are normal consumers, able to function productively, being fully socially integrated at work and home. Many people use illegal drugs frequently or occasionally without becoming dependent or allowing it to impact detrimentally on their lives. The economic model of human behaviour is seen to be applicable to drug consumption: drug consumers are no different to anyone else in reacting systematically to changes in benefits and costs. Miron and Zwiebel (1995) suggest that many drugs are less addictive than portrayed and that the negative health consequences of drug use tend to be overstated; problems are seen to relate to *excessive* consumption resulting from overdoses or adulterated doses. They further argue that little evidence supports the received wisdom that drug use has been a significant cause of declining labour productivity. Kaestner and Grossman (1995) use the standard economic approach to individual consumption choice to suggest that drug use is not a significant factor related to workplace accidents; employees who used drugs out of work did not allow this to impact detrimentally upon their work experience or performance. Further, Becker and Murphy (1988) suggest that even strongly addictive behaviour involves forward-looking utility maximisation with stable preferences. Whilst drug addicts and alcoholics may tend to be present- rather than future-oriented they do respond to changing relative prices, earning possibilities, and punishments. Prinz (1997) provides evidence which suggests that market forces work in the sense that users do respond to price signals: he found that higher drug prices reduced the number of drug-related deaths. Of course, there is a need to recognise, as Miron and Zwiebel (1995: 182) make clear, that 'it is remarkable how uniformly the utility from drug consumption is ignored in public discourse on drug policy'. Such utilities will remain hidden as long as drug users are reduced to irrational addicts.[14]

From this brief excursion, it is our contention that the emergence and development of workplace drug testing programmes over the last 30 years have mirrored wider societal prohibitionist discourse and practice, especially that surrounding demand side regulation and legislation. Simply put, the conventional view is one which presents illicit drug use as both costly and in need of complementary regulation in society at large and the workplace specifically. However, much evidence and discussion serves to challenge this orthodoxy, and in doing so, helps to further problematise both the basis and nature of much conventional evidence and prescription.

MAKING VISIBLE THE INVISIBLE: SOME CRITICAL ISSUES AND FUTURE RESEARCH DIRECTIONS

Throughout the above discussion we have attempted to problematise both the evidence and theoretical underpinnings within which workplace drug testing is embedded. In doing so our discussion has served to highlight a number of fundamental issues which need, in our view, further analysis and reflection. In this final section we endeavour to flag-up those core issues which remain unsettled and in need of greater research direction. We present these as questions, meriting further analysis and critical evaluation.

- *Is workplace drug testing necessary?* Much of the research carried out to date presumes that drug consumption is a harmful activity which results in direct and indirect costs to both the individual drug user and the wider collective (family, community, workplace and society). Economists (for example, Miron and Zwiebel, 1995; Stevenson, 1994; Prinz, 1997; Frey, 1997) increasingly emphasise that whilst all drugs tend to have negative effects on personal health these tend, first, to be overstated and exaggerated, and second, to be exacerbated rather than reduced by prohibition with its serious induced uncertainties of product quality. In addition, evidence on the negative impact of drug consumption by those in legal employment upon workplace activities remains largely unsubstantiated. There is, to date, insufficient evidence that such illicit drug consumption is responsible for lowering labour productivity and work performance or that it significantly affects the likelihood of workplace accidents. Drug consumption's impact on the significance, nature and extent of workplace absenteeism (in terms of individual and collective gains and losses resulting from absence compared with attendance) needs to be more directly explored and causally modelled. Where drug consumption involves absenteeism this may be for rational reasons: workers may perceive that by attending work they may be putting their livelihood and that of their colleagues at risk, so that it may be to the benefit of the organisation as a whole that they stay away.[15] The alleged large negative impact of, possibly widespread and increasing, drug use by the working population upon employees, employers, and customers, needs to be substantiated by a larger body of clear evidence rationalised by firmer theoretical underpinnings.

The traditional conventional wisdom linking drug use to the irrational addict engaged in crime and apart from the legal world logically implies that drug testing in the formal workplace is unnecessary. As it became increasingly apparent that substance abuse was more widespread than initially imagined and that it would include employees rather than just 'criminals', drug testing in the legal workplace appeared to have some role and justification. Where irrational addicts held down jobs it was seen to be important to carry out drug tests in order to safeguard their colleagues, employers, and customers, by identifying and, where necessary, removing them from the workplace environment. Once we recognise that drug users are rational, rather than irrational, we can no longer simply presume that such drug testing is necessary. Rational consumers of illicit drugs (and other commodities) are unlikely to risk their future consumption patterns and seriously jeopardise their livelihoods by allowing their consumption habits to significantly impact upon their workplace performance. As Kaestner and Grossman (1995: 60) maintain, in connection with their argument that drug use does not significantly affect workplace accidents, government and firms devote increasingly large sums to the eradication of drug use by employees yet this 'spending cannot be justified on the basis of the relationship between drug use and workplace accidents'. Likewise, Hecker and Kaplan (1989: 702) highlight the fact that organisations have concentrated their attention upon illegal drug testing *even though* 'alcohol is responsible for more than twice the costs in lost productivity and treatment'. Whilst drug testing is often portrayed as the sword most likely to cut the Gordian knot linking drug consumption to undesirable work behaviours, the expenditures committed to it, and the benefits accruing from it in terms of a reduction in detrimental workplace activity, must be shown to be justified. Greater research also needs to be carried out to demonstrate whether drug testing is actually advantageous to the workplace. In addition, its role as a potential disincentive to wider societal future drug consumption activity needs to be more firmly explored and established.

- *Is drug testing advantageous?* It is generally assumed by those who advocate drug testing that such an activity is worthwhile. But, as Miron and Zwiebel (1995: 189) argue, 'any particular policy towards drugs requires its own cost-benefit analysis' *including* the policy of drug testing. The benefits of drug testing are assumed to reside in such features as its ability to clearly identify drug users and remove them from the workplace by dismissal or discipline (punitive measures) or treatment (rehabilitation measures). The direct workplace benefits of such a policy relate to its reduction in the presumed negative impact of drug consumption upon employees, employers, and customers discussed earlier. There is the widespread expectation that drug testing will be a means to enhanced productivity and other desirable work patterns. The benefits from drug testing remain speculative in clearly distinguishing between the drug-consuming and non-drug-consuming employee, as does the belief in the application of the methods of drug testing to *clinically* distinguish between on-the-job and off-the-job drug consumption, and the occasional from the frequent user. Questions remain over whether drug testing should be applied narrowly or broadly; directed at some occupations or all; at some staff within an organisation or all; directed at current employees and/or new applicants; random or selective; voluntary or compulsory. Is drug testing an appropriate and effective screening or filtering device? Should employees receive advance notice of testing and will such pronouncements largely nullify the potential benefits from such testing? What is the most appropriate method of drug testing application? As Konovsky and Cropanzano (1993: 176) concede 'there has been a paucity of research examining the effectiveness of various testing programs'. In addition, those who support drug testing in the workplace neglect or play down other potential costs or losses associated with testing, including increased worker control and surveillance; reduction in employee rights and freedoms; and notions of fairness.

- *Is workplace drug testing a form of social control?* There are some who view blanket drug testing in the workplace as a beneficial, additional and direct micro weapon in the drugs war; it is seen as a successful factor helping to reduce the demand for drugs at a time when supply side policies against traffickers appear blunted.[16] Others remain concerned about the merits and consequences of drug testing in the legal arena. Hecker and Kaplan (1989) present workplace drug testing as a modern form of social control and scientific surveillance. They see this as moving us closer towards the 'Brave New Workplace' and are aware of the dangers posed by a widely adopted practice of workplace drug testing whereby 'One's own bodily fluids can tell tales, not about one's being impaired on the job, but about one's activities last Saturday night, or perhaps a week ago, or about other personal characteristics or medical conditions unrelated to work or to illegal drug use' (Hecker and Kaplan, 1989: 701). Such surveillance not only blurs the distinction or boundary between work and non-work activity but places a premium upon the latter not being detrimental to the former. The worker must not only be an appendage to a machine but constantly monitored to ensure their being a *healthy and productive* appendage. Whilst drug testing measures tend to be viewed as protecting the collective interests of all (employee, employer and customer alike), in a society where drug consumption is widely prevalent, they also provide an additional workplace control mechanism that *extends beyond* workplace activity, raising additional questions of workers' rights, freedoms and privacy.

- *Does drug testing threaten employee rights?* The emphasis upon creating and maintaining a drug-free workplace has implications for workers' rights. Drug testing helps to break down the on-the-job/off-the-job distinction (reducing the importance of much of the latter to that which *best serves* the former) and is often advocated as an increasingly vital policy of social (collective) welfare; it also, however, has potentially negative consequences for worker freedom and civil liberties. As Konovsky and Cropanzano (1993: 179) note: 'Although drug testing is an intrusive personnel selection and evaluation device and is often considered a threat to employee rights, much of the available data indicate that employees have surprisingly favourable attitudes toward drug testing.' Support in the workplace for such testing appears to be influenced by the perceived benefits rather than actual costs. Given our argument earlier, the social gains from drug consumption reduction appear to be overstated so that the social welfare claims of drug testing in the workplace may also be inflated. Sensitive civil liberty issues related to such matters as privacy (reduced by the increasingly fuzzy work/non-work distinction) and employee rights may have been undervalued. Within the US, where such drug testing has been increasingly applied, constitutional issues have been raised and worker rights threatened and possibly violated. Baumrin (1990) has explored such 'social welfare versus worker freedom issues' arising from drug testing and suggested that the former collective gains have not been substantiated whilst employee freedoms have been challenged with regard to punitive sanctions being applied against those who refuse to submit to test or test positive. Problems are seen to arise less with regard to the screening out of prospective employees or to the use of involuntary workplace drug testing which results in, at worst, employees receiving medical treatment, and arise more in relation to the application of punitive sanctions of dismissal or discipline. Such punitive sanctions are only appropriate where workers accepted *prior existent* drug-free rules. In a large number of cases the initial employment contract may have made no reference to drug testing or its possible sanction consequences. Just as US asset forfeiture (seizure) laws were intended to confiscate the property of major drug dealers and have had the unintended consequence of also hitting law-abiding citizens, so drug testing in support of a drug-free workplace may also result in the confiscation or seizure of livelihoods.[17]

- *Is drug testing fair?* Konovsky and Cropanzano (1993) argue that an important factor with regard to workers' reactions to drug testing relates to the question of the fairness of any drug testing programme. In particular, they argue that employees are concerned about *distributive justice* or the fairness of outcome of drug tests related to the sanctions applied and *procedural justice* or the fairness of the methods employed. Employees are becoming increasingly concerned about the explicit, especially punitive sanctions that may be imposed against them due to failure to submit to test or testing positive. They appear to be less worried where rehabilitation and treatment rather than discipline and/or dismissal is the likely outcome. Workers are also concerned with regard to how the drug tests are conducted and the results reached. Doubts remain over *just what, in fact, drug testing is supposed to be actually testing?* Is it, for instance, the workers and their workplace relations (obligations, performance etc.) or is it their lifestyle choices away from work (which may or may not have an adverse effect on their workplace relations)?

CONCLUDING COMMENTS: HAVE WE BEEN SOLD THE DRUG TESTING MYTH?

As we indicated at the beginning of this chapter, drug testing in the US has become a several billion dollar a year industry with the potential to grow ever larger. The disadvantages arising from employee drug consumption and the workplace connection have been asserted as significant but, as yet, remain both tentative and inconclusive. The advantages of a drug-free workplace, again claimed to be substantial, remain inconclusive. The benefits accruing from drug testing have been effectively hyped and sold to both the private and the public sectors. Expectations are high. We have suggested the need for a more sober approach: the benefits and costs of such testing need to be more carefully assessed and justified alongside alternative strategies. The drug testing industry may be partly engaged in perpetuating its own industry and generating an artificially high demand for its product by constructing a social problem myth of employee drug consumption being significantly detrimental to the workplace environment.

NOTES

1. Additionally, the drugs literature can also be charged with essentially glossing over the subject of workplace drugs use and regulation, favouring in its stead analysis of the dynamics of recreational and/or problem usage in predominantly non-work environs. Indeed, to draw upon this collection's theme, we would argue that workplace drug use and its regulation have remained an invisible issue within the drugs literature and popular discourse, especially within the UK. For example, in a recent review of the key issues affecting the drugs literature today, South (1997) makes no mention of drugs–workplace connections, nor identifies them as being trends or areas of concern for the drugs debate at the end of the twentieth century. Rather, through a review of postwar trends in drug use, a discussion of the control of drugs in Britain (and internationally), together with a review of the debates surrounding drugs, alcohol and crime, the primary focus of South's review article is that of debates affecting the visible and often so-called normalised activities and patterns of drug taking and of the formal regulatory practices of agents and agencies of criminal justice – namely the police, courts and prisons.

2. Indeed, given economists' preference to present participation in crime as illegal (rather than legal) occupational choice – with imprisonment characterised as periods of involuntary employment (see Stigler, 1970: 530) – this broad-based generalisation of workplace activity (not to exclude the illegal) serves to rationalise governments' proposals to drug test and monitor criminals. It is the extension of drug testing into the (illegal) workplace.

3. A number of writers fail to differentiate, in their discussion of workplace drug testing programmes and the number of employees affected, between licit and illicit drugs. Moreover, studies tend to focus upon the medium and larger organisations who are more likely to have testing mechanisms in place (Konovsky and Cropanzano, 1993: 171). Hence any figures should be read with caution and should be seen as indicative only.

4. See DuPont et al. (1995: 2); Macdonald and Wells (1994); and Macdonald and Dooley (1991) for a thorough review of these various mechanisms.

5. The specific data analysed includes that derived from the National Alcohol Survey, National Household Surveys of Drug Abuse, and the National Longitudinal Survey of Labour Market Experience Youth Cohort.

6. Drug use first became a substantial self-report focus of the British Crime Survey in 1992 and involved the use of an additional self-complete paper questionnaire, in which individuals were asked about their drug use over their lifetime, during the past year and within the last month. More recent surveys (conducted during 1994 and 1996) have involved a computerised system of self-completion, allowing for greater comparisons to be made across years and a

greater accuracy of response. Within both reports, cross-tabulations between drug use and employment status are provided, allowing for a number of generalised findings about illicit drug use within the workplace to be made.

7. From this discussion, it is clear that whilst there is some evidence and pattern of workplace illicit drug use, difficulties affecting both its measurement and definition remain, resulting in the need for caution when analysing data.

8. In doing so, it must be remembered: first, that these categories are ideal specific and there is, in practice, a great deal of overlap; second, that studies often focus upon measurement of only one or two areas of risk, and often fail to connect them in discussion or to broader areas of analysis; and third, that many studies often focus upon the impact of licit as opposed to illicit use. Finally, it should be noted that the overwhelming literature on the area of risk has been orientated towards the US.

9. Estimates of the financial cost of employee drug use have been put in the billions, although reliable estimates are difficult to achieve, and proving the causal relations even more problematic.

10. We have already detailed a number of problems associated with the study of drug use and the workplace. In addition to those detailed under *employee risk*, other problems concern the nature of causality, the involvement of other factors, types of data collection (through survey or testing), an individual's propensity to risk, and the limited nature of much analysis. Also with regards to the user, the amount and type of drug consumed, the frequency and method of usage and the degree of addiction remain critical.

11. The large increase in illicit drug prices has not resulted in a significant decrease in drug consumption (given that the demand for all drugs is relatively inelastic) but rather to an increase in illegal drug market revenue and incomes.

12. It has been estimated that around half of all murders in the USA are drug-related: the vast majority of these were the result of 'turf wars' over territory or 'economically compulsive' acts (stealing to pay for a drug habit). Evidence suggests that drugs prohibition has promoted drugs-related offences with the financing of drug consumption by such illegal means as prostitution and acquisitive crime. According to Stevenson (1994: 30–1) the value of drug-related theft in England and Wales in 1993 was almost £2 billion or 50 per cent of the total value of theft. A *Sunday Times* editorial (dated 8 March 1998) cited Jack Straw, the Home Secretary's claim that heroin-related theft alone costs this country more than £1 billion a year. Prinz (1997: 378), referring to German and American studies, has suggested that only around 20 per cent of drug consumption is financed by legal sources. Within a drug prohibition regime serious uncertainties remain with regard to product quality and the likely threats it poses for accidental poisonings and overdoses related to these adulterated, suspect, street commodities. Prohibition has effectively resulted in the surrender of the drugs market to gangster

cartels and is best characterised as 'sending lambs to the wolves' where potentially casual customers with an initial weak soft drug curiosity trade with suppliers interested in developing a dependency culture more reliant on a harder drug base.

13. There is the expectation that Keith Hellawell, Britain's 'drugs tsar', will recommend compulsory drug testing and treatment for burglars and other criminally oriented 'occupational' groups who are suspected of drug-related crime. It is to be hoped that work-based controls on drugs provide greater success than society-wide measures of enforcement; individuals would appear to be more clearly bound by a tangible employment contract than some intangible social contract.

14. It is interesting to note that since Becker (1968) and Ehrlich (1973) economists have applied their rational choice framework to criminal activity and presented participation in the illegal arena as normal occupational choice; we are all potential criminals if the price is right – it is simply a matter of weighing up the expected benefits and costs from illegal and legal participation. Given that such deviant behaviour is presented as normal rational choice, it is a small consistent step to view drug use as normal rational consumption choice based upon the net utilities it generates in comparison with alternative goods. This framework of economics provides a natural link between work (as normal choice between legal and illegal activity) and illicit drugs (as normal consumption choice with other commodities). It provides an extended and richer picture of drug consumption, focusing upon the addict, casual and occasional user, linked to employment, defined broadly to include illegal as well as legal activity. It can go beyond the conventional focus upon the irrational addict-illegal participation (crime) connection to explore the rational drug consumer-legal participation (workplace) connection. *The orthodox economic approach by presenting crime as illegal work can view the traditional approach to drugs as restricted to the special case of the addicted, frequent heavy user, participating in the 'crime workplace', rather than the more appropriate general case of the rational drugs consumer participating in both the legal and/or illegal workplace.*

15. It has long been recognised that coal miners who had too much to drink before a shift would often intentionally miss it.

16. In its attempt to control drug-related crime the New Labour administration appears intent on proposing to electronically tag drug addicts who have committed crimes and force them to receive medical treatment (*Sunday Times*, 5 April 1998). This can be viewed as a move to increase their monitoring and surveillance of the 'crime workplace'.

17. The drug testing of criminals also raises questions, although rights appear to be less of an issue here if sanctions are only treatment-based and the negative consequences of their actions are more clearly demonstrable.

REFERENCES

Alleyne, B. C., Stuart, P. and Copes, R. (1991) 'Alcohol and Other Drug Use in Occupational Fatalities', *Journal of Occupational Medicine*, 33, 496–500.

Axel, H. (1989) 'Characteristics of Firms with Drugs Testing Programs', in *Drugs in the Workplace: Research and Evaluation Data*, NIDA Research Monograph, No. 91 (Washington, DC: US Government Printing Office).

Backer, T. E. (1987) *Strategic Planning for Workplace Drug Abuse Programs* (DHHS Publication No. ADM-87-1538) (Rockville, MD: National Institute on Drug Abuse).

Baumrin, B. H. (1990) 'To Test or Not to Test? Social Welfare versus Worker Freedom', *Journal of Psychoactive Drugs*, 22(4), 485–7.

Becker, G. S. (1968) 'Crime and Punishment: an Economic Approach', *Journal of Political Economy*, 76(2), 169–217.

Becker, G. S. and Murphy, K. M. (1988) 'A Theory of Rational Addiction', *Journal of Political Economy*, 96(4), 675–700.

Becker, H. (1963) *Outsiders: Studies in the Sociology of Deviance* (New York: Free Press).

Blackwell, J. C. (1994) 'Drug Testing: the War on Drugs, Workers, and the Workplace: Perspectives from Sociology', in S. Macdonald and P. Roman (eds.), *Drug Testing in the Workplace*, Research Advances in Alcohol and Drug Problems, Volume 11 (New York: Plenum Press).

Bottomley, P. (1998) 'Drug Testing in the Workplace', *ACW*, March/April, 14–15, 20.

Bross, M. H., Pace, S. K. and Cronin, I. H. (1992) 'Chemical Dependence: Analysis of Work Absenteeism and Associated Medical Illnesses', *Journal of Occupational Medicine*, 34, 16–19.

Burt, M. R. (1981) 'Prevalence and Consequences of Drug Abuse among US Military Personnel: 1980', *American Journal of Drug and Alcohol Abuse*, 8, 49–439.

Campbell, D. (1997) 'Work Samples', *The Guardian*, 29 October, 6.

Confederation of British Industry (1986) *Danger – Drugs at Work* (London: CBI/Centre Point).

Crouch, D., Webb, D., Peterson, L., Buller, P. and Rollins, D. (1989) 'A Critical Evaluation of the Utah Power and Light Company's Substance Abuse Management Program: Absenteeism, Accidents and Costs', in *Drugs in the Workplace: Research and Evaluation Data*, NIDA Research Monograph, No. 91 (Washington, DC: US Government Printing Office).

Cullen, F., Van Voorhis, P. and Sundt, J. (1996) 'Prisons in Crisis: the American Experience', in R. Matthews and P. Francis (eds.), *Prisons 2000: an International Perspective on the Present State and Future of Imprisonment* (Basingstoke: Macmillan).

Delaney, T. J. (1987) 'The EAP Part of the Personnel Function', *Public Personnel Management*, 16, 359.

Dickinson, F. (1988) *Drink and Drugs at Work: the Consuming Problem* (London: IPM).

DiNardo, J. (1994) 'A Critical Review of the Estimates of the Costs of Alcohol and Drug Use', in S. Macdonald and P. Roman (eds.), *Drug Testing in the Workplace*, Research Advances in Alcohol and Drug Problems, Volume 11 (New York: Plenum Press).

Drugs Debate (1998) BBC Television, 27 April.

DuPont, R. L., Griffin, D. W., Siskin, B. R., Shiraki, S. and Katze, E. (1995) 'Random Drug Tests at Work: the Probability of Identifying Frequent and Infrequent Users of Illicit Drugs', *Journal of Addictive Diseases*, 14(3), 1–17.

Ehrlich, I. (1973) 'Participation in Illegitimate Activities: a Theoretical and Empirical Investigation', *Journal of Political Economy* 81(3), 521–64.

Fillimore, K. and Caetano, E. (1982) 'Epidemiology of Alcohol Abuse and Alcoholism in Occupations', *Occupational Alcoholism: a Review of Research Issues*, NIAAA Research Monograph 8 (Washington, DC: Government Printing Office), 21–88.

Financial Times (1998) 'Drug Demand', 11 March.

Frey, B. S. (1997) 'Drugs, Economics and Policy', *Economic Policy*, October, 389–98.

Goode, E. (1997) *Between Politics and Reason: the Drug Legalization Debate* (New York: St. Martin's Press).

Health and Safety Executive (1992) *Drug Abuse at Work: a Guide for Employers* (London: HSE).

Health and Safety Executive (1994) *Drug Abuse at Work: a Guide for Employers*, revised edition (London: HSE).

Health and Safety Executive (1998) *Drug Misuse at Work: a Guide for Employers* (London: HSE).

Hecker, S. and Kaplan, M. S. (1989) 'Workplace Drug Testing as Social Control', *International Journal of Health Services*, 19(4), 693–707.

Hingson, R. W., Lederman, R. I. and Walsh, D. C. (1985) 'Employee Drinking Patterns and Accidental Injury: a Study of Four New England States', *Journal of Studies on Alcohol*, 46, 298–303.

Hoffman, A. and Silvers, J. (1987) *Steal this Urine Test: Fighting Hysteria in America* (New York: Penguin).

Institute of Personnel Management (1986) *The IPM Guide on Substance Misuse at Work* (London: IPM).

Kaestner, R. and Grossman, M. (1995) 'Wages, Workers' Compensation Benefits, and Drug Use: Indirect Evidence of the Effects of Drugs on Workplace Accidents', *American Economic Review*, Papers and Proceedings, May 1995, 55–60.

Kandel, D. B. and Davies, M. (1990) 'Labor Force Experiences of a National Sample of Young Adult Men: the Role of Drug Involvement', *Youth and Society*, 21, 411–15.

Kandel, D. B. and Yamaguchi, K. (1987) 'Job Mobility and Drug Use: an Event History Analysis', *American Journal of Sociology*, 92, 836–78.

Kay, J. (1989) 'Workplace Drug-programmes in Britain: Does it Bake more Biscuits?', *Druglink*, November/December, 8–9.

Konovsky, M. A. and Cropanzano, R. (1993) 'Justice Considerations in Employee Drug Testing', in R. Cropanzano (ed.), *Justice in the*

Workplace: Approaching Fairness in Human Resource Management (New Jersey: Lawrence Erbaum Associates Inc.).

Lehman, W. E. K., Farabee, D. J., Holcom, M. L. and Simpson, D. D. (1995) 'Prediction of Substance Use in the Workplace: Unique Contributions of Personal Background and Work Environment Variables', *Journal of Drug Issues*, 25(2), 53–74.

Lewis, R. J. and Cooper, S. P. (1989) 'Alcohol, Other Drugs, and Fatal Work-Related Injuries', *Journal of Occupational Medicine*, 31, 23–8.

Macdonald, S. (1995) 'The Role of Drugs in Workplace Injuries: is Drug Testing Appropriate?', *Journal of Drug Issues*, 25(4), 703–22.

Macdonald, S. and Dooley, S. (1991) 'The Nature and Extent of EAPs and Drug Screening Programs in Canadian Transportation Companies', *Employee Assistance Quarterly*, 6: 23–40.

Macdonald, S. and Roman, P. (eds.) (1994) *Drug Testing in the Workplace*, Research Advances in Alcohol and Drug Problems, Volume 11 (New York: Plenum Press).

Macdonald, S. and Wells, S. (1994) 'The Impact and Effectiveness of Drug Testing Programs in the Workplace', in S. Macdonald and P. Roman (eds.), *Drug Testing in the Workplace*, Research Advances in Alcohol and Drug Problems, Volume 11 (New York: Plenum Press).

Martin, J. K., Kraft, J. M. and Roman, P. M. (1994) 'Extent and Impact of Alcohol and Drug Use Problems in the Workplace: a Review of the Empirical Evidence', in S. Macdonald and P. Roman (eds.) *Drug Testing in the Workplace*, Research Advances in Alcohol and Drug Problems, Volume 11 (New York: Plenum Press).

Millard, T. L. (1991) 'Combating Drug Abuse in the Workplace: Effective Intervention Strategies and Techniques', *Employee Assistance Quarterly*, 7(1), 45–56.

Miron, J. A. and Zwiebel, J. (1995) 'The Economic Case against Drug Prohibition', *Journal of Economic Perspectives*, 9(4), 175–92.

Newcomb, J. (1994) 'Predictors of Drug Use and Implications for the Workplace', in S. Macdonald and P. Roman (eds.) *Drug Testing in the Workplace*, Research Advances in Alcohol and Drug Problems, Volume 11 (New York: Plenum Press).

Normand, J., Salyards, S. D. and Mahoney, J. J. (1990) 'An Evaluation of Pre-Employment Drug Testing', *Journal of Applied Psychology*, 75, 629–39.

Prinz, A. (1997) 'Do European Drug Policies Matter?', *Economic Policy*, October, 373–85.

Ramsay, M. and Percy, A. (1996) *Drug Misuse Declared: Results of the 1994 British Crime Survey*, Home Office and Research Study, No. 151 (London: Home Office).

Ramsay, M. and Spillar, J. (1997) *Drug Misuse Declared in 1996: Findings from the British Crime Survey*, Home Office and Research Study, No. 172 (London: Home Office).

Ritzer, G. (1995) *The McDonaldization of Society* (London: Sage).

Ritzer, G. (1997) *The McDonaldization Thesis* (London: Sage).

Schottenfeld, R. S. (1989) 'Drug and Alcohol Testing in the Workplace

– Objectives, Pitfalls, and Guidelines', *American Journal of Drug and Alcohol Abuse*, 15(4), 413–27.

Sheridan, J. and Wrinkler, H. (1989) 'An Evaluation of Drug Testing in the Workplace', in *Drugs in the Workplace: Research and Evaluation Data*, NIDA Research Monograph, No. 91 (Washington, DC: US Government Printing Office).

South, N. (1997) 'Drugs: Use, Crime and Control', in M. Maguire, R. Morgan and R. Reiner (eds.) *The Oxford Handbook of Criminology*, 2nd edn (Oxford: Clarendon Press).

Stevenson, R. (1994) *Winning the War on Drugs: to Legalize or Not?*, Hobart Paper 124 (London: Institute of Economic Affairs).

Stigler, G. J. (1970) 'The Optimum Enforcement of Laws', *Journal of Political Economy*, 78, 526–36.

Sullivan, E. J., Bissell, L. and Leffler, D. (1990) 'Drug Use and Disciplinary Actions among 300 Nurses', *International Journal of the Addictions*, 25, 375–91.

Sunday Times (1998) 'Zero Tolerance' Comment and 'Drugs Tsar Targets Jails and Schools', 8 March.

Sunday Times (1998) 'Addicts Face Tagging to Curb Drug Crime', 5 April.

The Institute of Alcohol Studies (1993) *Testing for Drugs and Alcohol in the Workplace: Proceedings of a Conference held at Alliance House 20 June 1990* (London: Institute of Alcohol Studies).

The Observer (1998) 'Hair Test Identifies Army's Crack Troops', 25 January, 9.

Transport and Workers Act (1992) (London: HMSO).

University of Strathclyde (1997) *Alcohol in the Workplace: Results of a New Empirical Study* (London: HSE).

Walsh, D. C., Hingson, R. W., Merrigan, D. M., Cupples, L. A., Levenson, S. M. and Coffman, G. A. (1991) 'Associations between Alcohol and Cocaine Use in a Sample of Problem-Drinking Employees', *Journal of Studies on Alcohol*, 52, 17–25.

White, H. R., Aidala, A. and Zablocki, B. (1988) 'A Longitudinal Investigation of Drug Use and Work Patterns among Middle-class, White Adults', *Journal of Applied Bahavioural Science*, 24, 455–469.

Williams, J. (1998) 'Tinker, Tailor, Soldier, Smackhead: Doctors on Heroin, Nurses on Pills, Executives on Coke. How Serious is Drug Taking at Work', *The Big Issue*, 9–15 February, 14–15.

Zimmer, L. and Jacobs, J. B. (1990) 'Mapping the Drug Testing Industry and its Implication', in A. S. Trebach and K. B. Zeese (eds.), *The Great Issues of Drug Policy* (Washington, DC: Drug Policy Foundation), 219–26.

Zwerling, C., Ryan, J. and Orav, E. J. (1990) 'Costs and Benefits of Pre-Employment Drug Screening', *Journal of the American Medical Association*, 267, 91–3.

8 Watching the Workers: Crime, CCTV and the Workplace

Michael McCahill and Clive Norris

INTRODUCTION

The 1990s have seen a massive expansion of video surveillance in public space. All the major cities with a population over 500 000 boast city centre schemes, and there are in excess of 500 police and local authority schemes operating in high streets and smaller towns. However, while these developments have captured the headlines they have diverted attention away from another area where CCTV is increasingly extending its surveillance gaze: the workplace.

Although it is difficult to put precise figures on the extent of video surveillance in the workplace, it is possible to gain some indication from various business surveys. The annual survey of the business analysts Marketing Strategies for Industry (MSI) revealed the total CCTV market was £151 million in 1995 and £115.6 million in 1996 (*CCTV Today*, 1 January 1998: 20). However, as the 1996 MSI survey revealed, despite the massive investment in town centre systems, public and civil systems still only accounted for 22 per cent of the market with annual sales of £25 million. The remaining 78 per cent was dominated by the retail, commercial and industrial sectors which accounted for 33 per cent (£38 million), 30 per cent (£35 million), and 17 per cent (£17.3 million) respectively.

Other sources have estimated that, in the earlier part of the decade, the market was substantially larger. The BSIA, for instance, estimated that by 1993 as many as 150 000 CCTV systems had been installed in retail outlets, offices, schools and hospitals. According to Beck and Willis in the early 1990s around £300 million a year was being spent on CCTV systems of which public systems accounted for about £50 million annually. In total they estimated there may be more than a million cameras in use (Beck and Willis, 1995: 163). Not only, then, is workplace surveillance more extensive than public surveillance but it also appears to be growing rapidly. Hearnden's 1994 survey of the use of CCTV by small business which included the manufacturing, retail, commercial and transport sectors, found that just over half (51 per cent) of firms had installed CCTV over the last five years and only one-fifth (19 per cent) had been installed more than ten years ago. Hearnden estimates that the 'growth in the use of CCTV in the UK has averaged 25% each year since 1988' and 'in 1993 companies inspected by the National Approval Council for Security Systems (NACOSS) installed 1189 new CCTV Systems' (Hearnden, 1996: 20). Overall, it would not be unreasonable to 'guess-timate' that between 1990 and 1997 the total value of CCTV sales was between £1 billion and £1.5 billion. Moreover, the vast majority of this investment was in the private sector, monitoring commercial, retailing and industrial premises.

The growth of CCTV surveillance in the private sector can largely be accounted for by the increased recognition of the extent and impact of business victimisation. One of the most important elements of this growing awareness has been the finding of the surveys of the British Retail Consortiums' Retail Crime Surveys which first began in the early 1990s. The annual sweeps of the surveys have estimated the cost of crime for the retail trade in 1992/3, 1993/4, 1994/5, 1995/6 which they calculate to be £2 billion, £2.2 billion, £1.4 and £1.6 billion respectively. In 1995/6 this represented 1.13 per cent of total retail turnover and equated to £85 per household in the UK (Wells and Dryer, 1997). In 1995 a Home Office survey of crimes against retail and manufacturing premises estimated the average cost to be £800 per premises (Mirlees-Black and Ross, 1995).

In this context it is hardly surprising that Beck and Willis argue:

Crime is rapidly becoming one of the most influential factors in retailing. It is a cause of dramatically increasing insurance costs. It creates losses in revenue through lost stock and equipment. Not only does crime increase overheads, it impacts directly on the 'bottom line' of profitability. Retailers are increasingly advised to see their security departments and their strategies less in terms of 'preventing crime' and more in terms of 'protecting profit'. (Beck and Willis, 1995: 40–1)

However with this recognition comes the uneasy realisation that a significant proportion of losses are not due to the activities of customers or other external threats but are perpetrated by the companies' own workforce. The BRCS attributes one-third of all losses to staff theft equivalent, in 1992/3, to nearly £0.75 billion.

Despite the economic importance of these losses and the massive expansion of the surveillance capacity of private companies to monitor their premises and, by default, their customers, clients and workforce, there has been scant academic attention paid to the issue. The little work that has been carried out has focused very much on the issue of effectiveness (Gill and Turbin, 1998a, b; Hearnden, 1996; Beck and Willis, 1994). Thus, while there is now a fairly large and rapidly expanding literature on public CCTV surveillance (see Norris and Armstrong, 1999a, 1999b; and Norris, Moran and Armstrong, 1998 for a review) little is known about the contours of private sector surveillance.

In this chapter we draw upon a case study of the extent and impact of CCTV surveillance in one northern town. It draws on interviews and site visits to twenty-four retail and manufacturing businesses. Interviews were conducted with the security managers of seven department stores, six major high street retailers and eleven of the top twenty manufacturing concerns in the area and fieldnotes written up after each site visit. We start by documenting the use of CCTV to monitor the external threat posed by customers and burglars and other outsiders. We then turn our attention to how this same technology is increasingly targeted on the internal threat posed by the workforce not just as a means of preventing theft but increasingly as a general managerial tool. Finally we argue that although the elimination of workplace theft may seem unequivocally beneficial, the introduction of CCTV may not only disrupt the routine, but also informal practices of fiddling and pilfering. These, as we show, have historically been tolerated by management as a compensation for poor working conditions and low wages and their increased visibility and potential eradication may lead to a number of unintended and undesirable consequences.

MANAGING THE THREAT TO PROFITABILITY: MONITORING THE EXTERNAL THREAT

In all of the retail stores visited the primary purpose of the CCTV system is to act as a deterrent to shoplifting. The cameras are highly visible and are announced by a variety of signs declaring, in one way or another, that the store is under permanent video surveillance. In several of the stores this message was reinforced by large monitors sited near the entrance displaying live footage from the system to pointedly remind customers that video surveillance was in operation. In addition, the cameras have a major role in the prevention of cheque and credit card fraud which costs retailers over £20 million a year, and the Association of Payment and Clearing Services, which underwrites the transactions, a further £165 million (Beck and Willis, 1995: 38). To achieve this, cameras are located to record till transactions so that when, and if, fraud is detected the tapes can be searched to provide a visual identification. Finally, and not inconsequentially, the effect of such systems is to provide a visible deterrent against robbery from the tills and assault more generally. This is especially salient given that the BRCS estimates that over 120 000 retail workers are either assaulted or threatened with physical violence each year.

Not only are the cameras used as a deterrent to customer theft, fraud and assault but also as a means of training staff to recognise the characteristics of shoplifters and to help identify persistent and prolific offenders. For example, the security manager at one retailer holds monthly security meetings with members of staff where he shows them tapes of shoplifters in action to alert them to the 'body language'. This approach was echoed by another high street retailer:

We do show staff videos of prolific shoplifters shoplifting. I've got a tape downstairs that . . . every shoplifter, they are prolific, they're known around the town, they've got several offences against them. So we've got a compilation of shop thefts that we use which amazes the staff when they watch it. Because they don't realise it goes on on the shop-floor. (Security Manager, high street retailer)

In some stores this is taken a stage further and the staff are actively encouraged to view tapes and images to get to know the 'shoplifters' who are currently active in their stores. One security manager, for example, explained how his company now operates a Retail Crimes Operation (RCO) whereby photographic information is exchanged between the security personnel throughout the country. A news sheet is sent out once a week to all the company's stores listing offenders who are known to be currently active. The sheet includes 'mugshots' captured from the CCTV system and textual descriptions of locations, modus operandi etc. The security manager gives the following example of how this system works in practice:

For instance, just before Christmas we had a shoplifter, she was apprehended here for I think it was theft of about £190. She's from down South but she was staying in a caravan park . . . Following a Section 18 search on this caravan that she was staying in they found receipts from eighteen (of our) stores all over the country. So what we do we have a photographic facility in the control room where we can take any amount of stills from the video. We send these to Head Office to the collators . . . then they will distribute photographs or reports . . . to every store.

Indeed the CCTV control room of this store is covered wall-to-wall with the 'rogues' gallery which includes the suspect's name (if the security staff have a name), address, post code and known associates. The security manager explained:

I did an 'open-day' and everybody is like plastered on the wall. We had an open . . . well an 'open month' actually, inviting all the staff to come in and view the photographs

'cause obviously it's beneficial if they do see these faces . . .
It gives us more pairs of eyes on the shop floor and
they can contact security if they recognise anybody . . .
We have noticed with them being plastered on the wall,
we are getting familiar with the faces whereas in a book
they're looked at and then forgotten really. It's surprising how many people do spot them in other stores.

The attempt to make shop staff more vigilant and aware
of 'known' persons and 'shoplifters' in their stores is also being
practised by other stores. In a local chain of medium-sized
convenience stores the CCTV system involves round-the-
clock recording but no permanent monitoring. Only if an
incident occurs are the tapes reviewed and then sent to head
office where hard copy printouts can be made. Photographs
of known shoplifters are distributed to all the other stores
to be pinned on the staff notice boards frequently with the
message: 'This person is not allowed in our stores.'

Unlike the department store or high street retailers, the
industrial workplace does not want to encourage public access
to their sites; thus, rather than having multiple exits and
entrances the sites are completely fenced off and all traffic
channelled into one or two access points. On nine of the
eleven sites, the CCTV control room is situated at the entrance to the site which is usually just beyond an access
control barrier operated by the security officers in the control
room. At every site visitors must report to the control room
and sign a visitors' book. The control rooms on nine of
the sites are monitored on a continuous basis by private
security officials, i.e. 24 hours a day, 365 days a year. In
the other two sites one has a CCTV monitor placed in the
management office which is monitored by the management
periodically, and on the other site a private security guard
monitors the images at night time when the factory is closed.
A typical factory has around ten cameras including a combination of fully functional and fixed cameras. These cameras
are usually positioned to monitor the entrances, exits, perimeter fencing, car parks, bike sheds, contractor loading
bays and factory floor.

One of the common themes to emerge from all the interviews at the industrial workplace was the use of CCTV

systems to monitor the 'external threat' of intruders coming on to the site and for maintaining perimeter security. Unlike the retail sector this threat is not posed by customers but by burglars, dishonest contractors and unwanted intruders. For instance, at one major engineering firm who have a number of 'defence'-related contracts, the security manager explained that the CCTV system had been used most recently to monitor outside contractors (e.g. builders, roof workers) suspected of theft from the premises, 'peace camps' and 'vigils' outside the site, who might try and occupy the site and people tampering with cars in the staff car park. For most companies, CCTV was an integral part of the perimeter security arrangement, often linked to other alarm systems such as motion or infrared detectors, and could be used to quickly visually scan the scene of any alarm.

MANAGING THE THREAT TO PROFITABILITY – THE INTERNAL THREAT

In the retail sector the primary justification for the installation and expansion of CCTV systems has been the external threat posed by shoplifters, fraudsters and violent customers. Once such technology is in place it inevitably means that, by default, workers also come under the cameras' gaze. However, default had turned to design in five of the seven department stores and the CCTV systems were explicitly used to monitor staff for the purposes of preventing staff theft in three locations: at the tills, in the cash office and in the loading bays. As one security manager described:

> There's one [a camera] in the stock room, one in the store counting office where they do all the cashing-up, all the others are on the shop-floor or the stairways. The one in the cash office is to stop staff theft. Because there's thousands of pounds in there all on the table where they count it up. In some stores they've had money go missing so it's like a deterrent.

Although in all five stores the main purpose of having CCTV cameras in the cash office is to act as a deterrent against staff theft, as several security managers explained, it also provided a measure of security for the staff if there was an attempted robbery. The cameras are also used to monitor the cleaning staff and those working on the loading bays:

> We look for people sneaking in, drivers dropping one item and taking one back, staff coming on to the loading bay who shouldn't be there, because they're not supposed to come on here unless they have specific business there, looking for collusions, things like that . . . Collusions between drivers and our guys. (Security manager, department store)

> My predecessor had someone who was lifting things out of the stock room, pinching things, and they video'd them actually taking it out the stock room. And we do company searches so later on they did a search and they had the goods on them. He was dismissed and I think the police were called as well. (Security manager, high street retailer)

> Sometimes I come in early to watch the cleaning staff, to make sure they're not taking anything off the shelves, and to do a couple of searches. (Security manager, high street retailer)

The use of CCTV to monitor shop staff in the retail sector, however, is primarily used to monitor staff working the tills. All the department stores have CCTV cameras located on the shopfloor and these are perfectly placed to monitor till procedures. This was demonstrated on several occasions and showed that the operators had the ability to zoom in with such clarity that a customer's signature could be clearly read on the video monitor. In many of the retail stores the tills are now linked to stock control computers in an electronic point of sale (EPOS) system. This enables management to look at the electronically recorded takings from each till and compare it with the actual cash taken. If there are any discrepancies, since each member of staff has to individually log into the system before ringing in a transaction, mistakes can be isolated to an individual or, if more than one person has been using a till, a group of individuals. As one manager explained, at the press of a button he could now get a printout of all the expected and actual takings of each till and could see that:

> this till took £72 900 in takings and was £20 down, that's not a lot, that's 0.03% of takings. But look at that one that's 0.16% down so that's worth investigating . . . (we) would start in the Accounting Office where they would go through the readings and see if a cheque has not gone through properly or something like that. Then if they don't find anything they might ask me to go through it, and usually it's human error, you know, they've given change for twenty pound instead of a tenner or something. But then if you get an ongoing problem week in week out then you know something might be up. For example, a few months ago we had a kid upstairs on electrics who had an unusual number of 'price over-rides' (where an item is bar-coded through the till but no money is taken, usually on prescriptions) so we decided to watch him on camera. It turns out that members of his family were coming in and he was putting kettles through at thirty quid a time and not charging for them. We caught him on camera and he received an instant dismissal.

Two retail security managers revealed they also use covert (i.e. hidden) cameras to monitor shop staff suspected of internal theft. One stated that he used a covert camera which he moves around the store when the need arises, for instance, to monitor shop staff suspected of theft and also to cover various blind spots that the overt CCTV system can't reach. Another security manager reported he has used a covert camera on the loading bay where a night cleaner was caught on camera stealing chocolates. This member of staff received an instant dismissal.

The security controller of the chain of convenience stores also uses covert cameras to monitor shop staff suspected of internal theft. The company has a team of 'mobile store detectives' who travel from store to store to carry out various operations on behalf of the security controller. The security controller says:

we also have other systems where we'll actually go and get ourselves in a room in a store and monitor. Wire up various covert cameras and monitor from within the store. I mean I've got a video tape with a number of incidents on that we've compiled which basically shows various thefts taking place where staff have stolen money out of the tills, given goods away without taking payment for them etc. So, you know, we do have a number of colour cameras for that particular function as well. I think, you know, it's worthwhile spending a bit extra on colour cameras. But we've got about, at any one time we could have covert camera systems in five or six of our stores if we wish to, 'cos we have that many cameras at our disposal . . . The staff don't know about it. It's for detection purposes.

In the industrial workplace while the CCTV systems play a central role in maintaining perimeter security and excluding the undesirable, the presence of cameras on the shop floor is, unlike in the retail store, unambiguously targeted at the worker.

On other sites, with less sophisticated CCTV systems, the cameras are used by the management mainly as a deterrent. The manager of a food processing factory, for example, described how he installed four internal cameras to reduce 'shrinkage'. The cameras are all fixed and the images are not monitored on a permanent basis in a CCTV control room. There is a monitor in the production director's office and he monitors the images periodically. The manager of the factory believes that the main function of the CCTV system is to deter theft as he explained:

We had a little bit of stealing going on in the stores area and we've just swung a camera around to take that area in. Again it's prevention more than anything else, we tell them what we're doing and er . . . because alright, you want to catch the beggar that's doing it, but primarily you want to stop people from doing it. I find that cameras are more of a deterrent than anything else. I mean if you're catching people stealing that's not the course of the exercise. The course of the exercise is to stop people from doing it in the first place.

He also makes sure the staff know that they are being watched in order to maximise the deterrent effect of the CCTV system:

> Well they know they're on film. We brought every member of staff upstairs and showed them what we could see and what was being recorded, because every camera point is being recorded on a separate film you see. We make a big fuss about making sure that they know the cameras are there. To some extent we have re-trained people, or trained people to sort of put in their mind that these cameras are there, they're under surveillance.

However, if the cameras do not deter the culprits then disciplinary intervention can be used as the following example shows in a case where a worker was in an 'unauthorised area':

> Well generally when the tapes run through or if it's spotted live then the person's brought to book with it. They're brought upstairs and asked why they were there, and if they deny it they can't 'cos we've got it on tape. And that compounds it 'cos they've lied you see. And they'll get a warning, it'll go down as a disciplinary ruling.

In the food processing plant it was the management themselves that monitored the images displayed by the CCTV system or who reviewed tapes retrospectively after an incident had occurred. However, on the other ten industrial sites the CCTV systems are monitored by private security officials rather than the management themselves. This means management must rely on the security personnel for any information concerning internal theft and other misdemeanours. The CCTV operative employed by a frozen foods company explained how, if he spotted anything, he would report the incident to the management who would then deal with it:

> if somebody's actually spotted on site and we think they're a worker all we've actually got to do is get the Managers together and they'd be able to tell us who it is. The only one we've had is with the No Smoking Policy that we've got on site. We actually spotted some people round the back there (the S.M. zooms in to a corner at the back of

a building) smoking at night time. I mean the cameras are light sensitive so when you light a match or take a draw of a cigarette it actually lights up like a torch. And we actually caught him on the camera . . . we informed the management and the next morning they came and reviewed the tape. There was only one forklift driver who was round there that particular night and they showed him the tape and sacked him.

Internal theft was a particular problem for one security manager employed by a local manufacturer. The cameras on this site were introduced only eight months ago. Three of the cameras monitor the two main entrance points and the staff car park. The other seven cameras are all situated inside the factory to cover 'vulnerable areas' and were introduced to reduce 'shrinkage' as he explained:

People have broken into there to steal microwaves. We've had people walking through the main gate with heavy bags. A lot of drills have gone missing. We've even had people riding off on bikes with big carpets under their arms. . . . in terms of preventing people from stealing, the law doesn't always back you up . . . you can search vehicles and bags but not the person. We were losing stuff in the curtain store and the cameras put a stop to that. But that lasted about two weeks. Now they wait until the curtains are out of the store room and then they steal them. People are more dubious though, they know certain areas are covered and it has stopped the theft of big stuff like carpets. But in factory life they (the workers) know everything that's going on before you do . . . if the cameras are there (nods towards an imaginary camera) we'll stand here.

Improving Worker Performance

Store managers involved in some sites volunteered information about CCTV being used initially to target staff suspected of dishonesty, but then unexpectedly proving to be more valuable in checking whether staff were meeting company requirements, for example compliance with till procedures or rules relating to refunds and exchanges.

The use of CCTV as a more general managerial tool in the retail sector was mentioned by five of the security managers interviewed. In one store the company had produced a document which is distributed to all the security managers and store managers in the country. This protocol document is designed to enable the management to gain maximum benefit from the CCTV system which, it states, 'should be thought of as a valuable management tool, not just a means of deterring and identifying shoplifters or protecting staff and customers'. The document lists the following uses of CCTV as a management tool:

- When contractors are in the store ensure a camera is concentrated on areas of the store they are working in or the main entrance/exit point in the store.
- On a supervisor's day off, it may be relevant to record that particular area of the store.
- Recording work groups with consistent poor till out-turns will aid identification of poor procedures and therefore training needs required.
- Recording store opening/closing/deliveries/cashing up procedures may highlight opportunities for improvement.

In two of the department stores the management are trained to use the cameras and it would normally be the management themselves who would monitor the staff to ensure they were complying with company procedure. In one store the security manager would sit in the control room himself and then report to the store manager:

> We do operate a system where I watch the cameras. In the CCTV operative's breaks I'll watch the cameras and we look for various things, Customer Service, till operations, till procedures, everything you can think of really that you can't stand on the shop-floor and watch. I suppose it's a bit of an 'eye spy' really. (Security manager, high street retailer)

The security managers in three other stores said that the CCTV system was particularly useful for what they described as 'Customer Service':

> Yes with Customer Service it's just that the staff are being

polite, friendly and are smiling. It's not really a security point of view but it's something that we do exploit the CCTV system for. It's just from a commercial point of view really. Fitting rooms as well, just check the fitting room queues aren't getting too big. Correct procedures again in fitting rooms where the items are counted as they're going in, they're counted as they're going out, you know. It's not always practised that. (Security manager, high street retailer)

A lot of stores also use it like a 'management aid' 'cos erm . . . we do a thing here called *Selling the (. . . .) Experience*, it's all about Customer Care and everything. It's how you are with your customer. You know, your eye contact and all things like that. And I know in some stores they watch a member of staff, how they are on the counter and with the customer and things. (High street retailer)

As well as watching the body language of the shop staff to make sure they are 'polite' and 'friendly' with customers, the cameras can also be used to monitor the productivity of the shop worker. For example, the management may decide to watch a member of staff for a period of time to see if they are attending to customers or are standing around and talking to their friends:

this system is also used as a management tool. There's a very big emphasis, obviously because of declining resources and personnel, placing the key personnel within different departments, and the personnel function would use this (CCTV) to see if people are adhering to that. I mean, you know, people standing together and not noticing customers and things like that. (Security manager, town centre department store)

We have like consultants and they're supposed to approach customers to see if they need help. Management can watch them and make sure they are actually approaching people and saying: 'Do you want any help with the word processors?' They're worth a lot of money if you get a good sale on them. (Security manager, high street retailer)

In another store the management would actually monitor how many times a shop worker stopped customers to ask them if they were interested in a particular product as the security manager explained:

> I mean they don't do it like all the time but they can say: 'Oh we'll watch so and so for an hour, see how many people she approaches in an hour, or see if she stands talking to her friend', things like that.

In the industrial workplace, managers described how, in addition to the prevention of shrinkage, the system was used to monitor compliance with health and safety regulations, time keeping, access restriction, unauthorised breaks and so on, as one security manager described:

> We monitor the loading bays. Loading and unloading, it's amazing what you can pick up. Exactly who's doing what with fork lifts and the like . . . are people damaging goods going on to the lorrys? Are they damaging trailors? Are they driving forklifts as they should be? We've picked up bad driving practices but they were dealt with. It was brought to my attention that something had gone on and I was then able to go back to the tape and find it on the tape and challenge the person concerned with it. So I say to them 'what have you been doing?' And they say, 'I never did that'. So I say, 'oh yes you did, look'.

In nine of the eleven industrial sites visited the CCTV system was used to monitor the workforce. However, the use of CCTV on these sites is, like any other system, shaped by the people responsible for operating the systems. Thus, while a CCTV system may be installed for the purpose of the general managerial control of the workforce, whether or not the system is used in this capacity depends to some extent on how the introduction of this technology fits in with existing social practices and informal rule systems in the workplace. For example, on ten of the eleven sites the management do not observe the workforce themselves. This means that they must rely on the security personnel to inform them of any worker malpractice. However, as the following extract from the researchers' fieldnotes shows, the security personnel are not always willing to do this:

Dave, the CCTV operator, says 'we've had workers lifting stuff over that fence'. He then flicks over to camera number six, which is monitoring the office in the general office block. He says, 'stuff has gone missing from the offices here'. Dave tells me that he would never report any of these activities to the management. His reluctance to do so is partly to do with the fact that he identifies with the workers rather than the management, and partly to do with the fact that he is also involved in the workplace 'fiddle'. As he explains: 'There's no way I'm gonna grass on anyone. If I do my job it would cause a lot of bad feeling when it got back to the staff . . . anyway perks are part of the job. If I go to someone and say "have you got a washer for my tap", they'll say to me, "here, have a new tap".'

Dave went on to tell me about a management purge on unauthorised parking. This was another issue on which he sided with the workers rather than the management:

It's the same as when the management asked us to put parking stickers on the workers' cars because of unauthorised parking on the site. It caused a bad feeling between meself and the lads. If someone comes off the site with a lampstand and I stop and search them and they say, 'I've got a gate pass', I say, 'fair enough'. One or two of the workers are funny with security, but the majority are alright. If they treat us alright we treat them the same.

The inability of technological systems to penetrate existing social practices in the industrial workplace was also found on a visit to a large pharmaceuticals factory as the following extracts from fieldnotes shows:

The site is protected by a perimeter fence and all traffic, on entry and departure is channelled through two manned security points. Various members of the security team were present in the control room when the site was visited and some of them chipped in with a number of 'CCTV stories'. One of the CCTV operatives zoomed in on the local public house and said: 'we've had some fun outside there on Saturday nights'. He went on to describe how on one occasion a night-shift worker had unwittingly set off an audible alarm in the control room when he crossed an infra-red beam whilst 'nipping over the wall for a pint and a game of snooker in the local'. This was regarded as a good laugh by the security team. The security guard who told me the story turned to the security manager and said, 'We didn't report him though did we gaffer?' The security manager smiled and shook his head.

On two of the industrial sites the security managers showed us how they had used covert cameras to monitor workers suspected of theft. On both sites these operations were set up in the security managers' personal offices. This meant that they did not have to rely on the CCTV operatives to inform them of any worker malpractice. On the first site the use of covert surveillance was prompted by a spate of office thefts. As a result, the security manager has installed several dummy cameras in 'easily identifiable places' in the corridors of the general office block simultaneously however, he has installed eight 'pin-prick lens' cameras in strategic places around the building:

> When we arrive at the security manager's office he opens a wardrobe to reveal the hidden monitor and multiplexer which has the capacity for 16 cameras overall. Steve (his deputy) splits the screen into eight pictures and shows me how the system enables them 'to track staff throughout the entire building, covering all the corridors and all floors'. The security manager says, 'the system cost two and a half thousand pounds, but was well worth it. We didn't catch the rogue thief (who had been stealing staff property) but the stealing has stopped.' They talk enthusiastically about some of the CCTV equipment in the office saying things like, 'this one's the best . . . it can pick out a fly on the wall'. When we left the office the manager stated that he had also had trouble in the general office block with the 'vending machine thief'. Apparently someone had been emptying the vending machines of goods. He was caught on film after they decided to place covert cameras directly above the vending machines. On our way out of his office he nodded towards the wood panelling on the ceiling directly above a vending

machine which had a tiny hole where the pinhole camera had been placed.

On another site the security manager had recently invested in some highly sophisticated covert monitoring equipment which was kept in his office. The researchers' fieldnotes describe how the system works:

> The security manager describes the system as a 'digital motion detector'. This system is set up on his desk and runs on a computer. It is linked to an adjacent building by microwave. He explains how it works by drawing a white-shaped rectangle on the screen the same size as the exit door on the building opposite his office. The member of staff suspected of stealing from this building would have to leave via this exit. The S.M. says that when someone walks out of this door it will trigger an alarm on the monitor and the image will be recorded. This works, he says, by picking out light change and colour change. If the S.M. misses the alarm it doesn't matter because an 'alarm log' stores all the images which he can view at a later date. He goes on to show me the last six alarm calls from the previous evening which he reviewed earlier that morning.

DISCUSSION

As we have already noted, employee theft is estimated to cost businesses around £750 million annually and represents between one-third and one-half of all retail losses. It would appear then, on preventative grounds alone, intensified surveillance of workers is unequivocally justified in an attempt to stem these losses. While we do not take issue with this pragmatic justification, we believe it is necessary to consider some of the wider issues that arise from this intensification of surveillance.

Intolerable Theft or Acceptable Fiddle?

The estimated size of losses attributed to employee theft should immediately alert us to an important issue: workplace theft cannot be blamed on a few 'rotten apples'. In many industries and retail concerns it is a widespread and commonplace activity which has a long historical pedigree and has become embedded in a range of informal organisational structures and practices. For instance, Ditton's study of the Wellbread Bakery and its salesmen found fiddling to be endemic and practised by 'most, not just a few salesmen' (1977: 9). Similarly, Zeitlin (1971) found that over 75 per cent of employees participated in 'merchandise shrinkage'. These findings have been confirmed by a number of studies in a range of settings such as among dock workers (Mars, 1974) and hotel workers (Mars and Nicod, 1981; Gill, 1996).

Moreover, these studies suggest that, within limits, fiddling, including employee theft is tolerated, accepted and even encouraged by management and that, rather than seeing it as theft, it is regarded as a 'legitimate' perk. For instance in Gill's study she found that according to one ex-security manager:

> Fiddling was part of the fundamental fabric of the hotel trade. He explained that the habits had been accepted over the years and that they had become so ingrained that they were difficult to challenge. He found strong evidence that certain managers were fiddling. . . . [However, when he told the general manager nothing was done] . . . and for a long time he had to turn a blind eye to misdemeanours and finally came to the conclusion that his position was untenable. (Gill, 1996: 131)

Similarly Mars' (1974) study of dockworkers shows how management implicitly condoned pilfering by the dockers. These losses were tolerated by management as long as they stayed within acceptable limits as they constituted an established perk which guaranteed that work was done efficiently and effectively.

While it would be tempting to see the toleration, and even tacit encouragement, of such practices as irrational, this informal economy of fiddles and hidden rewards may not have entirely negative consequences for management. First, to try and break such practices may lead to a considerable amount of staff resistance, resentment and labour unrest, none of which is likely to be good for business –

especially if it results in high staff turnover. Second, the monetary value of the thefts may constitute a significant proportion of an individual's total income. This is especially so in the retail and service sectors with notoriously low rates of pay. If wages can be routinely increased by fiddling then, although this represents a drain on profitability, it may be less of a drain than the blanket payment of higher wages. Indeed, since these additions to income are achieved with no tax, national insurance or pension contributions from the firm and, in some cases, losses can be recouped from insurance they may result in considerable savings. Third, as Ditton and Brown (1981) have argued, the existence of an informal economy consisting largely of stolen goods derived from the workplace may contribute to overall social stability by making those who feel 'relatively deprived' in the formal wage market see themselves as 'relatively prosperous' when informal rewards are added. And, as all good Durkheimians know, the trick of social stability is to make people believe that they 'deserve what they get and what they get is what they deserve!'

If we now return to the issue of CCTV in the workplace we can begin to see how it may be highly disruptive of the tacit assumptions governing the exploitation and distribution of what Mars and Nicod (1981) term the 'hidden rewards' of work. The nature of these workplace fiddles is that they are largely 'hidden' from view; even so they are not completely invisible, but tolerated. Management, by 'turning a blind eye' or 'looking the other way' can facilitate tacit acceptance and absolve themselves from the disruption that would ensue from moral condemnation. Thus, one of Gill's managers reported 'The problem with the (hotel) is that a lot of staff have been here for so many years ... someone like me will get crushed. Not that I am turning a blind eye, but I have a mortgage' (Gill, 1996: 131). Of course, management itself may be also on the fiddle and therefore unwilling to 'rock the boat'.

The introduction of CCTV systems, however, means that 'visibility' of a whole range of working practices is increased, and with the video recorder the potential is available for public replay. In this situation, 'turning a blind eye' becomes more problematic. The lexical and moral constructions which label certain practices as 'fiddles' and 'perks' find that such ambiguity is hard to maintain when the evidence of workers helping themselves to the stock is replayed for all to see. Since such subterranean practices cannot be defended publicly as 'just a fiddle' they inevitably become recast as an unequivocal case of 'theft'.

What is at stake here is that if we are to understand the impact of CCTV in the workplace it is necessary to attend to its broader organisational significance and consequences.

First, if the unintended consequence of CCTV is to disrupt the informal economy of rewards from work this may well have implications for the formal economy. Workers may seek other means of maximising income such as pushing for higher wages and engaging in more confrontational industrial relations. At the level of the individual firm re-strictions of such practices may also lead to the losses of experienced and otherwise 'trustworthy' staff, who will seek employment with rivals where 'fiddling' is still possible.

However, as we have seen, there is no simple relation-ship between the imposition of CCTV surveillance and the eradication of workplace deviance. Surveillance systems are mediated by social actors who bring with them their own values and beliefs and these may be more in tune with the occupational culture of the shopfloor than of management. Given the low status and pay of security guards and their likely class backgrounds, it is hardly surprising that they may not identify their interests as in line with manage-ment. Thus where management delegates surveillance to others, there is no guarantee that the systems will be used as intended, and through tacit acceptance the security guards will 'turn a blind eye' or more collusively ensure that the cameras are positioned so as not to capture specific events.

Second, one of the unintended consequences of the de-ployment of CCTV in the drive against retail theft, is that the possibilities of using the system to extend general managerial control can soon become realised and practised. In this way CCTV becomes an instrument of 'disciplinary' power exercised through the architecture of the panopticon, allowing management to see everything without ever be-ing seen themselves. And as we have seen this enables a honing-in on the minutiae of shopfloor workers' presentation of self. In the name of 'customer service' employees' gestures, facial expressions and body language all become subject to the disciplinary gaze. The power of this gaze not only enables management to intervene on the basis of the evidence from the cameras, but also, and more effectively, the employee becomes the 'bearer of their own surveillance'. The 'anticipatory conformity' that this induces in employees presents management with an extremely powerful managerial tool (see Lyon, 1994: 133).

However, as Beck and Willis argue, if CCTV is used mainly as a general managerial tool rather than for its stated purposes of monitoring customer and staff theft, then 'the high level of staff confidence in CCTV could evaporate if they felt they were being misled in this way' (1995: 193). The question of the perceived legitimacy of surveillance is central and is raised even more starkly by the increasing use of covert cameras with all the implications of invasions of privacy, the use of unethical and deceptive practices, and breach of trust. If such activities become public, they may lead to a backlash, calling into question the right of management to place their workforce under such intensive and omnipresent surveillance. In which case we may not be surprised if CCTV becomes the cause of crime rather than its cure as employees sabotage the surveillance systems. This has already happened at two workplaces in our sample.

The security manager at one industrial site, for example, described how some of the CCTV fuse boxes had been 'tripped out in suspicious circumstances'. The other act was less subtle as a CCTV operative in a food processing factory explained:

> We did try putting internal cameras in one of the Tea Bars, but it was only there for about fourteen hours and somebody nicked it . . . there was quite a lot of thefts and damage to the tea machines and sandwich machines. People putting their hands in and moving the stuff across so they could get an extra sandwich and then breaking into the machine itself. So we had a camera on the wall overlooking the vending machines. Obviously they didn't like it being in there so they took it. The cabling is still there if we need to use it again.

REFERENCES

Beck, A. and Willis, A. (1994) 'Customer and Staff Perceptions of the Role of Closed Circuit Television in Retail Security', in M. Gill (ed.), *Crime at Work: Studies in Security and Crime Prevention* (Leicester: Perpetuity Press), 185–202.

Beck, A. and Willis, A. (1995) *Crime and Security: Managing the Risk to Safe Shopping* (Leicester: Perpetuity Press).

Beck, A., Gill, M. and Willis, A. (1994) 'Violence in Retailing: Physical and Verbal Victimisation of Staff', in M. Gill (ed.), *Crime at Work: Studies in Security and Crime Prevention* (Leicester: Perpetuity Press), 83–101.

Clarke, M. (1990) *Business Crime* (Cambridge: Polity).

Ditton, J. (1977) *Part-Time Crime: an Ethnography of Fiddling and Pilferage* (London: Macmillan).

Ditton, J. and Brown, R. (1981) 'Why Don't they Revolt: Invisible Income as a Neglected Dimension of Runciman's Relative Deprivation Thesis', *British Journal of Sociology*, 32, 521–30.

Gill, K. (1996) 'Fiddling in Hotel Bars: Types, Patterns, Motivations and Prevention', in M. Gill (ed.), *Crime at Work: Studies in Security and Crime Prevention* (Leicester: Perpetuity Press), 125–38.

Gill, M and Turbin, V. (1998a) 'CCTV and Shop Theft: Towards a Realistic Evaluation', in C. Norris, J. Moran and G. Armstrong (eds.), *Surveillance, Closed Circuit Television and Social Control* (Aldershot: Ashgate Gower).

Gill, M. and Turbin, V. (1998b) 'Security Measures and Risk in Retailing: Customer and Offender Perspectives', in M. Gill (ed.), *Crime at Work: Increasing the Risk for Offenders, Volume II* (Leicester: Perpetuity Press).

Hearnden, K. (1996) 'Small Businesses' Approach to Managing CCTV to Combat Crime', *International Journal of Risk, Security and Crime Prevention* 1(1), 19–31.

Henry, S. and Mars, G. (1978) 'Crime at Work: the Social Construction of Amateur Property Theft', *Sociology*, 12, 2 May, 245–63.

Lyon, D. (1994) *The Electronic Eye: the Rise of Surveillance Society* (Cambridge: Polity Press).

Mars, G. (1974) 'Dock Pilferage', in P. Rock and M. McIntosh (eds.), *Deviance and Social Control* (London: Tavistock).

Mars, G. (1982) *Cheats at Work: an Anthropology of Workplace Crime* (London: Allen and Unwin).

Mars, G. and Nicod, M. (1981) 'Hidden Rewards at Work: the Implications from a Study of British Hotels', in S. Henry (ed.), *Can I Have it in Cash?* (London: Astragal Books).

Mirlees-Black, C. and Ross, A. (1995) *Crime against Retail and Manufacturing Premises: Findings from the 1994 Commercial Victimisation Survey* (London: Home Office Research and Statistics Department).

Norris, C. and Armstrong, G. (1999a) 'CCTV and the Rise of the Surveillance Society', in P. Carlen and R. Morgan (eds.), *Crime Unlimited: Questions for the 21st Century* (London: Macmillan).

Norris, C. and Armstrong, G. (1999b) *The Maximum Surveillance Society: the Rise of CCTV* (Oxford: Berg).

Norris, C., Moran, J. and Armstrong, G. (1998) (eds.), *Surveillance, Closed Circuit Television and Social Control* (Aldershot: Ashgate Gower).

Wells, C. and Dryer, A. (1997) *Retail Crime Costs Survey 1995/96* (London: British Retail Consortium).

Zeitlin, L. R. (1971) 'A Little Larcency Can Do a Lot for Employee Morale', *Psychology Today*, 5, 22, 24, 26 and 64.

9 Making Visible the Invisible?

Peter Francis, Pamela Davies and Victor Jupp

Having digested the breadth, range and focus of the particular chapters contained within this volume the reader should by now be acutely aware of the complexity of the task we set ourselves. Also, having contracted, collated and edited the various contributions over the past year or so, we are also now much more aware of the complexity of the task we set ourselves! To recap, that task was to critically review a range of acts and events taking place at the end of the twentieth century which in our view remained to a greater or lesser extent hidden, and to map their particular contours under the generic title *Invisible Crimes: Their Victims and Their Regulation*.

On completion of this task we are satisfied with the eventual outcome, albeit with a number of provisos attached. First, we would like to reiterate the *nature and manner* in which we deconstructed the term 'invisible crime', and of the subsequent characteristic features detailed. These features were discussed under seven ideal typical headers – no knowledge, no statistics, no theory, no control, no politics, no research and no panic! As we went on to suggest 'Although expressed in what may appear "simplistic" and "headline" fashion, such features . . . help provide a means of categorising and characterising a wide range of acts and events which remain invisible in everyday life' (pp. 5–6). These features were aimed at organising our thoughts around why it was particular acts and events remained hidden at the end of the twentieth century. The reader may be able to detail a range of other characteristics of invisibility, and such features may be no less instructive than those that we finally agreed upon. Our use of the seven features detailed arose through our own reading of the material on the areas in question and a desire to be as clear and concise as possible.

Second we would like to reiterate the necessity to focus upon these identifying features both *independently* and *interdependently*. Thus, particular acts or events described as 'invisible' may not necessarily exhibit all seven features, and those that do will probably not do so to the same degree. Rather, as we again argue in Chapter 1 'such features constitute a template with which to assess relative invisibility. The elements of this template (knowledge – statistics – theory – research – control – politics – panic!) can be viewed as independent of one another but there is also the potential for interaction and for mutual reinforcement' (p. 6). Third, the reader should also be aware of the importance given to both *space* and *time* in constructing the strength and patterning of these particular features. That is, the extent to which these seven features are able to help organise thoughts around the 'invisibility' of a particular act or event is dependent upon their historical and comparative social, economic and political contexts.

The template and features in no way exhaust the characteristics of particular acts and events we know little about, but rather are indicative. Our justification for using them remains that they are extremely useful in providing a vantage point from which to, first, *map* the contours of a particular hidden act or event; second, to develop *understanding* about particular acts or events; and third, to *explore* why they remain hidden/invisible at particular historical times. Three examples drawn from the various contributions discussed within the three sections of this volume help illustrate these points, and in doing so highlight the merits of the template discussed, as well as outline variations in the nature, form and contours of particular types of 'invisibility'.

The first example is taken from Part I of the collection and Chapter 2 by Hazel Croall on white-collar crime. For some readers, the inclusion of this contribution in this current volume may seem rather strange given the range of academic inquiry into the area over the recent past (see Nelken, 1997a for a thorough discussion here). However, as Croall argues, despite more that half a century of research and theorising about white-collar crime, it remains invisible in many different respects. As she argues 'Offences are typically concealed within occupational and organisational routines, are difficult to detect by victims, observers or law enforcers, and few offenders are tried and sentenced in open court' (p. 29). In contrast to some of the other contributions, this example of white-collar crime is neither a feature solely of late modern society, nor is it problematic solely due to its location. Rather in part its 'invisibility' arises from a neglect from within the criminological mainstream itself, and a continuing reluctance to embrace it fully. In part also it is a result of a historical failure to focus upon the criminal act rather than the person doing it. Thus for Croall, whilst such acts and events go on, and whilst we know that they take place, there is a real need to make further visible both the processes and consequences associated with them.

A second example can be found in Part II of the collection, and in the contribution by David Wall. In his chapter the focus of the analysis itself – cybercrime – remains 'invisible' at the end of the twentieth century. Because of the relative youthfulness of cybercrime as an issue, little knowledge about it exists. There is also a paucity of statistical data and research development on the area – unsurprising given that Mann and Sutton (1998: 207) state in a recent contribution to the debate surrounding what they term 'netcrime' that 'there are few writers specialising in the field of high technology crime'. Certainly the theoretical imagination surrounding cybercrime, as Wall highlights, remains in its infancy, contested and open to criticism; while measures of regulation and control are for the most part adapted from the more traditional regulatory armoury already in place. As a result, developments so far have attempted to 'chart' and unpack this previously unknown criminological territory, and to make visible what has, for the most part, remained invisible. The purpose of such work, therefore, has been to explore the boundaries and characteristics of cyberspace and cybercrime, as a precursor to develop further knowledge and understanding. Wall's contribution both in this present volume and previously (Wall, 1997) highlights the nature of the developing work being undertaken in this area.

Our third and final example is taken from Part III and concerns what Francis and Wynarczyk identify as the 'invisibility' of workplace illicit drug use. As is generally acknowledged, especially within western democracies, the use of drugs in society is anything but 'invisible' at the end of the twentieth century (see South, 1997a). Indeed some talk of it being 'normalised' (Parker et al., 1995, 1998) although this view has recently come under criticism (see Newburn and Shiner, 1996). In Britain alone, and following the lead of the US, a 'war on drugs' style campaign has been initiated against both supply and demand side variables and factors, spearheaded by a vocal and powerful 'drugs tsar' and backed by a range of educative, preventative and regulatory powers and measures. Certainly the authors would not deny that there has been some measure of panic about the use of illicit drugs, fuelled by political muscle and an array of data derived from mountainous piles of research, theoretical development and journalistic licence. Indeed it is probably safe to suggest that knowledge of illicit drug misuse is anything but invisible today.

Yet, such knowledge of illicit drug use and its consequences is confined to particular times and spaces – such as the street and school as well as particular individuals – namely the young and males. In contrast, the workplace has remained, until recently, invisible, especially within the academy of universities and research organisations. Thus, although there is some statistical data and research evidence on workplace illicit drug use, as Francis and Wynarczyk argue, the paucity and/or inconclusive nature of it is terrifying. Certainly the evidence, counter-argument and analysis, remain poor. Hence as the title the authors set themselves – 'Regulating the Invisible?' – the act of taking drugs and its control may not be invisible *per se*, but such events within particular times and spaces – namely the workplace and related environs – along with the consequences of such acts, are.

These three examples go some way towards drawing out the relative usefulness of the seven ideal typical features discussed in Chapter 1 and of their interaction and relations over time and in space, as well as highlighting and locating the various contributions within the title of this present collection. A further three points can be made in order to highlight the variety of permutations possible. In doing so, discussion will focus upon examples of invisible

236   *Peter Francis, Pamela Davies and Victor Jupp*

crime, invisible victimisation and invisible regulation. With regards the invisibility of *crime*, sometimes it is the act which is relatively common, being something which violates the criminal law, and attracting a range of legal sanctions; and it is the *location* which is in some way responsible for the 'invisibility'. Croall, Davies and Jupp, Levi, McCahill and Norris, and Francis and Wynarczyk offer discussions around this theme. Often the invisibility *itself* is a consequence of new technologies, environs and situations, as Wall highlights so convincingly. And sometimes, that which is taking place is not necessarily seen as 'criminal' given that it does not constitute criminal law violation. Steve Tombs offers a thorough analysis here with regard to health and safety 'crimes', while Levi and Croall both raise further important points for discussion around this theme. And lest we forget – often this mixture of elements combine.

With regards 'invisible victimisation', Croall offers an excellent discussion of how the recipients of so called 'invisible crimes' often remain neglected or invisible, as does Wall; while Francis and Wynarczyk critically discuss victimisation in terms of employee, employer and customer risk. Throughout these discussions, what becomes apparent is the limited understanding of much victimisation – what Walklate (1989) refers to as that which goes on behind our backs. Invisible victimisation often occurs because we do not *know* or appreciate when we are victimised; because *others* have not understood how their actions may victimise someone; or because it has not been *defined* as victimisation in the formal sense. As Wall succinctly highlights with regards cybercrime, although its generalisability is abundantly clear, invisibility derives from the fact that it 'will be some time before a comprehensive sociology of cyber-victimisation can develop, especially as most of the discussion of cybercrimes has tended to focus upon the deviant act rather than either the deviant group or the victims' (p. 127). Similarly, with regards to white-collar crime, Croall suggests the need for a more systematic analysis of aspects of victimisation than that which is often provided.

Finally, various contributors highlight the complexities surrounding 'invisibility' and regulation and control. Certainly, in many cases there is a range of preventative, regulatory and enforcement strategies, policies, mechanisms and procedures in place, as all of the contributors to the book make clear. That said, often these may operate 'invisibly' in that we do not know the *processes* involved; in some cases it can be the *consequences* of such regulation which remains 'invisible'; while in other cases the *appropriateness* and/or *effectiveness* of the measures remain hidden. In each of these cases, whether to a lesser or greater extent, the unifying theme is that of 'invisibility'. An example of invisible regulation is provided by McCahill and Norris regarding the introduction of CCTV within the retail sector, the sole aim of which is the tracking, watching and apprehending of the culprit. Sometimes it is the act which is invisible (for example employee theft rather them customer) and sometimes it is the response (employees unaware that they too are under surveillance). As many of the chapters highlight, often it is a combination of both the invisibility of the act and the response.

The discussion and list of examples of invisibility could go on. In putting together this volume, as we stressed in Chapter 1, we are in no way suggesting that this collection and its contents should be seen as exhaustive of invisible crimes, victimisation and regulation. Far from it! We are aware of a number of hitherto neglected acts and events which have been explored, thus exposing and uncovering them for further research development, theoretical understanding and critical analysis. The examples discussed here have been chosen to highlight the variety of actions and events and times and spaces involved. In each case the nature of their 'relative invisibility' is exposed. The first three examples focus upon neglected areas traditionally labelled as crimes of the powerful (Pearce, 1976). First, Stan Cohen (1996) and more recently Nigel South (1997c) have drawn attention to 'crimes against humanity'. In doing so, Cohen highlights the nature of the invisibility thus (Cohen, 1996: 489):

> It would be ludicrous to claim that Western Criminology over the past decades has completely ignored the subject of state crimes or the broader discourse of human rights.... The subject has often been raised and then

its implication conveniently repressed. This is a process strangely reminiscent of my substantive interest in the sociology of denial: how information is known but its implications are not acknowledged.

Whilst many of us have knowledge of the area of 'crimes against humanity' (one needs only open a broadsheet newspaper on the subject), Cohen highlights how its invisibility is neither constant nor continuous, and is determined by broader influences at both the level of agency and structure. A second example is that of environmental destruction. Recently, Nigel South (1997a, 1997b), amongst others (see *Theoretical Criminology*, 1998), has drawn attention to the need for the development of a green criminology able to explore, understand, prevent and possibly eradicate environmental devastation. As South (1997a: 116–17) argues:

> it is recognised by many commentators in other social and natural science disciplines, and yet rarely in criminology, that the earth and its resources are being wasted. Twentieth-century industrial society has over exploited the planet and its resources through processes in which human beings become commodities in chains of production and distribution, and profit is put before sense or sensibility. In these processes, multiple and numerous crimes, violations, deviations and irregularities are perpetuated yet go largely unchecked.

In South's work, invisibility arises from the ever-powerful expansion of capitalist knowledge and productivity. Our final example is that of political crime (Hagan, 1996) including crimes committed by government. In highlighting the paucity of the literature on the subject – less than twelve books – Hagan (1996: 9) raises two particularly articulate questions about political crime which are especially relevant in the context of this present volume: 'what unknown horrors lie in wait in the twenty-first century, and how well will social scientists be able to isolate, define and explain the critical variables associated with them?' Various other explorations of invisible crimes can be found in the recently published *New European Criminology* (Ruggiero, South and Taylor, 1998).

In contrast to these global areas and issues, but certainly of no lesser contemporary relevance and importance is the work conducted by feminists, as well as by radical and critical social scientists into the private sphere including the home as well as particular hidden areas of the public sphere, and often involving women, the economically marginalised and ethnic minorities. Four examples serve our purpose well here: Stanko's (1998) personal journey into making visible the crimes which affect women's lives such as private violence; Mooney's (1993) work on domestic violence; Bowling's (1993) and Witte's (1996) exploration of racial violence and the state's response; and Nick Davies' (1997) wonderful account of 'the shocking truth about hidden Britain' – entitled *Dark Heart*. Indeed, Davies (1997: vii) highlights well the nature and location of much of this invisibility when he states that:

> Outwardly all the land marks of normality would remain clearly in sight. There would still be rows of red brick terraced houses with televisions in the front rooms and cars waiting outside by the kerb; there would be crowds of people tracing the paths of their regular routines, buying and selling and building their futures – all the symptoms of an orderly community. But at some point it was as if I crossed an *invisible frontier and cut a path into a different country.* (emphasis added)

In contrast to these various explorations, save for the contribution by Wall, our exploration of 'invisible frontiers' focuses upon the workplace. Croall draws upon a critical reading of the literature on white-collar crime; Davies and Jupp's contribution focuses upon the invisibility of workplace crime; Levi focuses upon the regulation of fraud; Francis and Wynarczyk upon the testing of workplace illicit drug misuse; and McCahill and Norris on surveillance at work. Moreover, whilst Wall's contribution focuses upon cybercrime and therefore is in many respects unbounded by conventional time and space it can be interpreted as involving workplace acts and events, given that the vast majority of workplaces are computer-orientated. The choice of the workplace as a site for investigation was deliberate. Despite the limited work which has been conducted on this area, it is clearly the case that too little remains known, not only regarding the nature and extent of 'crimes' which take place within the workplace, but also of their causes, offenders, victims and of the various regulatory and preventative mechanisms of control in place. And this criticism is not directed purely at academic and research organisations. It is also directed at the various research funding bodies, alongside broader government departments, agencies and institutions. Indeed, as we made clear in Chapter 1, it is no coincidence that on election to government in May 1997 New Labour focused its resources in the sphere of law and order for the most part on those acts and events deemed visible and/ or a nuisance mostly in the public sphere. New Labour's intention was to get people from welfare to work, rather than uncovering the neglected and hidden side of employment itself.

In reiterating some of the more characteristic features which we have argued categorise the various contributions to this volume a number of recurring themes arise. These themes go to the very heart of why particular acts and events remain to a greater or lesser extent invisible. They require, in our opinion, greater attention from criminologists and critical social scientists if neglected actions and events are to be given the future consideration they deserve. That means there is a need to refocus or dismantle and rebuild the criminological telescope if hitherto invisible acts and events are to be explored; if such acts are subsequently to be criminalised (or not as the case may be); if related victimisation is to be acknowledged and victims are to receive the appropriate support and attention; and if mechanisms of enforcement, regulation and legislative enactment are to be effectively developed and evaluated. However, in giving attention to these themes, there is a danger that undue attention is directed at one and at the expense of others. Each theme discussed below requires adequate exploration and consideration both independently and interdependently. There is also the danger that knowledge will be repressed or manipulated to serve particular ends; as the quotation from Cohen above highlights. It is therefore important that any investigation is able to critically and reflexively develop, rather than being constrained by particular organisational ideals or institutional funding arrangements. After all, these themes raise important issues regarding doing research itself (see Jupp et al., 1999). In the remaining pages of this concluding chapter we offer some provisional discussion of them. In doing so our aim is to highlight their nature and form, alongside placing them on the agenda for future exploration and analysis.

The first is methodological. As each of the various contributions to this volume makes clear, what is apparent is the paucity of conclusive empirical evidence on the value, form and extent of the activities under review. Related to this point is the over-reliance on means of measurement which are unsuitable to the task in hand. The two most frequently cited sources of evidence in the various contributions are crime statistics (compiled by the police or businesses and organisations themselves) and crime surveys. While official criminal statistics detail some activities discussed here – drugs, fraud and some white-collar activities for example – their inability to map all contours of criminal activity has been seriously exposed, for example by Tombs in relation to health and safety crimes and Wall in relation to computer technology crime. Similarly, Croall details the problems of industry-specific statistics, while the appropriateness (or otherwise) of crime surveys to uncover much that is hidden in the workplace has been highlighted by Francis and Wynarczyk. Indeed, each of the authors highlights more generally the need for an holistic and sophisticated methodology to uncover that which is at present invisible. To explore much crime which is 'invisible' requires in-depth exploration of both the processes and mechanisms associated with it; neither of which is achievable solely through those traditional methods detailed above.

The second recurring theme is theoretical, and arises from a reluctance of much traditional criminology to embrace broader theoretical developments beyond the 'criminological mainstream', an over-reliance on description rather than analysis, and in some cases a neglect of gender, race and class also. Most of the contributions highlight the problematic nature of much theoretical developments here. With regards to the reluctance of criminology to explore new worlds, Wall highlights how cybercrime and its interpretation poses a considerable challenge to the discipline of criminology, while Croall highlights the need for victimology to embrace more fully an understanding of white-collar victimisation. In both variations the point being made is the need for criminology to 'open up' to broader debates taking place. While we would agree with Nelken (1994) in stressing caution in embracing theoretical fads from parent disciplines such as sociology and politics, we would also agree with Sparks (1997) and Walklate (1998) that the theoretical base of criminology has much to learn from broader debates in social policy and social theory (see Francis, 1999). Certainly it would benefit from a greater comparative angle also (see Nelken, 1997b). The second strand of this recurring theme concerns an over-reliance on what we would see as description rather then analysis. In some cases this can be understandable, where criminologists are exploring – Wall, and McCahill and Norris all explore relatively uncharted territories and thus a level of description is necessary; although they also attempt theoretical contextualisation. However, as the various contributions argue throughout this volume, all too often theory building and modelling are neglected or at best only partially acknowledged. Thus without the necessary theoretical development and associated reworking and refinement, the usefulness of the earlier investigation becomes somewhat questionable. Finally, as many of the contributions have made clear, there is also a neglect of gender, race and class in exploring invisible crimes, their victimisation and regulation (see Stanko, 1998). This theme also connects closely with the third: that surrounding the nature and appropriateness of much policy and practice.

A number of contributors, and not just those located firmly within Part III, detail the nature and form of policy and practice. As regards white-collar crime, Croall highlights the complexity of debates surrounding law enforcement, sentencing and the role of the criminal law; Levi revisits and reviews developments in the regulation of fraud; McCahill and Norris explore the surveillance of employee workplace theft; while Francis and Wynarczyk investigate developments in workplace illicit drug testing. Despite the array of areas under exploration, the recurring theme that arises concerns the appropriateness and effectiveness of policy statements along with regulatory procedures and practices. Moreover, this is compounded by the nature of evaluating their efficacy and effectiveness. In part, it seems to us, there is a need to locate and explore policy and practice within broader critiques of the late modern capitalist state, its institutions and control. Certainly there is a need to explore their consequences – both intended and otherwise – and their impact. Francis and Wynarczyk clearly highlight the need for caution in travelling down the workplace drug testing road, drawing attention to a range of possible unintended consequences along the way; while more generally each of the contributors stresses the need for theoretically informed and evidence-led policy and regulatory practice.

The extent to which the latter is possible depends to some extent on the fourth and final recurring theme highlighted by the various contributions – that of the nature, form and impact of power and politics. Individually and collectively each of the contributions in this volume highlights and explores the impact and consequences of power and politics. Whether it surrounds the wish of particular organisations to ensure the 'invisibility' of criminal activity and of victimisation in order to protect their 'image' and stockmarket position; the power of organisations to allocate, award and refuse financial grants to organisations and individuals to undertake research; the ability of an industry to generate sufficient concern over particular activities to ensure the purchase of the latest regulatory armoury of equipment; the strength of the media to expose particular acts and events or otherwise; or the power of government to legislate, decriminalise and/or suppress information, power and politics remain key to exploring the invisibility or otherwise of particular acts or events. It is therefore essential that research into hidden and invisible crime, victimisation and regulation explores these channels and avenues, and investigates their relations to the broader academy in terms of, for example, who gets research funding, why and in what capacity. Failure to do so, we would argue, fails to get to grips with the central feature of this volume, the relative lack of knowledge of particular acts and events and of the reasons as to why this is.

In summary, throughout this collection such themes have

recurred in various guises in different places and in different contexts. They are not exclusive to those areas under exploration here, nor are they particularly new in that they have not been stated before. Nevertheless they remain; and while they do, numerous acts, events and activities continue to remain hidden, neglected or in our words 'invisible' – be they crimes and criminal activity, victims and victimisation and/or regulatory mechanisms and practices. Not only is there a need to continue to explore the various areas reviewed, alongside those other neglected or hidden areas, there is also a need to explore how and in what ways our understanding of these areas has developed, and of how and in what ways our knowledge of them has been constructed. Surely these areas remain the task of any critical and reflexive criminology today. We hope this volume in some way contributes to this task.

REFERENCES

Bowling, B. (1993) 'Racial Harassment and the Process of Victimisation: Conceptual and Methodological Implications for the Local Crime Survey', *British Journal of Criminology*, 33(2), 231–49.

Cohen, S. (1996) 'Human Rights and Crimes of the State: the Culture of Denial', in J. Muncie, E. McLaughlin and M. Langan (eds.), *Criminological Perspectives: a Reader* (London: Sage in association with Open University Press).

Davies, N. (1997) *Dark Heart: the Shocking Truth About Hidden Britain* (London: Chatto and Windus).

Francis, P. (forthcoming 1999) *Contemporary Theories of Crime* (London: Sage).

Hagan, F. (1996) *Political Crime: Ideology and Criminality* (Needham Heights, MA: Allyn and Bacon).

Holdaway, S. and Rock, P. (eds.) (1998) *Thinking About Criminology* (London: UCL Press).

Jupp, V., Davies, P. and Francis, P. (eds.) (forthcoming 1999) *Criminology in the Field: the Practice of Criminological Research* (London: Sage).

Mann, D. and Sutton, M. (1998) '>>Netcrime: More Change in the Organisation of Thieving', *British Journal of Criminology*, 38(2), 201–29.

Mooney, J. (1993) *The Hidden Figure: Domestic Violence in North London* (Middlesex University: Centre for Criminology).

Nelken, D. (ed.) (1994) *The Futures of Criminology* (London: Sage).

Nelken, D. (1997a) 'White Collar Crime', in M. Maguire, R. Morgan and R. Reiner (eds.), *The Oxford Handbook of Criminology*, 2nd edn (Oxford: Clarendon Press), 891–924.

Nelken, D. (1997b) 'Understanding Criminal Justice Comparatively', in M. Maguire, R. Morgan and R. Reiner (eds.), *The Oxford Handbook of Criminology*, 2nd edn (Oxford: Clarendon Press), 409–36.

Newburn, T. and Shiner, M. (1996) *Young People, Drugs and Peer Education: an Evaluation of the Youth Awareness Programme*, Drugs Prevention Initiative Paper 13 (London: Home Office).

Parker, H., Measham, F. and Alridge, J. (1995) *Drugs Futures – Changing Patterns of Drug Use Among English Youth*, Monograph No. 7 (London: ISDD).

Parker, M. Aldridge, J. and Measham, E. (1998) *Illegal Leisure – The Normalization of Adolescent Recreational Drug Use* (London: Routledge).

Pearce, F. (1976) *Crimes of the Powerful: Marxism, Crime and Deviance* (London: Pluto).

Ruggiero, V., South, N. and Taylor, I. (eds.) (1998) *The New European Criminology* (London: Routledge).

South, N. (1997a) 'Control, Crime and "End of Century Criminology"', in P. Francis, P. Davies and V. Jupp (eds.), *Policing Futures: the Police, Law Enforcement and the Twenty-First Century* (Basingstoke: Macmillan).

South, N. (1997b) 'Late-Modern Criminology: "Late" as in "Dead" or "Modern" as in "New"', in D. Owen (ed.), *Sociology after Postmodernism* (London: Sage).

Sparks, R. (1997) 'Recent Social Theory and the Study of Crime and Punishment', in M. Maguire, R. Morgan and R. Reiner (eds.), *The Oxford Handbook of Criminology*, 2nd edn (Oxford: Clarendon Press), 891–924.

Stanko, E. A. (1998) 'Making the Invisible Visible in Criminology: a Personal Journey', in S. Holdaway and P. Rock (eds.), *Thinking About Criminology* (London: UCL Press).

Theoretical Criminology (1998), Special Issue: For a Green Criminology (London: Sage).

Walklate, S. (1989) *Victimology: the Victim and the Criminal Justice Process* (London: Sage).

Walklate, S. (1998) *Understanding Criminology: Current Theoretical Debates* (Milton Keynes: Open University Press).

Wall, D. S. (1997) 'Policing the Virtual Community: the Internet, Cyberspace and Cybercrime', in P. Francis, P. Davies and V. Jupp (eds.), *Policing Futures: the Police, Law Enforcement and the Twenty-First Century* (Basingstoke: Macmillan).

Witte, R. (1996) *Racist Violence and the State* (London: Longman).

Index

Abbas Gokal 153, 159
accidents (*see also* Disasters) 81,
    88, 178, 184, 185, 187, 188,
    194, 195, 196
Al Fayed 151
Alleyne, B. C. 183
Asil Nadir 164
Attorney General 146, 150
Audit Commission 161
Axel, H. 172

Backer, T. E. 180
Bank of Credit and Commerce
    International (BCCI) 31,
    148, 153, 157, 159
Barings 31
Barlow, J. P. 159
Barlow Clowes 153
Baumrin, B. H. 199
Beck, A. 208, 209, 210, 211,
    229
Becker, G. S. 194, 203
Bennett, T. 68
Bergman, D. 94
Blackwell, J. C. 173, 185, 189,
    190, 193
Blue Arrow 150, 152, 158, 159
Boesky/Guinness 155
Bottomley, P. 177
Bowling, B. 239
Box, S. 36, 77, 80, 127
Braithwaite, J. 55, 62, 65, 69,
    92, 109, 160
Brett, Lord Justice 165
British Crime Survey 9–11, 30,
    61, 181, 201
Bross, M. H. 184, 185
Burt, M. R. 185
business ideology 84, 96

Calavita, K. 145
Campbell, D. 168, 174
CBI 177

CCTV and surveillance 21,
    208–31, 237
Cohen, S. 22, 56, 237, 238, 240
Companies Act 1989 150, 162
Company Directors'
    Disqualification Act 1986
    (CCDA) 162
Conservative government 21,
    98, 146
corporate manslaughter 80
County NatWest 150
Court of Appeal 150, 152
crime control 141–231, 198,
    201, 219–25, 228–30
crimes
    armed robbery 68
    assault 211
    blue collar 154
    bribery 145
    burglary 68
    business 69
    conventional 37, 83, 87, 109
    corporate 77, 83, 87, 143,
        150, 151
    corruption (anti-corruption)
        59, 145, 146
    cybercrimes (*see* cybercrimes)
    definitions of 55
    domestic violence 239
    economic 67, 77
    élite 154–5, 158
    embezzlement 143
    employee fraud 164
    environmental 3
    expressive 67
    fiddles, fiddling, fiddly work
        7, 59, 62, 211, 223, 225–30
    financial 154
    green crimes 3
    harassment and violence 65,
        239
    health and safety 23, 77–104,
        241

insider dealing 143
instrumental 67
international 158
organisational 144, 156, 161
pilfering 62, 211, 226
political 238
property 173
prostitution 202
racial 239
robbery 211, 215
shoplifting 211–14
statistics 8, 16, 78, 93
survey 9–11, 241
tax evasion 158
theft 62, 143, 160, 202, 210,
 211–12, 214–19, 224–30,
 237
violent 173, 190, 211, 239
white collar 29, 55, 66, 111,
 127, 156, 160–5, 233, 234,
 236, 239, 241, 242
Criminal Justice Act 1987 144,
 147, 149
criminal statistics 8, 93, 241
criminals 191, 203
 blue collar 143
 burglars 68, 210, 214
 corporate 77, 83, 87, 152, 161
 fraudsters 151, 159, 161, 164,
 214
 high status 63, 65, 152
 middle class 63, 65, 143
 shoplifters 164
 upper class 63
 white collar 143, 148, 160,
 164, 165
 working class 65
criminology 169, 232–44
 conventional 14, 55
 critical 96–9
 feminist 15
 green 3
 mainstream 14
 postmodern 15
Crouch, D. 184
Crown Prosecution Service (CPS)
 146, 147, 148, 151, 152
cybercrimes 4, 20, 105, 234,
 236, 239, 242

hate 125
 obscenity 123
 pornography 124
 regulation of 128
 spying 116
 stalking 125
 terrorism 114
 theft – cyber-cash, cyber-credit,
 cyber-piracy 117
 trespass 113
 victims 127
 violence 125
cyber-punk 114
cyberspace 106, 234
cyber-victimisation 127

Davies, N. 239
deaths at work 78
Delaney, T. J. 180
Department of Trade and
 Industry 145, 147, 148,
 150, 155, 162, 163
deconstruction 12–13, 63
Dickinson, F. 177, 180
DiNardo, J. 185, 186
Director of Public Prosecutions
 (DPP) 145, 146
disasters
 Herald of Free Enterprise
 sinking 31, 39
 King's Cross fire 31
Ditton, J. 62, 67, 226, 227
Drug Free Workplace Act
 1988 174
drugs 161–207, 235, 241
 crimes 7
 debate 177
 investigations 156
 misuse 177
 screening 171, 173, 174, 176,
 188, 190, 191
 testing 168, 171, 172, 173, 175,
 176–8, 179, 187–8, 191,
 192, 194, 195–203, 243
 trafficking 156, 160, 189,
 191, 192, 198
 tsar 203, 235
DuPont, R. L. 172, 180, 201
Durkheim 227

E Coli 39
economic
  crimes 68, 77, 202
  marginalisation 239
Economic and Social Research
  Council (ESRC) 99
economists 203
economy
  and crime 191, 194
  'black' 58
  hidden 59
  market 58
  shadow 58
Ehrlich, I. 203
Electronic Point of Sale System
  (EPOS) 215
employee
  rights 169, 198–9
  risk 178, 183–4, 195–6, 202,
    236
employer risk 183, 184–6, 188,
  202, 236
employment and crime 57,
  168–207
enterprise culture 44
ethnicity 239
Etzioni, A. 83
Europol 156
expressive crimes 67

feminist criminology 15, 239
feminist postmodernism 15
fiddling 7, 59, 62, 211, 223,
  225–30
fiddly work 60
Fillimore, K. 179
Financial Services
  Authority 149, 164
Financial Times 190
Fisse, B. 160
folk devil 23
Foster, J. 68
fraud 19, 88, 241
  credit and cheque 211
  investigation and prosecution
    145–57
  regulating 19, 143–67
  trials 152
  tribunals 152

Fraud Investigation Group 146
Fraud Squad 145, 154, 158
Fraud Trials Committee 1986
  146
fraudsters 151, 159, 161, 164,
  214
free enterprise 44, 85
Frey, B. S. 192, 193, 195

gatekeepers 16, 95
gender 63
Giddens, A. 107
Gill, K. 226, 227
Gill, M. 61, 210
Globalisation 20
Goldman, L. 89
Goode, E. 173, 189
Gottfredson, G. 109
Greenberg, S. 125
Guinness case 150, 152–3, 159,
  164

Hagan, F. 238
harassment 239
  racial 65
  sexual 65
Harding, P. 59
health and safety 171, 175,
  177, 222
  crimes 23
  statistics 10, 78, 93
  victims 90
Health and Safety at Work
  (HASAW) Act 81
Health and Safety Commission
  (HSC) 78
Health and Safety Executive
  (HSE) 10, 78, 80, 177,
  186
Hearnden, K. 209, 210
Hecker, S. 177, 196, 198
Heidensohn, F. 63
Henry, S. 59
HM Customs & Excise 149
hidden economy 59, 226–7
Hingson, R. W. 184
Hirschi, T. 109
Hobbs, D. 68
Hoffman, A. 172

Home Office 168
Consultation Paper 152
Hough, M. 9, 61

informal economy 226–8
Inland Revenue 149
insider dealing 143
Institute of Personnel
  Management 177
Internet 106, 129
Invesco-Mims 164
invisibility 5, 178–9, 180,
  195–200
invisible crimes 178, 227,
  232–44
  features 6–23
  regulation of 46–9, 168–207
  victims 40–2

Jenkins, A. 59
jury
  trials 152
  verdict 146, 150–1

Kaestner, R. 172, 174, 185, 196
Kandel, D. B. 185
Konovsky, M. A. 171, 172, 173,
  183, 194, 197, 199, 201
Kramer, R. C. 96

Labour government 22, 85
Labour Party 21
Law Commission 81
Lehman, W. E. K. 176, 177,
  180
Leonard, M. 63
Levitt, Roger 150, 160, 163
Lewis, R. J. 183
Lyon, D. 229
Lyons, J. 159

MacDonald, R. 60
MacDonald, S. 172–6,
  183–8, 191, 201
Maguire, M. 68
Mangan, M. 125
Mann, D. 234
market economy 189–90
Mars, G. 59, 62, 226, 227

Martin, J. K. 178, 179, 180,
  181, 183, 185, 186
Maxwell, R. 150, 153, 157, 158,
  160, 164
pensions fund fraud 31, 148
Mayhew, P. 9, 61
media 22–3, 85
method/methodological 183,
  187, 241
Milken, M. 155, 163
Millard, T. L. 177
millennium 169
Miron, J. A. 191, 194, 195, 197
Mirrlees-Black, C. 209
money laundering 144
Mooney, J. 239
Morgenthau, R. 157
Murdoch 163
Mutual Legal Assistance
  Treaties 157

Naffine, N. 58
Nelken, D. 60, 95, 233, 242
Newcomb, J. 179, 180, 182
Newburn, T. 235
New Labour 22, 203, 240
Normand, J. 184, 185

Oakley, A. 63
occupational fatality 82
Ostrich Farming Company 162

panic 22
Parker, H. 235
Parnes, A. 159
Pearce, F. 80, 84, 96, 237
perks of the job 223, 226, 228
pharmaceutical industry 62
Pickholz, 145
pilfering 62, 211, 226
police
  attitudes to fraud 154–5
  co-operation 156
  officers 158
policing of fraud 161
political
  agenda 20, 23
  crime 238, 243
  pressure 154

pornography 123, 124, 129
postmodernism 15
Poveda, T. 144
Presley, Elvis 120
Prinz, A. 189, 194, 195, 202
Private Eye 163
Production Order 149, 150
Prosecution of Offences Act
　1985 148
Punch, M. 16, 42, 65, 69

radical criminology 239
Ramsay, M. 181, 182
regulating
　cybercrimes 128
　fraud 19, 143–67
　the invisible 168–207
regulation 141–231, 234, 237
　legal regulation 18–20, 46–9
　self regulation 46–9
regulatory
　enforcement 19
　justice 160–5
　practices 19, 187, 188
Ritzer, G. 175
robbery 211, 215
Ronson, G. 159, 164
Roskill Committee 157
Roskill, Lord 146, 147
Rosoff, S. 155
Rossbacherm, H. 145
Ruggiero, V. 42, 239

Saunders, Ernest 155, 159
scandals 87
Schottenfeld, R. S. 175
Scottish Office 79
security 211–19
self-report studies 11
Serious Fraud Office (SFO) 20,
　144, 147–54, 157, 158
shadow economy 58
Shapiro, S. 155
Sheridan, J. 185
Simon, D. 144
site of crime 38, 66
Slapper, G. 79
Smart, C. 15
Smith, S. 58

social class 65
social control 198, 219–25,
　228–30
South, N. 3, 201, 235, 237, 238
Sparks, R. 242
Stanko, E. A. 239, 242
statistics (*see* criminal statistics)
Steele, H. L. 130
Stevenson, R. 191, 192, 195,
　202
Stigler, G. J. 201
Sullivan, E. J. 185
surveillance 169, 198, 203, 208–31
　see also CCTV and surveillance
Sutherland, E. 32, 44, 65

Theft Act 1968 165
twentieth century 169, 232,
　234, 235, 238

UBS Phillips & Drew 150
unemployment and crime 57,
　181
United Nations 190

victimisation 236, 242
　business 209
　cyber-victimisation 127
　knowledge of 6–8
　location of 40–2
　multiple victimisation 38
victims 144
　corporate 154, 161, 240
　health and safety 90
　multiple 38
　surveys (*see* British Crime
　　Survey)
virtual reality 105

Walker, George 150
Walklate, S. 236, 242
Wallace, J. 125
Walsh, D. C. 185
Weisburd, D. 143
Wells, C. 88, 151, 209
Wheeler, S. 165
White, H. R. 185
white collar crime (*see* crimes;
　criminals)

Widlake, B. 148
Williams, J. 168, 172, 174
Wilson v Clinch 1879 165
Witte, R. 239
women and crime 63
work
  definitions of 56
  drug taking at work 168–207
  non-work 198–9
  workers 208–31
  workplace 208–31, 235,
    239–40, 241

deaths 82
regulation 168–207
risks 170, 183–6

Young, L. F. 114

Zedner, L. 127
Zeitlin, L. R. 226
zero tolerance 83, 173
Zimmer, L. 173
Zimring, F. 145
Zwerling, C. 184, 185